Deaths in (

Caring for Peo

# Deaths in Custody: Caring for People at Risk

*Edited by*

Alison Liebling

Whiting & Birch Ltd

mcmxcvi

Published by Whiting & Birch Ltd,
PO Box 872, London SE23 3HL, England.
*USA:* Paul & Co, Publishers' Consortium Inc,
PO Box 442, Concord, MA 01742.
*British Library Cataloguing in Publication Data.*
A CIP catalogue record is available from
the British Library
ISBN 1 871177 85 5 (cased)
ISBN 1 871177 86 3 (limp)
Printed in England by Ipswich Book Company

# Contents

# Acknowledgements

Special thanks are due to Julia Braggins, Director of ISTD, and to Carol Martin and Gail Bradley, also of ISTD, for their organisational skills, patience and team-work in the translation of an idea into practice. Thanks also go to Nic Groombridge, Irene Frost, Elaine Player, David Neal, Martin McHugh and Tim Newell for their work on the organising committee and throughout the busy days of the conference. Many thanks to New Hall, for graciously hosting us. Generous sponsorship was gratefully received from the Prison Service of England and Wales, the Department of Health, the Prison Service of Northern Ireland and the Home Office Programme Development Unit. Ian Dunbar, formerly Director of Inmate Administration, accepted our invitation to chair the conference proceedings, and did so with his usual flair and warmth. It is a fitting signal of his devotion to improvement in prison affairs that he should choose to spend the final days of his distinguished career fulfilling such a task for us.

My colleagues at the Cambridge Institute of Criminology played a role in the support of our conference by hosting an informal welcome address and tour of the Radzinowicz Library. Three of our MPhil students - Mary Bosworth, Patricia Connell and Uji Chiemeka smoothed procedures throughout, to our delight and relief. Terry Waite kept a full dining hall in silence as he shared with us some of his own experiences in solitary confinement - we thank him for his openness on such a relevant and serious occasion.

Maureen Brown deserves our continued thanks for her patient secretarial and other support. For 'technical assistance', thanks are due to Peter Hutchinson for the use of his scanner and to Andrew Pauza for the translation of various discs into Mac language. I am also grateful to David McDonald for his helpful comments on the introduction and to Leonie Howe for help with proof reading.

Trinity Hall hosted a dinner on the eve of the conference for those speakers and participants who arrived on Easter Monday. Many thanks are due for the relaxed and intimate setting in which we began our discussions.

Finally, for kind words at the right moment, I would like to thank Samantha Sherratt, Kathy Biggar, Jonathan Steinberg, and the third year law student who said in passing, 'Your conference has changed my life'. May she continue to feel the urge to understand and improve.

A.L.
Institute of Criminology, Cambridge
June 1994

# Introduction

*Alison Liebling*

The second International conference on Deaths in Custody was held at New Hall in Cambridge, in April 1994. There were significant changes, in tone, atmosphere, interest and outcome from the first conference held in March 1991 at Canterbury (see Liebling and Ward, 1994). Our Conference Co-Ordinating Group had sought a broad representation from as many countries as possible, but held as an important orienting principle the search for examples of progress and change, of good practice and of hope for the future. Such an endeavour was not intended to detract attention from the urgency and tragedy of the issues so pertinently raised during the first conference. Far from it. Our respective commitment to the understanding and prevention of deaths in custody required a serious look at possibilities for change as well as the outlaying of the various problems faced. To some extent, it was a major achievement of the first conference that its tone was so chilling. Much has been acknowledged in official and policy arenas in its wake. It was in order to reflect and build upon this recognition by those in official circles of the seriousness and complexity of the problem of prison suicide that a slightly different tone was sought this time. How far this orientation was (and will remain) appropriate, we will be interested to learn.

Perhaps this introduction can begin with the most important conclusion to emerge from the 1994 conference. One of the most positive themes to emerge from our final deliberations, both in groups and during a final plenary panel discussion, was the need for this collection of people from such diverse fields and countries to remain in touch. The conference topic united a wide range of individuals with a strong sense of commitment to continuing their work in this area. Many expressed the need for a forum or federation to belong to. We discussed this idea in detail, but did not arrive at a plan for the future. One unresolved question is the precise area of interest: some participants at the conference felt that suicide and suicide risk in prison was a large enough topic in its own right; others felt that the relationship between suicide and other deaths in custody was important and that the two broad areas were inseparable. Two commitments were made: that ISTD would devote a Special Issue of their journal, *Criminal Justice Matters* to deaths in custody in the near future. In addition, a third conference would be seriously considered for 1997 at which the question of establishing a network or federation might be more formally raised. The possibility of an occasional Newsletter is also being considered. These issues will remain on our agenda until then, and we would welcome suggestions and opinions on these matters in the meantime.

The sense of a common purpose and interest between diverse groups was a powerful message throughout this conference. Here were an assortment of academics, practitioners, volunteers, prisoners, campaigners and others from many different countries and backgrounds, with a single commitment: to articulate the significance of basic human values in the context of custody, to insist upon the treatment of all with dignity and respect; at the very least, to raise the standards of care in institutions, and to ask searching and honest questions about the purposes and necessity of such institutions and about the nature and context of those groups who find themselves incarcerated. Issues of social justice were raised at the same moment as issues of individual need.

In this volume, most of the papers presented at plenary sessions during the conference are included, in more or less the order of their presentation. Several of the contributors to seminar and workshop sessions have also submitted written papers, for which we are grateful. We are especially pleased to have received a contribution from one of the serving prisoners who gave workshop presentations; more on this below. Absent, as ever, are the discussions, feelings and ideas expressed throughout the proceedings. Some of these are hopefully reflected in this introduction. The remainder will doubtless recur and persist, and may become topics in their own right at the next conference.

Part One begins with an introduction by Ian Dunbar, who opened and chaired the conference and who represented the prison service commitment to and interest in our conference theme. Many of us shared the mixed feelings of sadness at his retirement and yet delight at his choice of the right moment to depart. It is a tribute to his own tremendous work in this field and in the prison service more broadly, that he could leave at the same time as the launch of the new prison service suicide awareness training strategy for England and Wales. For his decision to end his service at our conference, and for all he has done to improve both thinking and practice in the prison service and amongst its commentators, we record our thanks.

Professor Rod Morgan has been professionally embroiled in issues relating to prison conditions and particularly in relation to deaths in custody for many years. His experience and involvement - for example as an Assessor to Lord Justice Woolf's enquiry into the 1990 prison disturbances, and as an expert advisor to Amnesty International and the Council of Europe Committee for the Prevention of Torture and Inhuman and Degrading Treatment or Punishment - are reflected in the broad and challenging introductory plenary session which set the agenda for all that was to follow. He reminded us, importantly, that both the general and the international nature of the topic should remain in sight in order for us to arrive at a satisfactory understanding of it. Conceptually, its various strands - suicide, execution, murder, unlawful killing, death from natural causes, and the various institutions incorporated under the general heading of 'custody' are related, and it is at this level that we should develop both any theoretical understanding but also any realistic and effective preventive strategy which may reduce the number of such deaths. He called upon the international community to abolish the death penalty, to prohibit 'extra-judicial executions' and to employ a minimum use of custody in conditions which are compatible with care, accountability and normalisation.

Professor Gethin Morgan, Chair of Mental Health at the University of Bristol, talked of suicide and institutions - in particular, of psychiatric institutions. The term has been tarnished by the very persuasive historical attack made on all total institutions during the 1960s and 1970s (cf. Goffman, 1961) and on psychiatry (Laing, 1960; 1967; Foucault, 1967; 1977; and for example, Szasz, 1963; 1970) throughout the same period. He outlined the psychological state of the suicidal: 'The hurt, anguish, soreness, aching, psychological pain' which so little research truly captures or expresses and which so few professionals can acknowledge or respond to adequately. Managing the guilt of those who work with the suicidal is a fundamental step towards changing these poorly articulated attitudes which can sometimes confirm the despair of the desperate. The 'give and take of talk' was here raised and repeatedly echoed in later presentations, in discussions and in questions.

Alison Liebling, Senior Research Associate at the Institute of Criminology in Cambridge and David Neal, formerly head of the Suicide Awareness Support Unit in Prison Service Headquarters, presented the collective outcome of five years of research, policy development and practice innovation which has culminated in the launch of a radically different approach to the suicide problem in prisons in England and Wales away from the reactive, defensive and largely medical approach which was so much the focus of heartfelt criticism at the last conference and towards a multi-disciplinary, supportive and innovative approach to suicide risk. With some trepidation, those responsible for policy development within the prison service welcomed the very generous response which came forward from police representatives at the conference: that on paper at least, and in training material, policy and in overall strategy, the police may have lessons to learn from the prison service, so marked have been the strides taken forward in recent years. The inevitable question of the effectiveness of the new approach in reducing the rate of prison suicide was seriously examined: how can such a change be properly evaluated, what are the outcome and process measures, and how far does a context of increasing suicide rates amongst vulnerable groups in the community act against such an improvement? How and when, and to what extent, does the introduction of 'aspirational' policy make itself felt in the daily lives of those who live and work in prison? These were large and ambitious questions, which will doubtless also recur.

The paper presented by Louis Blom-Cooper, QC, reflected his influential role as Chairman of the Mental Health Act Commission between 1990 and 1994. He raised the question of the nature of inquiries following from the deaths of detained patients or prisoners and asked whether the coroners' inquest can adequately fulfil the need for an accountable and open system of inquiry in such circumstances.

All such deaths should be treated as problematic and require thorough investigation, he argued. He suggested that internal inquiries, whose reports should be made available to interested parties, should always be carried out. All such deaths - and the results of each subsequent inquiry - should be reported to the Mental Health Act Commission, who should monitor these inquiries and attend inquests. This comprehensive inquiry should be separate from the inquest, which is not a satisfactory arena for such an investigation. He gave examples of such inquiries and concluded that 'every death prompts inquiry' - legislation should require that they satisfy the needs of families, the public, and of justice.

It was interesting to note during the discussion which followed this plenary session that the Australian Royal Commission (see below) looked closely at the coronial systems of the Australian States and Territories and recommended sweeping changes to bring such legislation up to date. As a result, a number of States and Territories have now substantially re-written their coronial legislation, introducing procedures aimed at ensuring that thorough, independent inquests are conducted into all custodial deaths (see Royal Commission into Aboriginal Deaths in Custody 1991, *National Report* Elliott Johnston, Commissioner, Volume I AGPS, Canberra pp.109-181).

Part Two begins with an important contribution from one of the several Australian participants at the conference on the impact of the Royal Commission into Aboriginal Deaths in Custody (see Biles and McDonald, 1992). David McDonald, a Senior Criminologist at the Australian Institute of Criminology in Canberra gave us a comprehensive, articulate and powerful outline of the work of the Commission, the most expensive Royal Commission in Australian history. He gave us a concise history of its achievements, its limitations and the underlying issues which it sought to address. The Royal Commission into Aboriginal Deaths in Custody was established in 1987 by the Commonwealth of Australia, Australia's six State Governments and the Northern Territory of Australia. It investigated the deaths of Aboriginal and Torres Strait Islander people which occurred in custody throughout Australia during the period 1 January 1980 to 31 May 1989, and the social, cultural and legal factors which had a bearing on those deaths. During this period, 99 such deaths occurred in police, prison and juvenile detention centre custody. Thirty-seven of the deaths were by natural causes, 30 were by hanging, 23 were from injuries and 9 were from the use of alcohol and/or other drugs. No individual custodial staff were found to have caused any of the deaths by deliberate violence or brutality, but many of the deaths were found to have been the result of system failures and/or the failure of custodial officers to exercise their duty of care to people in their custody.

The Royal Commission made 339 recommendations in its final National Report and almost all were accepted by the Australian Government. The recommendations cover both aspects of the criminal justice system and the underlying issues relating to Aboriginal disadvantage and their gross over-representation in custody. David McDonald discussed with us the impact of the Report, arguing that Aboriginal organisations have generally rejected the Royal Commission's findings and are frustrated at what they see as the inadequate implementation of many of its key recommendations. The Australian Institute of Criminology is monitoring deaths in custody in Australia and has reported that the incidence of custodial deaths has continued to rise and that changes in the patterns of such deaths have been observed. All hope that a fuller implementation of the Royal Commission's recommendations will occur and will lead to a reduction in custodial deaths and to the improvement of the well-being of Australia's indigenous people.

Brian Wade and Paul Etheridge, Chief Inspector and Police Sergeant respectively, gave us an outline of a recent review of cases of deaths in custody within the Metropolitan Police District. The review led to improved guidelines for officers having to identify vulnerable persons in their custody, their medical care and the training of staff, particularly in relation to the high proportion of cases where alcohol or drug use is suspected. 216 deaths have occurred in the Metropolitan Police District between 1983 and 1993. In 117 of these cases, alcohol has featured as a contributory factor in coroners' reports. Dr Irene Sagel-Grande of the Criminological Institute of the State University of Leiden in The Netherlands echoed these dangers in her presentation on deaths in police custody in Dutch police-cells. Only recently has the Dutch National Ombudsman repeated his call of several years ago to the Minister of Justice for the introduction of a national registration for deaths and attempted suicides in police cells. The data is now being collected. Research is also being carried out into the type and quality of care provided for arrestees held in police custody in the Netherlands.

We were very pleased to have what turned out to be our most overcrowded workshop from the Northern Ireland prison service, presented by Stephen Pope, formerly Head of Regimes Planning Branch at the Headquarters of the Northern Ireland Prison Service Headquarters, and Bob Cromie, the Governor of the only Young Offenders Institution in Northern Ireland: Hydebank Wood in Belfast. Stephen gave us a well illustrated 'tour' of the Northern Ireland prison system and a resumé of some of its distinct features and problems. Bob followed this introduction with a case study of his establishment's history and approach to the problem of suicide and self-injury. We were disappointed not to be able to include this paper in our collection. We very much hope that they will find the opportunity to write up their work for publication elsewhere.

Dr Sheila Gore, Dr Graham Bird and Dr Sheila Burns have contributed a chapter based on the presentation by Dr Gore at the conference of a paper on HIV Epidemiology in prisons in Scotland, based on her team's ongoing work with the Scottish Prison Service. The chapter reviews past and planned work in the UK and shows how HIV surveillance in prisons fits into national unlinked anonymous testing programmes. It includes a detailed design for monitoring HIV sero-conversions in prison, prisoners' risk behaviours and their use of harm reduction measures on offer.

We had several contributions from representatives of the various 'Listener schemes' now in operation in 50 prisons in England and Wales (see Davies, 1994 for an overview) during our conference. The most formal, and the most welcome in the light of our various and unavoidable omissions in the published version of the last conference in 1991, was the very well attended workshop presentation by Kathy Biggar, formerly Samaritan Liaison Officer for the Prison Service, 1990-1993 and now Senior Probation Officer at Wandsworth prison, Margaret Bray, a branch Samaritan, and Marc Carolissen and Len Eustace, both serving prisoners at HMP Wandsworth, and both experienced Listeners. The written version of this presentation inevitably omits much of the power and spontaneity of this particular workshop, which was both moving and light-hearted in places, but this contribution, written by Kathy and Marc stands in its own right as a first account of the evolution of the scheme from the two groups most directly involved in its development and implementation: the Samaritans and prisoners. It is a tribute to the quite exceptional work carried out by Kathy and those she has carried with her that Listener schemes are now evolving so rapidly and successfully in prisons in England and Wales, despite the very real difficulties such schemes face. We very much hope that her new role 'back in the field' at Wandsworth prison consolidates rather than diverts her commitment to these schemes and all that they represent.

Listener schemes are being evaluated nationally by a team including Michael Jennings, a chartered forensic psychologist at Styal prison and a co-presenter of one of our workshops on women in custody at the conference. Mike and Wendy Ratcliffe outlined some of the specific features of suicide risk amongst women in custody. They looked at whether there are special features of suicide risk for women prisoners, for example the particular significance for women of lack of contact with the family and especially children and their relatively higher levels of anxiety and depression.

In Part Three of this volume, and at the risk of repeating the structure of the last conference too closely, we have contributions from two of the leading spokesmen on suicide prevention and deaths in prison. We invited Lindsay Hayes, Assistant Director of the National Centre on Institutions and Alternatives, Massachusetts and Joseph Rowan, Executive Director and Chair of Juvenile and Criminal Justice International of Minnesota, USA, to give plenary presentations on the prevention of suicides in custody on the last morning of the conference. Both Joe and Lindsay are difficult to beat in terms of their respective commitment and dedication, their experience, and their enthusiasm for unravelling what can appear to be a tangle of insurmountable problems. Both gave realistic but inspiring presentations which focused on the all important theme of attitudes. What Lindsay called 'local' and 'universal' negative attitudes impede the sensitivity which professionals and practitioners might otherwise bring to clues, events and communications which so often precede a suicide. He gave us examples of large state facilities in New York and Texas which have drastically reduced their suicide rate despite increases in the size of their prison populations. The key impetus for change, he argued, has been litigation, followed swiftly by effective inquiry and then regulation, training and inspection. Knowing where to look - to system changes and attitude changes - may help to remove some of the intransigent obstacles to effective suicide prevention.

Joe Rowan, who has contributed so much to training in suicide awareness, both in the USA but also throughout the world including most recently in England and Wales, Scotland and Northern Ireland, has worked for fifty-two years with adults, juveniles and families in healthcare, suicide prevention and in corrections. His paper characteristically gave an impressive international overview of suicide prevention efforts and strategies, highlighting areas where good practice, innovation and training have led to significant reductions in the suicide rate. He illustrated the importance of good, strongly led but participatory management, of training which covers motivation, attitude and philosophy (MAP training), of total health screening and of teamwork. He raised the important question of the positive influence of female staff working in establishments for male prisoners - and of the importance of commitment from individuals who make it their mission to secure the necessary time, resources and training to make a difference. His own influence in this respect has been, and continues to be immense. We look forward to seeing him again.

There are inevitable dangers in any attempt to approach the subject of deaths in custody positively. The words 'complacent' and 'self-congratulatory' were aired from one or two quarters at moments during the conference. Many of us who are struggling with our conflicting instincts both to work slowly but constructively within a system and yet who sometimes feel tempted to reject and challenge it more forcefully, drew some comfort from the broad spectrum of interest groups represented at this conference and the common voice with which many seemed to be speaking. That there was guarded pride in some of the progress made over the last three years, for example in the presentations by the prison services of England and Wales and by Northern Ireland, was a welcome aspect of the conference, tainted as this pride inevitably was by a clear sense of the difficulties of the road ahead and, perhaps most recently, of the changing climate of our penal politics. How far the future will reflect our worst fears, we may reflect at the next deaths in custody conference.

# Part One

# Deaths in Custody

# One

# Deaths in custody: Caring for people at risk

*Ian Dunbar*

INTRODUCTION

I welcome you all to what I am sure will prove to be an important, stimulating and productive conference in an area which is of major concern to us all.

The ISTD held the first 'Deaths in Custody' conference in Canterbury in March 1991. It was, like today's, international, but it was smaller and more expensive. It was intense and disputatious. As an aspect of death in custody, suicide was a highly disturbing and contentious issue inside and with out the Prison Service in England and Wales. Many participants still recall it as a bruising experience but the general perception was that there was a shared commitment at the end to achieve something constructive and long lasting.

The ISTD has planned this conference as an opportunity to share among delegates any progress which has been made since then and to identify those further issues which still remain and need to be addressed. An important part of our work over the next three days is to share experience so that it is more readily available across all participating countries.

Suicide, whilst a major concern of many of us here because of our responsibilities and interests, is but one aspect of death in custody and the programme has been designed to explore all deaths in custody. Our first speaker will set the scene and explore issues of care and accountability regarding all deaths, no matter how they occur.

The organisers have had to set a ceiling of 170 participants and to encourage a wide participation have limited the numbers of those from the Prison Service who can attend. That the conference has been oversubscribed demonstrates the interest which this topic arouses in society at large. We have members from England, Wales, Scotland, Northern Ireland, Republic of Ireland, Australia, Belarus, Bophutatswana, Canada, China, Greece, Hungary, Israel, Netherlands, Poland, Slovakia, Ukraine and the United States.

The Conference has been financially supported by the Department of Health, the Home Office Programme Development Unit, and the Prison Services of England and Wales and Northern Ireland. Present are those from academia, the health service, police, special hospitals, various prison services and a small group of prisoners.

We are all here on a personal basis and all have a shared concern about deaths in custody. We want to take our thinking and practical responses forward because we are dissatisfied with the level of deaths in custody which occur at the present. We want to see the care of people, for whom we are responsible, improved.

I want to encourage a supportive and cooperative atmosphere rather than one which is contentious, antagonistic or confrontational. We are here because we share our concern and my hope is that at the end of the conference we will all better understand, not only each other, but also those who are at risk and therefore may become better able to care for them. All participants in the conference from the Chairman down are here because we feel responsibility for this problem; it is a heavy responsibility.

We share experience, in the knowledge that no matter what improvements have been made many more are still needed. It is a balance between challenge and support, between sharing of intellectual concepts and emotional responses which will enable us to help, for example, those officers on the landings and supporting staff better to understand these ideas and principles and to put these concepts into practice.

When people are dealt with in institutions, they lose many of the freedoms you and I most value and most need. They are also totally dependent on others for meeting and obtaining basic, everyday needs, they are de-skilled and de-roled. Trust becomes an invaluable, but oft times, rare commodity, all too often replaced by anxiety and fear. I know from my experience in running prisons how important it is to create a safe and a fair environment, 'balancing' as Lord Woolf has said, 'custody and control and humanity and justice'.

In the institution normality assumes a different guise from that with which we are familiar. Even the positive, altruistic gesture can be viewed with suspicion. In these circumstances any death achieves a significantly horrifying and traumatic dimension.

When death occurs, it is shocking - inside or outside an establishment. When it happens inside it is even more so and whether from natural or other causes, friends, relatives and staff have a strong desire to know how? why? Could it have been prevented? Could I have done more? Stress, anxiety, guilt, anger, hostility and despair are all present. I have experienced this myself as governor.

We all share a concern that more can be done and I welcome chairing this conference in the belief that the interchange of ideas and the experience of members and lecturers will further that concern and ultimately help reduce the problem.

I have seen a sea change in the way the Prison Service in England and Wales has approached this issue and involved staff, Samaritans and prisoners, in the process. It is about the exemplification of one of our values, caring for those in our custody.

# Two

# In the hands of the state: Care and accountability

*Rod Morgan*

INTRODUCTION

It is important at the outset that we remind ourselves of two things. First, 'death in custody' is an international concern: we should not be too parochial in the way that we approach it. Second, our concern is with 'deaths in custody', not about a particular form of death in custody. In the United Kingdom 'deaths in custody' tends to prompt a focus on suicide, and this emphasis is understandably, and appropriately, reflected in the balance of papers in this collection. However, 'deaths in custody' will signify very different issues for observers from different jurisdictions. In this paper I want to try and chart some of these varied preoccupations and attempt to show how, conceptually, they might be linked to preventive mechanisms. Let me start by defining some terms.

## FORMS OF CUSTODY

Our context is custody, no matter what form that custody takes, imposed with the authority of the state. This will normally be custody determined by the police or as a result of a court order in a prison. But we should not forget juvenile institutions or mental hospitals nor custody at the behest of immigration authorities. In many countries custody may also be at the hands of the armed forces.

We shall be largely concerned with institutions, but not

exclusively so. In the same way that in England and Wales the provisions of the Police and Criminal Evidence Act 1984 concern custody from the moment of arrest (or what in other jurisdictions is sometimes termed 'apprehension'), so custody should be construed as a condition rather than a location. By custody we mean restraint of liberty and submission to the authority of the state and this condition begins before the person in custody arrives at a designated institution.

This distinction is important because it is a regrettable fact that in many countries persons taken into custody by the police or army are not immediately taken to designated places of custody and may never be taken to such places. Further, in some countries the agencies of the state are less than honest as to where persons in custody are held. In most European jurisdictions we are able, happily, to rely on information from justice ministries to the effect that there are 'x' number of prisons or police stations, at 'y' locations and that 'z' number of persons are either detained therein, or have been detained during a particular time period. We take the truthfulness of such statements more or less for granted. But such assumptions are not warranted everywhere. Secret locations are resorted to and 'disappearance', temporarily or permanently, is a technique of repression or state terror now widely employed by many governments (Amnesty 1993, Appendix IX; Amnesty 1994).

FORMS OF DEATH

It may be useful to distinguish five causes of death in custody each of which raise different analytical and preventive issues. It may also be useful to cite examples of what we are talking about. In doing so we should avoid a trap. The examples are no more than illustrative. The phenomena which should concern us are legion. They are certainly not confined to distant places to which we may feel morally superior.

*Death by authorised execution*

Though the international trend is marginally still towards abolition of the death penalty, either in law or practice (Hood, 1989, distinguishes between countries which have abolished the death penalty and those which, though retentionist, appear to have ceased carrying out executions) it is still the case that slightly more than half the countries in the world retain capital punishment. Moreover in some countries, as is well known, there is a counter trend (this includes countries which, though retentionist in law, appear to have been abolitionist in practice, but have now resumed executions– see Hood 1989, 8). In 1993 the United States executed the largest number of persons, 38 (*Overcrowded Times*, February 1994), since the reintroduction of the death penalty in 1976. In 1992 executions were resumed in Pakistan and last year Belize and Trinidad followed suit. The Jamaican Government has stated its intention to resume executions as has the Philippines. In countries like Afghanistan, Albania and Saudi Arabia, public executions are regularly being held and in China it is not possible to know the extent to which the death penalty is being resorted to, but it is estimated to run well into four figures (Amnesty International 1993, pp 15-17).

I doubt that this issue will receive much attention in the rest of this collection of papers. Most European jurisdictions now regard the death penalty as a matter of history. But it is not invariably the case. Several former Warsaw Pact countries, including some that are joining the Council of Europe, retain the death penalty. There is no room for complacency. Nor should we forget the degree of human anguish which this form of state violence entails nor our own constitutional connections with it. In November 1993 we were forcibly reminded of the fact by the Privy Council judgement in the case of *Pratt and Morgan*.

Earl Pratt and Ivan Morgan were jointly convicted in Jamaica in January 1979 of a murder committed in October 1977. They were sentenced to death. Fourteen years later they had still not been executed. Throughout that time they were housed on death-row, along with more than two hundred other prisoners, in St Catherine's Prison, near Kingston. Of the more than 250 prisoners on death row at the end of November 1993, 23 had been awaiting execution for more than ten years and 82 for more than five years.

The Privy Council ruled, in a vitally important judgement, that to await death over an extended period– they decided five years– amounts to inhuman and degrading punishment and that henceforward any death sentence not carried out within five years should be commuted to life imprisonment. Consider briefly a little of what Pratt and Morgan's fourteen year-long agony of suspense entailed.

The death-row cell blocks at St Catherine's, like death-row cell blocks elsewhere, provide a highly restrictive regime for their condemned inhabitants (Amnesty International 1993a, 2-3). They live in darkness without natural or electric light in their cells. A single naked bulb provides a dim light on each landing. There is no work, no recreational programme, no medical facilities– no doctor has visited St Catherine's Prison in two years– and the prisoners are locked into their cells for practically the whole day, except when they are allowed out in small groups to walk in an adjacent restricted compound. Mattresses and blankets are not provided, though most death-row prisoners appear to acquire them during their long years of incarceration.

After unforgivable delays and convoluted procedures lasting eight years (of which the Privy Council was highly critical) the first warrant of execution for Pratt and Morgan was issued on 12 February 1987 for execution on 24 February. On 23 February the Governor General of Jamaica issued a stay of execution. During this period Pratt and Morgan were held in the condemned cells next to the gallows by the gatehouse. The prisoners claim they were not told of the stay of execution by the governor until 45 minutes before the execution was due to take place. The governor denies this: he maintains that he told them the previous evening (Ibid. 9) The appellants' case having been unsuccessfully reconsidered a second warrant of execution was issued on 18 February 1988 for execution on 1 March. Again the prisoners were held in the cells next to the gallows. Again the execution was stayed on the preceding day: on this occasion we do not know when the prisoners were told. Following further appeal proceedings a third warrant of execution was issued on 18 February 1991 for execution on 7 March, though this time, appeal proceedings having commenced which led eventually to the Privy Council judgement, the executions were stayed on 28 February.

Thus on three occasions in fourteen years, during which time fellow prisoners *were executed*, Pratt and Morgan were moved to the gallows cells there to await their imminent end. It is difficult to contemplate a more slow-burning mental torture. Though I concur with the Privy Council that any jurisdiction which provides for the death penalty must provide for means of appeal, which will necessarily take time– the Privy Council considered that it should be expeditious and should not normally take more than two years to exhaust– it is difficult to see that the agony of waiting over one, two or three years, would constitute less mental torture than that resulting from having to wait twelve, thirteen or fourteen years. The Privy Council judgement in the case of *Pratt and Morgan* makes plain for all to see, except those who would deny all humanity to convicted serious criminals, the procedural indefensibility of the death penalty itself, no matter what delay is involved in carrying it out.

The extreme alternative to these prolonged inhumanities is not discernibly better. In Russia, as I understand it, the where and how of executions has in the past been a state secret. Those awaiting death are not told when they will be shot.[1] It is done suddenly, when they do not expect it. Which presumably means that prisoners under sentence of death live in permanent expectation that every guard with whom they have contact may suddenly shoot them when their back is turned.

These two examples illustrate extremes. There is no acceptable way of carrying out the death penalty.

## Death at the hands of custodians

This takes a variety of forms. It ranges from killings covertly organised by the state, to killings connived at by the state to killings by rogue state servants.

I deliberately began with 'authorised execution' because of the phenomenon of extrajudicial execution, a form of death which sometimes occurs after victims have been taken into custody but not necessarily in places of custody. By extrajudicial execution I mean an execution 'carried out by order of a government or with its acquiescence' (Amnesty 1994, 86). It is a form of death distinguishable from justifiable killings in self-defence, or deaths resulting from the use of reasonable force by law enforcement officials, or killings in time of war which are not forbidden by international laws regulating armed conflict (Ibid.). It comprises murder by the state or murder condoned by the state.

I will not dwell on the mass killings in recent history of literally hundreds of thousands of people, many of them in custody– in Indonesia, Cambodia, Uganda and Iraq. There is not space here to range so widely. Let me be more focused and concentrate on the 1990s. Amnesty International has recorded 'disappearances' in more than thirty countries since 1990 and has received reports of known or suspected extrajudicial executions in over sixty countries during the same period (Ibid, 93). British forces and the British Isles are not strangers to this issue. The Gibraltar shootings are recent and allegations persist that on occasion the security forces in Northern Ireland have deliberately killed suspected members of armed opposition groups rather than arrest them.

This is certainly a phenomenon which persists within the European community of nations. I need say nothing about current events in Bosnia where the killing of persons in custody has undoubtedly been widespread. Let me rather refer to the less well-publicised position in Turkey, a member state of the Council of Europe, a signatory of the European Convention of Fundamental Human Rights, the first country in Europe to sign the Convention for the Prevention of Torture and Inhuman or Degrading Treatment or Punishment, and currently an applicant to join the European Union.

Turkey is facing a major problem. The Turkish Government is combating, particularly in the South East of the country now under emergency rule, armed guerilla units of the Kurdish Workers' Party (PKK) whose objective, originally at least, is the creation of a secessionist Marxist Kurdish state. Since 1984, when the conflict began, it is estimated that at least 10,000 people have been killed. There is no doubt that terror tactics, which includes extrajudicial executions, are being employed by both the Turkish security forces and the PKK in those rural areas which both parties seek to control. Two things need to be made plain about the position in Turkey, however.

First, the Turkish authorities are killing suspects or Government opponents not just in hot blood during armed combat but in cold blood in custody. Suspects, including community leaders and leading politicians, are being taken into custody by the security forces or the gendarmerie and after being interrogated and tortured their bodies are being disposed of in open country or beside roads. When found they bear the marks of torture, their eyes and hands and feet are sometimes bound, their limbs broken, their skulls crushed or their bodies bullet-ridden (Amnesty 1994, 58). It is of course claimed by the Turkish authorities that these assertions are false, at best the product of unverified rumour and at worst the collusive design of PKK propaganda and biased NGOs whose alleged concern for human rights is one-sided, blind to the human rights implications of terrorism. This defence has now been shown to be unsustainable. The Committee for the Prevention of Torture (CPT), the Council of Europe Committee set up under the Torture Convention in 1989, and the delegations of which have right of access to any place of detention in a member state (for detailed assessments see Evans and Morgan 1992; Morgan and Evans 1994), have shown conclusively that the use of torture in police custody is widespread in Turkey– electric shock treatment, Palestinian hanging, *falaka*, beatings and so on. The CPT has also shown that police headquarters buildings contain torture rooms

*11*

designed for the purpose and that the victims of torture are not just suspected terrorists or government opponents but ordinary petty criminals (Council of Europe 1992). There is a culture of police violence in Turkey which anyone taken into custody can reasonably expect to suffer.

This is true of many countries as anyone who saw the recent Channel 4 fly-on-the-wall documentary series *Karachi Cops* must now be aware. The Pakistani police officers portrayed in the programme had no compunction about beating suspects taken into custody on camera, or off camera but within recording distance: the screams of suspects apparently caused the police who appeared in the programmes no embarrassment. The same applies elsewhere in the Indian Sub-Continent and in many other jurisdictions. Police rough handling, brutality or systematic use of torture is widespread. It is expressly forbidden by law in all these countries but precious little is done to prevent it and its existence is generally understood and in many quarters condoned if not openly approved of.

Wherever torture or brutality in custody is widespread it will occasionally result in death, either by 'accident' or by intention, the immunity from accountability enjoyed by custodians being used to cloak the ultimate abuse of power. This has repeatedly been the outcome in South Africa, for example, where, under Apartheid, the police and the security forces operated within a culture which encouraged officers to do everything in their power to act against those perceived as the 'enemy'. There is overwhelming evidence of the use of extra-judicial executions and the occurrence of deaths in custody as a result of torture and brutality at the hands of the police and the security forces in South Africa up to the present day (Amnesty International 1992), as the Goldstone Commission has somewhat belatedly recognised (Goldstone Commission 1994).

Elsewhere, though there may be a culture of institutional staff violence, death at the hands of custodians is more the outcome of rogue state servants, exploiting their power over detainees and sheltering behind inadequate accountability mechanisms. Let me cite one or two examples.

Consider first the case of John Pat who died in the juvenile cell of the police lock-up at Roebourne, Western Australia in September 1983, aged 16. This was one of the most controversial deaths in custody which led eventually to the appointment of the Royal Commission into Aboriginal Deaths in Custody which reported in 1991 (Royal Commission 1991a). John Pat died as a result of a torn aorta and multiple rib fractures sustained either during a fight with the police or as a result of an assault on him by the police after he had been arrested and taken to the lock-up (Royal Commission 1991b). Whatever the cause and timing of the fatal injury, the Royal Commission found unequivocally that: responsibility for the fight lay with police officers who had been drinking and who acted in an 'ill-advised, unprofessional and provocative' manner (Ibid, 15); Pat was twice assaulted by police officers back at the lock-up (Ibid. 17); evidence about the events were deliberately suppressed by the police (Ibid. 19); and, when an investigation was put in hand, an investigation which initially failed to treat the incident as one of potential homicide, the officers involved failed to co-operate with it (Ibid. 21). Five police officers were subsequently charged with manslaughter. They refused to answer any questions or to give evidence in court. All were acquitted by an all-white jury. The Solicitor General for Western Australia recommended against further charges being laid because of the difficulties of proof but he thought that there was ample evidence for internal police action against them (Ibid. 248). No disciplinary action was taken against the officers, an outcome the Royal Commission found to be 'most unsatisfactory' (Ibid, 249) yet the senior investigating officer who made that decision went on to become the Commissioner of Police for Western Australia.

Similar events have occurred in this country. Recall the case of Barry Prosser who died in Winson Green Prison, Birmingham on August 18 1980. The jury at the subsequent Coroner's Court found that he had been unlawfully killed. Eighteen months later three prison officers, including a prison hospital officer, were tried for his murder. They were acquitted and left Leicester Crown Court to the applause of prison officers in the public gallery. The events were shocking. No one, then or since, in the Prison Service or out, has entertained any doubt that Prosser was killed by prison officers unknown. But the guilt of the officers responsible could not be proved and other prison officers at Birmingham closed ranks to protect the culprits.

Barry Prosser was a manic depressive and had previously been hospitalised. He was remanded in custody to Winson Green for medical assessment with a view to making a s.60 order under the Mental Health Act 1959. He kept fellow prisoners awake on his wing by banging on his door. He was moved to what were then known as 'the pads'– unfurnished 'strip' cells– in the hospital wing and there, a few days later, he was killed. The pathologist who conducted the post mortem told the Coroner's Court:

> It is perfectly plain that he had been assaulted and very severely assaulted. He must have been held down by some people while another or others struck him. (Coggan and Walker 1982, 33).

In particular he had suffered a terrible blow to the stomach which had ruptured his stomach and torn the base of his oesophagus. The pathologist speculated that:

> If he had been lying on his back a heavy man dropping with his whole weight on to the unprotected abdomen, perhaps with feet, could have been responsible for the injuries' (Ibid, 33).

He also had 'bruises around both eyes, on his hands, elbows and hips, on the genitals and anus, his thighs, knees and ankles'.

He was locked in his cell throughout the material time. Only prison officers had access to him. At some stage, in the early evening, the hospital officer in charge of the hospital wing, possibly because Prosser was being a nuisance, decided that he should be quietened and, with the assistance of two other officers, they entered his cell. Only they knew what they did. But shortly thereafter the hospital officer called a prison doctor and wrote in the journal:

> This man has gone completely berserk. He is shouting and screaming and is very disturbed. He is hallucinating. Thinks he is being beaten to death. He has been going this way continuously for three hours. Dr Ali, please advise. (Ibid, 36-7).

Dr Ali attended. He did not examine the prisoner. He merely looked at him through the small spy-hole. Prosser's face was contorted. All he said was 'Water, water'. Whatever had happened, Prosser was in a state of shock. Dr Ali prescribed an injection of 50mg Largactil and left the hospital. Shortly thereafter an unusually large 'heavy mob' was summoned. Eleven officers attended, in addition to the hospital officer and two others who had already intervened. When they rushed Prosser they were surprised that he offered no resistance. He was not shouting. He was silent and immobile. The hospital officer injected him with the Largactil while the others held him. A few hours later he was dead. The officers' explanation for his terrible injuries? Self-inflicted. Like their Australian counterparts in the John Pat case, the three accused officers declined to enter the witness box at their trial and they were acquitted. Barry Prosser was unlawfully killed by prison officers in an English prison and no one was convicted for his murder.

I am not satisfied that the Prosser case represents a bygone British age. In the case of Patrick Alexander, a schizophrenic prisoner who died in Brixton in October 1989 after having been removed by at least six prison officers from his cell to a strip cell not unlike that in which Barry Prosser died, the jury returned a verdict of 'lack of care' not 'unlawful killing'. I have little option but to defer to the judgement of the pathologist and dentist who gave evidence at the inquest that the fracture of his lower spine was not the result of someone jumping on his back and the two teeth found embedded in the back of his throat could easily have been dislodged (*Guardian*, 10 April 1990). Nevertheless you will forgive me if I wonder how such injuries to a mentally disordered prisoner could have been the outcome of 'control and restraint' techniques skilfully applied with the minimum force necessary. And in the case of Omasase Lumumba, who died in Pentonville in October 1991, on this occasion having been removed by six prison officers from his cell to the punishment block, the jury did return a verdict of 'unlawful killing'. They found that he died as a result of 'improper methods and excessive force in the process of control and restraint' (*Independent*, 5 August 1993). But, as I understand it, no prosecution is to be pursued, it having been found impossible to identify the fatal assailants. The code of silence that prevented justice being done in the case of Barry Prosser is clearly not dead.

Finally, let me take a recent and as yet unresolved case. On 31 October 1993, four prisoners on death row at St. Catherine's Prison, Kingston, Jamaica– the same prison and cell-block where Pratt and Morgan were still being held– were shot dead by prison warders. It is not clear what happened: the Jamaican police are still investigating the matter. The prison authorities initially claimed that the prisoners had taken one or more warders hostage and say that at least three prison officers were injured.

However, it appears that the prisoners were shot in their cells through the bars of their cells and that no prison officers received serious injuries. 'It is difficult', as the Amnesty report on the incident puts it, 'to see how the inmates could have been shot in such a confined space without injuring warders' if warders were still being held hostage (Amnesty 1993a, 5-6). Moreover, it must be a matter of concern that two of the dead prisoners had reported receiving death threats from prison officers only three weeks previously, that other prisoners in the cell block maintain that one of the dead prisoners was pleading for his life when shot, and that there has been a history of deaths at the hands of officers at St Catherines in recent years. Another death row prisoner died from a fractured skull in 1989 after being beaten by officers with batons. No inquest was held for three years and though four warders were charged with murder in 1992, their trial has yet to take place. Three more prisoners died allegedly after being beaten by officers in May 1990. Amnesty has been unable to discover whether any action has been taken against officers in connection with this incident (Ibid. 8-9) but there is some evidence of a group of rogue warders at St. Catherine's who employ excessive force against prisoners and the reports of the Jamaican Ombudsman repeatedly refer to the lack of action by the prison authorities in response to allegations of ill-treatment.

In many prison systems there is a culture of staff violence which is matched only by an absence of effective staff accountability. In answer to the age-old question– *Quis custodiet ipsos custodes*? Who guards the guards?– the answer appears often to be: No one.

## Death at the hands of other detainees

There is little scope for rose-tinted spectacles when viewing the realities of custodial life. One of the essential 'pains of imprisonment' has always been that of living with other prisoners (Sykes 1958). Life in prison, ironically, is typically insecure. The prisoner is subject to the depredations of his or her fellows. The solidarity of prisoners, like the much vaunted solidarity amongst thieves, is largely chimerical. Bullying, sexual exploitation, racketeering in scarce commodities backed up by violent enforcement– these are the oft-cited characteristics of many closed institutions (Bunker 1980). And to the extent that this is the case, it follows that the duty of care which rests upon the state includes pre-eminently the duty of the state to protect individual prisoners from their fellow prisoners.

Death at the hands of fellow prisoners is most likely during disturbances, when scores are settled and pecking-orders are often brutally reinforced. Further, the employment by staff of 'underground' modes of control appears to develop or maintain precisely the same techniques among prisoners, often leading to an amplifying spiral of violence. During the riot at the New Mexico Penitentiary at Santa Fe in 1980, a prison which, according to the subsequent inquiry was brutally run (see Colvin 1982), 36 prisoners were killed, as many as 200 prisoners were beaten or raped and 90 given drug overdoses. St Catherine's Prison, Kingston, Jamaica, has also been characterised as much by prisoner on prisoner violence as staff on prisoner violence. In June 1991 four prisoners were killed by fellow prisoners during disturbances and a fifth reportedly died later of his injuries. The deaths were initially thought to be simply the product of inter-gang rivalry, but allegations later emerged to the effect that warders paid and armed prisoners to take out other prisoners who were witnesses in impending staff corruption trials (Amnesty International 1993a, 9).

In England and Wales, thankfully, deaths at the hands of fellow prisoners are relatively rare events. But we should not allow the fact that the media initially exaggerated and sensationalised the events at Strangeways Prison Manchester in April 1990– you will recall that some newspapers initially reported that between twelve and twenty prisoners were dead– to minimise the brutality of what occurred. One prisoner subsequently did die of his injuries and no one should have any doubt of the terrifying nature of the events. They were sufficient to make at least one Rule 43 prisoner try to hang himself rather than fall into the hands of the mob baying for his blood (Woolf Report 1991, para 3.201-3.205) and I can report interviewing victims of the Strangeways violence several weeks after the event who had scarcely slept since, such was the horror of the riot and the actions of some prisoners during the course of it. Ensuring security from fellow prisoners is as important an aspect of the duty of care which falls upon the prison authorities as the accountability owed by prison staff.

Further, it would appear that the British literature on prison life has under-stated the insecurity which prisoners experience with regard to their fellow prisoners. The recently published National Prison Survey records that nine percent of prisoners report having been assaulted by another prisoner in the previous six months (Walmsley et.al. 1992). King and McDermott (forthcoming) report a slightly higher figure of 12.5 per cent of prisoners who say they have been assaulted by other prisoners in their current prison (it is not clear over what average time periods). However, as King and McDermott's more focused study demonstrates, these aggregate figures mask significant differences between prison and different prisoner groups. They found that black prisoners were more likely to report having been assaulted than white prisoners and the reported assault rate in the maximum security prison in which they worked was more than seven times as high than in the open prison. In Gartree almost a third of King and McDermott's respondents reported having been assaulted by a fellow prisoner and 12.9 percent said they had been sexually assaulted. In both the National Prison Survey and King and McDermott's surveys approximately a fifth of all prisoners reported that they did not feel safe from being bullied or injured by other prisoners.

*Death by suicide*

I shall say little about this form of death because the subject has been exhaustively reviewed in recent years (HMCIP 1990; Liebling 1992, 1994) and it is the focus of attention of most of the other papers in this collection.

Let me highlight only the connection with the issue I have just covered and that which follows, namely, deaths from natural causes. Prisoner suicide is sometimes precipitated by aggression and threats from fellow prisoners and it is usually associated with the miserable lives which prisoners have led prior to their incarceration. It frequently signals a life which, for one reason or another, has for the victim been reduced to the basics of animal existence. The humanity of the individual has been mentally tortured to the point of nothingness (see Scarry 1985) such that there is no wish to exist. I will illustrate the point briefly by reference to Lee Waite who at the age of 18 hanged himself in Feltham in August 1991.

At the inquest into Lee's death it appears, though none of this was said to be known to the officers responsible for the cell block in which he was housed, that Lee was repeatedly bullied during his short time at Feltham. His trainers and watch were taken from him during association. The pathologist found bruising to his buttocks and his anal passage was bruised and torn. She gave evidence that this sexual attack, which might have been carried out with a snooker cue, must have happened on the evening before he committed suicide, and must have been very painful: she would have expected him to have screamed. But the staff had apparently heard nothing and knew nothing (Howard League 1993, 6).

Careful reading of successive reports from the Chief Inspector of Prisons reveals that bullying is rife in many of our young offender and low security institutions (see HMCIP 1990, 1992, for two recent examples). Indeed the Chief Inspector's Inquiry into the riot at Wymott Prison last September revealed in the three month run-up to the riot no fewer than 17 assaults by prisoners on fellow prisoners were referred to the police for investigation. As one prisoner told the Inspectorate:

> I have never experienced a more frightening or barbaric place... The whole prison was a battleground... everyone knew about the drug problems... but no one, staff, education, probation and the inmates themselves, seemed to care about what was going on (HMCIP 1993).

Little wonder that in such environments prisoners reach the point of ultimate despair. Particularly if their life outside appears to them to have little meaning. The Royal Commission in Australia found that 30 of the 99 deaths of Aborigines under investigation resulted from hanging (Royal Commission 1991, Vol 1, 4). The life histories of most of these individuals make grim reading. Unemployed, separated from their families, uneducated and without qualifications, often chronic alcohol or substance abusers. Many of these victims would not have expected to live long in the so-called community had they not taken their own lives in custody.

*Death from natural causes*
Deaths from natural causes will occur in custody as they occur everywhere else: they are statistically to be expected. The rate at which they are to be expected will largely be dependent on the character of the population in custody– its age, gender, socioeconomic class, employment status, and so on– rather than what happens in custody. We should remind ourselves that in most jurisdictions the experience of custody is generally transitory. In England and Wales, for example, custody before charge in a police station averages between five and six hours (Brown 1989), and custody post-charge before a court appearance is usually only overnight. The vast majority of persons committed to prisons are there for days, weeks or months rather than years. Even when it comes to the sentenced population, of those in custody the longest, approximately 85 per cent are released within twelve months of receipt, when parole is taken into account (Morgan 1994, 903).

In most jurisdictions prisoners are typically male (usually 95 per cent) and young. The median and the modal age of prisoners in England and Wales, for example, is 25 or 26 years. Only some 400 out of 48,000 prisoners are over 60 years of age (Ibid, 909). Given this age distribution, the rate of natural deaths should be low. However, as we are all aware, custodial populations are generally unrepresentative of the population at large and the social character of custodial populations generally corresponds with indicators of bad health and poor life expectancy. I doubt this point needs underlining. The National Prison Survey for England and Wales, for example, indicates substantial over-representation of homelessness and unemployment prior to imprisonment and experience of community care during childhood (Walmsley et. al. 1992). Other surveys of the prisoner population indicate substantial proportions suffering from various mental disorders and, just as important from a physical health standpoint, high levels of substance dependency or abuse (Gunn et. al. 1991; Dell et. al. 1991). Custodial populations are invariably recruited from the most socio-economically marginal sections of the community, relatively deprived nutritionally, often dependent on drugs and alcohol, generally likely to have suffered the least satisfactory housing and often prey to the physical ailments and health risks that accompany a poor quality of life. The suicide rates for such populations in the community tends also to be high.

A stark example of this phenomenon is the position of the Aboriginal community in Australia, a group grossly over-represented in the custodial population, both in police stations and prisons. As one of the commentators who has done much to publicise the plight of the Aboriginal population has argued, the factors involved in Aboriginals dying in custody are the same factors which lead them to die outside.

'Some are dying from petrol sniffing or alcohol poisoning. Many are succumbing to diseases associated with squalor and poor nutrition. Some are being killed on the road or in brawls associated with alcohol abuse. An Aboriginal man and women in Australia in the late 1980s has a life expectancy seventeen years less than his or her white fellow Australian' (Graham 1989, 15).

These poor health factors were explored in detail by the Royal Commission. The Report revealed that the discrepancy in death rates between the Aboriginal and total Australian populations is greatest in the age range 35-44 years and that circulatory and respiratory diseases, including heart diseases, physical injuries and poisoning, largely account for these differences (Royal Commission 1991, Vol 3, 139-140). These factors critically affect the risk of death in and out of custody. Childhood malnutrition, with its legacy of impaired growth into adulthood, obesity in adulthood and its association with diabetes, sexually transmitted diseases including AIDS, hepatitis B, TB, psychotic mental disorders– all these conditions, in addition to alcoholism and petrol inhalation, contribute significantly to Aboriginal morbidity and mortality (Ibid. 140-2). What the Royal Commission analysis revealed is that the large number of Aboriginal deaths in custody was primarily the consequence of the over-representation of Aboriginals in custody. In fact, given the high death rates for Aboriginals generally, their death rate in prison was lower than that to be expected for Aboriginals generally, though the death rate in police custody was higher than that expected (Ibid. 148). And it is at this point that one moves to the question of whether the quality of health care in custody is adequately related to the typical health needs of the custodial population. As far as police custody in Australia was concerned, it clearly was not.

Finally, both in relation to the Australian data and the situation elsewhere, we should remember that for a substantial minority of persons, perennial custody is a feature of their impoverished lives. The revolving door between hostel life, rootlessness and rooflessness, police custody, prison custody and, often, mental hospital. As spectacular as their over-representation in custody, is the far higher recidivism rate of Aborigines in Australia compared to non-Aborigines– almost twice as likely to reoffend and subsequently to be incarcerated (Broadhurst and Maller 1990). For many of the persons whose deaths in custody the Royal Commission individually investigated, custody was a regular, distressing and depressing part of the downward spiral of their lives. The same is true in England and Wales.

Let me conclude this typology of death with a recent case from France which possibly provides a suitable bridge to a brief consideration of the duties which fall on custodians. On 11 December 1993 a Gabonese prisoner died of starvation in the Bois d'Arcy Jail, Yvelines in the Departement of Versailles. He had been sentenced to four months imprisonment for an immigration-related offence. He shared a cell with a fellow black Gabonese who the authorities later described as 'disturbed' (*Le Monde*, 5 and 6 January 1994). He was never visited. When received into prison he weighed 53.6 kilos. When he died, three months later, he weighed 30.6 kilos. When his cell was examined following his death, there were found in his cupboard 15 baguettes. No one apparently had noticed that he was not eating but wasting away. I suppose we must say that he died from natural causes. Or was it suicide? It was certainly, as one prison officer was reported to have said, 'a death due to indifference'.

This French case illustrates a general theme. The five-fold typology I have outlined is not intended to be watertight and is far from watertight. Prisoner-on-prisoner or staff-on-prisoner violence may lead to suicide. And many so-called natural deaths are the result of a lack of care that can sometimes reasonably be typified as constructive murder or even genocide. In some countries such descriptions are not exaggerations.

## CARE AND ACCOUNTABILITY

In keeping with the international and generalised approach I have adopted from the outset, let us try to establish principles and delineate conceptual connections with which to develop a preventive framework for the different categories of death in custody outlined above.

First, deaths in custody are best avoided by our taking an abolitionist stance. In the case of certain categories of death in custody– authorised executions, extra-judicial executions and 'disappearances'– there is no alternative but for the international community and individual states to prohibit such punishments and actions in law. The death penalty is still recognised by many states as a lawful and desirable penalty whereas extra-judicial executions and 'disappearances' are generally unlawful. What is lacking is the political will or ability to ensure that the perpetrators of such acts are treated as criminal offenders, brought to justice and punished with sanctions commensurate with the gravity of the offence. It must be regarded as constructive murder to order or request someone to carry out an extra-judicial killing, to provide intelligence or weapons or other material assistance to enable the deed to be carried out, or to cover up the crime by falsifying records and so on. Further, police and security forces must be instructed that they have a duty to refuse to carry out instructions to engage in such acts and that the fact that they were instructed to do so will not constitute a defence.

All deaths in custody will best be avoided by our employing the *minimum use of custody*: employing summons rather than arrest; providing community care rather than institutional settings for the mentally disordered; granting bail, conditional or unconditional, more generously; using community penalties rather than imprisonment. It may also mean decriminalising certain offences. In Australia, for example, Aborigine deaths in custody occurred mostly in police custody, it was in police custody that Aborigines were most over-represented and their most frequent instant and past offence was drunkenness. It was not sufficient merely to decriminalise drunkenness– indeed in some states that measure alone actually served to increase the use of police stations on grounds of personal protection without the need to complete paperwork. What was needed were alternative facilities, detoxification centres, shelters and so on (Royal Commission 1991, Vol 3).

The *minimum use of custody* principle also means limiting the *duration* and *depth* of custody: setting custodial time limits for those refused bail; achieving the general reduction of sentencing tariffs; increasing the proportion of prisoners held in low security categories and accommodation; and so on.

The use of custody will continue, however, and, in my judgement, defensibly so. In which case we have to establish how the use of custody can be made compatible with *care* and *accountability*.

Persons in custody are peculiarly vulnerable and dependant. I will not spell out the case for vesting positive rights in prisoners and mental hospital patients: that case has been eloquently and in my judgement persuasively expounded elsewhere (Richardson 1985, 1993). Nor will I detail the case for providing powerful safeguards to protect detainees in police custody: I shall take those arguments more or less for granted. I shall simply assert that because of the peculiar vulnerability of persons in custody, because they are in the hands of the state, because the state exercises complete control over them, it follows that the state should take responsibility for them and owes a correlative duty for their care. In England and Wales the prison authorities owe a common law duty of care to prisoners to take reasonable care for their safety (see Livingstone and Owen 1993, Chapter 3). I do not think that duty is yet interpreted in an adequately robust manner and I think there is a case for stipulating more precisely what those duties should comprise and what standards of care should be met (Morgan 1993). Nevertheless the state's duty exists in embryonic form.

This duty includes the duty to exercise control over and take responsibility for the actions of prisoners one to another. This goes to the heart of the issue of prisoner-on-prisoner violence. But it has to be conceded that there are difficult issues to resolve and the principles I have outlined may sometimes be in conflict. The case of *Palmer* illustrates the dilemma.

Palmer was stabbed in the stomach by a fellow prisoner who had been convicted of three murders. The assault took place in a workshop where both men worked. The assailant was said to be 'very dangerous to anybody in the prison, staff and inmates'. But the judge refused to rule as negligent the decision of the prison authorities to let the offending prisoner work in association:

> Those in charge of prisoners have a difficult task. Clearly, except in extreme cases, of which obviously there are some, those responsible for prisoners cannot keep prisoners permanently locked up or segregated from other prisoners. In addition it is necessary, or certainly desirable wherever possible, to provide suitable employment for individual prisoners.

Whether the judge in *Palmer* weighed the conflict between the duty of care and the need to ensure the minimum use of custody correctly I cannot say. But it is clear that there sometimes is a conflict between the duty of care and employing the minimum depth of custody which will not easily be resolved.

Perhaps more easy to assess is what I take to be the duty to ensure that the standards that prevail in custody are at least commensurate with those that prevail in the community and that they are adequate to meet the needs of the custodial population. The first part of this equation we may term *normalisation* (King and Morgan 1980) and regrettably the standard is often not met. Consider the case of *Knight*.

Knight committed suicide in prison. It was acknowledged that the psychiatric services available in the prison, where many prisoners were mentally disturbed, were not up to the standard that would be required in an outside hospital. But the judge held that the standard of care provided for a mentally ill prisoner detained in a prison hospital was not required to be as high as the standard required outside. Prison hospitals performed different functions and the duty of care had to be tailored to these different functions. Psychiatric hospitals had a duty to cure whereas prison hospitals had a duty to detain and prevent patients injuring themselves. The standards had to be assessed relative to the resources available to medical staff in the prison. It had to be acknowledged that 'resources available for the public service are limited and that the allocation of resources is a matter for parliament'.

Whatever the relative standards now attained in prison health care units the decision in *Knight* seems to me to be a lamentable one. No adequate standard by which prison hospitals are to be judged was specified. And the suggestion that prison hospitals should not be judged by the same standards that apply in the community seems to suggest that prisoners forfeit not just their liberty but their right to medical treatment equal to that which they might receive in the community. In this sense we lack, as many countries lack, the application of a constitutional doctrine of the sort that is applied in the United States. In the United States it is no defence to the charge that prison conditions are unconstitutional– generally that they breach the 8th Amendment prohibition of cruel and unusual punishment– to say that the prison authorities lacked the necessary resources to make them better. The state is not obliged to keep citizens in custody. It chooses to do so. And if it chooses to do so then it is under an obligation to ensure, by providing the necessary resources, that the conditions in which prisoners are held are constitutional. In England and Wales, to take the example illustrated in *Knight*, it is a matter of policy that mentally disordered persons are kept in prison rather than in hospital. The government has failed to institute measures or to provide resources to ensure that it is not so. How then can it be right to assess prison hospitals by standards different from those that apply in outside hospitals?

In conclusion, a few words about the relationship between care and accountability. One cannot be accountable to someone unless it is absolutely clear as to what one is accountable *for*. That means that effective accountability requires the specification of standards and that the implementation of those standards is recorded and monitored. It follows that accountability is necessarily a multi-faceted concept and mechanism. The chain of accountability is as strong as its weakest managerial link.

I suggest, therefore, that effective accountability has *political*, *legal*, *managerial* and *operational* dimensions. One dimension is unlikely to work without the other. All serve to reinforce the other. Law is certainly not enough not least because in many jurisdictions there is a disastrous gap between the law in the books and the law as it is applied.

*Political* accountability, to a democratic body, stands at the apex of the *managerial* accountability chain whereby senior personnel ensure that standards are met, instructions are followed, decisions are made according to given criteria, and so on. Political accountability will comprise a balance between its explanatory form (ex post facto explanation as to why discretion was exercised in a particular way) and its directive form (were instructions followed and, if not, should sanctions be applied?). There is need for *legal* accountability also. In England and Wales we have moved quite far along the legal dimension in relation to police custody by means of the Police and Criminal Evidence Act 1984. I do not say that the system is without its problems. There are certainly critics aplenty (see McConville et.al. 1991; Sanders 1994) – but the safeguards now in place for suspects in police custody meet those that have been stipulated by the CPT (Council of Europe 1991), they are arguably superior to those provided in many other European jurisdictions (see Council of Europe 1993, for example) and the CPT has been relatively complimentary about police custodial arrangements in England and Wales (Council of Europe 1991a).

The same cannot be said about conditions in some British prisons, which the CPT has described as 'inhuman and degrading' (Ibid, para 57). I suggest that there remains a distinct absence of legal accountability with regard to our prisons (Morgan 1993) and though the Woolf report provides an agenda for reform, current developments do not augur well for their implementation. As far as *operational* accountability is concerned– by which I mean that services operate in such a manner that their delivery is transparent both to those that consume them and the public at large – all forms of custody present obvious difficulties. But it is not impossible to achieve greater transparency and a good deal has been done in recent years to ensure that the hidden world of custody is opened up to greater public scrutiny. In addition to the rights of suspects specified in the Police and Criminal Evidence Act– the right to have a third party informed of one's detention, the right to legal advice, the provision of 'appropriate adults', etc– we have introduced lay visitors to police stations schemes (Kemp and Morgan 1990). And, in relation to prisons, there is to be appointed an independent Prison Ombudsman and we have removed the compromising disciplinary duties of boards of visitors so that, hopefully, they will in future act more single-mindedly and credibly as 'public watchdogs'.

But ultimately the provision of adequate standards in custody, and the development of a caring environment within them will depend on integrating the services provided in custody as closely as possible with those that are provided in the community (the essence of *normalisation*) and by developing high standards of professionalism among custodial staff. Custodial institutions must be neither cultural or physical enclaves. This proposition lay at the heart of the Woolf recommendations that there be developed 'community prisons'. That prisons should be located close to prisoners' community ties, that visiting and other contact arrangements should be more generous and humanely organised and that community agencies should be involved in the delivery of prison services (NACRO 1994).

Most deaths in custody are the consequence of despair borne of a sense of total rejection within an impoverished environment that seems to offer no hope. Prisons are not, by their very nature, positive places. But they need not be places of total despair. They can be places providing reasonable standards in which to live and work. They can by their arrangements safeguard human dignity. They can ensure that contact with the outside world is facilitated and maintained. They can provide opportunities for prisoners to think positively about their future beyond the walls. And they should. Not least because most prisoners are in custody for a relatively short time and because the purpose of custody is supposed to be crime prevention. If, as the Woolf Report underlined, prisoners leave prison alienated and disaffected then the prison will have subverted the central purpose of the criminal justice system of which it is a part (Woolf Report 1991, para 10.19).

In the pages that follow there is much discussion about the prevention of deaths in custody, suicides in particular, by screening prisoners to identify risk and take special preventive measures. Such programmes are no doubt necessary. However, our capacity to predict risk is for the most part poor. Most deaths in custody are best prevented by ensuring that the quality of prisoners' lives is raised generally and that the duties on the state to care and be accountable are developed and rigorously enforced. It is a sad truth that in many parts of the world justice stops at the prison gates and there is an almost complete lack of accountability on the part of custodians. It follows that in my submission preventing deaths in custody is for the most part not a medical issue which can be reduced to questions of individual pathology. It is very largely a question of asserting and safeguarding human rights.

**Note**
1. Personal communication from Professor Roy King, University College, Bangor, North Wales.

# Three

# Suicide and institutions

*Gethin Morgan*

The word institution has been criticised a great deal. The Oxford Dictionary defines it as follows:

> An institution is an establishment, organisation or association, instituted for the promotion of some object, for example one of public or general utility, religious, charitable, educational etc. For example, a church, school, college, hospital, asylum, reformatory, mission, or the like.

The word is indeed now tarnished. In psychiatry it is equated with totalitarian authority and loss of freedom for the individual. And so it may be. But as someone who has worked as a psychiatrist for many years I have watched the way in which the good in institutions can be jettisoned, ignored and rubbished. I refer especially to the old style Victorian mental asylums. Of course some people were damaged by them and one example of this is the institutionalisation process involving loss of personal dignity, autonomy and drive. But that should not mean that the whole system was necessarily bad. The attack on the psychiatric institution began some thirty years ago and I quote Enoch Powell:

> There they stand isolated, majestic, imperious, brooded over by the gigantic water tower - the asylums which our forefathers built with such immense solidity to express the notions of their day. Do not for a moment underestimate their powers of resistance to our assault.

Now in psychiatry any collection of inpatient beds of more than a very modest size is regarded in a pejorative way as an institution. We need to look very hard at the positive and negative aspects of such organisations whether they are hospitals or prisons and the main focus of my paper of course will be with regard to suicide prevention. First of all some facts. There has been much debate about whether suicides are mentally ill. Comprehensive studies in the community suggest that the great majority are unwell from the psychological point of view (Barraclough et al., 1974).

Table 1
Symptoms in 100 Suicides (During last one month)

| | |
|---|---|
| Looked Miserable | 69 |
| Insomnia | 76 |
| Taking Hypnotics | 64 |
| Weight Change | 66 |
| Looked Anxious | 60 |
| Complained of Sadness | 53 |
| Weight Loss | 53 |
| Difficulty in Working | 47 |
| Pessimistic/Hopeless | 43 |
| Anorexia | 44 |
| Less Social Activity | 40 |
| Self-Reproach | 36 |
| Poor Concentration | 35 |
| Weeping | 39 |

In institutions we meet of course selected samples. Undoubtedly in prison for example the proportion of suicides who may be regarded as mentally ill is probably very much smaller than those found in psychiatric hospitals. Lifestyle problems feature much more prominently in the prison group. In one series of 300 prison suicides only one third had a previous history of psychiatric contact and one quarter had previous psychiatric admission. I think we can safely assume however that whether in prison or otherwise we can expect the individual who proceeds to commit suicide to exhibit some kind of distress which we ought to be able to respond to appropriately. The proportion of suicides occurring in individuals who appear perfectly well at the time is undoubtedly very small, probably less than 10 per cent as it occurs in the overall community. This has obvious implications for healthcare professionals and personnel in the prison service with regards to suicide prevention.

The recent increase in suicide rates in young males may have relevance to the increase in suicide amongst the prison population. Dooley's analysis of 300 suicides amongst prisoners in this country reveals the increased susceptibility to suicide amongst those on remand compared with the general population. 47.1 per cent of all prison suicides occur amongst those people who are on remand whereas only 11.1 per cent of the overall prison population are remand prisoners (Dooley, 1990a).[1]

Overall in the community suicide rates in males are greater than those in females by about approximately 3 : 1. In prisons this ratio is 10 : 1. In analysing this of course the total number at risk in each sex must be taken into account.

### METHODS USED

Availability of agent clearly dictates the pattern of methods used in various settings. In the community the most recent picture in males reveals the use of car exhaust as the most common method, closely followed by hanging. In females overdose of drugs remains the most common method.

Table 2
Main Methods of Suicide 1989-1990*

|  | Males | Females |  |
|---|---|---|---|
|  | % | % |  |
| Car Exhaust | 30 | 11 |  |
| Self Poisoning | 15 | 42 |  |
| Hanging | 28 | 17 |  |
| Firearms | 5 | 1 |  |
| Drowning | 2.5 | 6 |  |

Source: *OPCS*

In Dooley's series of prison suicides some 90 per cent were by hanging, usually from window bars.

### CAUSES OF SUICIDE

There is general agreement that many different kinds of factors play a part in leading to suicide interacting together in a pattern which varies from one individual to another.

Table three illustrates the main categories of causes which are involved. Healthcare professionals of course focus particularly on the personal factors of illness and personality vulnerability although the full significance of these can only be evaluated in

Table 3
Causes of Suicide

| | |
|---|---|
| *Sociodemographic*: | Elderly |
| | Minority Ethnic Groups |
| | Social Context |
| | Cultural (attitudes) |
| | Employment |
| *Events*: | Loss |
| | Imprisonment |
| *Access to Means*: | Domestic Gas |
| | Firearms |
| *Personal*: | Illness (physical, mental) |
| | Personality |
| *Process of care* | |

the context of socio-demographic variables, life-events and access to the means used. Moreover the process of care which we bring to bear on persons who receive our help needs to be scrutinised on the assumption that the establishment of codes of practice, the acquisition of specialised skills and our willingness to learn from experience may all contribute significantly to suicide prevention. Much consideration has been given to the possible causes of the dramatic increases which have occurred in suicide rates among young adult males. Is it possible for example that young males have more ready access to motor vehicle exhaust fumes than do females? Links with unemployment are not easy to disentangle, certainly in terms of trends with time. Also relevant may be the large increases in alcohol and substance misuse related deaths in young adult males, both of which have been greater in males during the past two decades. Ease of access to method used is illustrated by the coal-gas story of the 1960s in the United Kingdom and of course access to fire-arms in the United States of America. The debate concerning antidepressant drugs is the modern counterpart of access to method.

### THE MENTAL STATE OF THE SUICIDAL

In those who are mentally ill we can expect to find the relevant characteristic symptoms and signs. Thus the very depressed individual will tend to have a profound sense of hopelessness about the future with marked self-blame and a schizophrenic illness might cause florid disorders of thinking in the form of delusional ideas as well as hallucinatory experiences. The common state of mind whatever the underlying cause is one of despair, narrowing of thinking into a polarisation which involves seeing the future as a choice either between death or a few unacceptable alternatives. There may be marked ambivalence right to the very end and this is a very important theme to exploit in reaching out to suicidal persons. Edwin Shneidman has described the basic fundamental mental state of the suicidal individual as Psychache in the following terms:

> The hurt, anguish, soreness, aching, psychological pain in the psyche, the mind. It is intrinsically psychological - the pain of excessively felt shame, or humiliation, or loneliness, or fear, or angst, or dread of growing old, or of dying badly, or whatever. When it occurs its reality is introspectively undeniable. Suicide occurs when the psychache is deemed by that person to be unbearable.

I think he makes an important point, that is, however we may construe the diagnosis the final common pathway is the same, and to be understood through the eyes of each individual personality.

### PROBLEMS OF ASSESSMENT

I now come to the second major part of my paper and first of all I want to say something about attitudes to suicide prevention. Extended discussion with healthcare professionals quickly reveals a variety of attitudes to the problem of suicide prevention and its feasibility. Many of these are negative. They signify a degree of reservation and lack of resolve which though not yet studied systematically nevertheless needs to be addressed effectively, otherwise the challenge of suicide prevention is compromised. It is perhaps not surprising that given the many clinical hazards which may complicate the assessment and management of suicide risk the response should be mixed in this way. There is little reward in suicide prevention because we can never be certain when it has been achieved. This has been expressed elegantly by George Murphy:

> If suicide prevention is successful the patient will live. A suicide will have been prevented. Yet to quantify this effect is impossible. It is important to realise that the absence of a suicide generates no data. Thus we can

never prove what has been accomplished. Yet we can hardly doubt that it occurs.

Several negative attitudes are commonly expressed and I will discuss them briefly in turn

*Suicide is a private and personal matter and whether or not to commit it should be left for each individual to decide*

This implies that others should not attempt to intervene. I suggest that such a view is inappropriate, certainly with regards to the role of healthcare professional if only because the patient is highly likely to be ambivalent about suicide and may well be testing our resolve before making a final decision about whether or not to proceed with it.

*Not all suicides can be prevented. By focusing on those which occur we merely accentuate the guilt feelings of those who did their best under difficult circumstances, yet failed to prevent a suicide*

A co-ordinated campaign to improve suicidal prevention strategies should not in any way imply that all suicides are preventable and need not accentuate guilt in those who have been involved with patients who proceed to commit suicide.

*There is no prospect of reducing suicide rates unless adverse economic and social factors are dealt with and these are not within the power of healthcare professionals or others to influence*

Although adverse economic and social factors are undoubtedly relevant to the aetiology of suicide if only contextually, the important and almost universal role of illness and personality variables cannot be denied. To these should be added the way in which we regard suicide and the clinical procedures which are used in trying to prevent it.

*It is not feasible to expect healthcare professionals to contribute to a reduction in suicide rate when suicide is such a rare event*

Is suicide such a rare event as to mean that it is unreasonable to expect us to detect those individuals who are seriously at risk and so distinguish them from other key persons? It has been estimated that a general practitioner might see just one such patient a year. Yet comparison in inception rates reveals that the incidence of suicide is no less than that of common diseases such as multiple sclerosis, ulcerative colitis and Crohn's Disease.

Table 4
Incidence of Disorders per 100,000 Population

| | |
|---|---|
| Crohn's Disease | 7.1 |
| Ulcerative Colitis | 10-12 |
| Multiple Sclerosis | 0.5-9.5 |
| Suicide in England and Wales | 7.4 |

Comparison of morbidity should take into account the wake of emotional distress in relatives and key others following a suicide. Suicide in medical practice may be relatively uncommon because doctors have been so vigilant in trying to prevent it and the ultimate statistic should not be used in a negative way.

*Persons who commit suicide are reluctant to seek help before the event*

As a generalisation, this is not true. Current research has demonstrated that about half of persons in the community who proceed to commit suicide have made some contact and sought help some time during the previous month.

Table 5
Suicides: Contact with Services

| | Avon 1959 (Seager & Flood) n=325 | Wessex 1974 (Barraclough et al) n=100 | Avon 1992 (Vassilas (& Morgan) n=144 |
|---|---|---|---|
| | % | % | % |
| Under 35 years | 16 | 11 | 37 |
| In Previous Month: | | | |
| Mental Illness Service | 16 | 18 | 21 |
| General Practitioner | 41 | 59 | 38 |
| Any NHS Contact | 46 | 69 | 46 |

There is no reason to believe that persons in prison are likely to behave differently. It has to be admitted however that young men are no more likely to seek help than do controls of the same age and this poses a very severe challenge to our suicide prevention strategies. Whether the willingness to turn for help amongst young men in prison is of the same magnitude remains uncertain.

CLINICAL SKILLS AND THE PROCESS OF CARE

It is clear that suicide may be caused by a wide variety of factors, some personal, others demographic or situational which interact in different ways depending upon the individual concerned. Some of these are not readily accessible to the influence of those responsible for delivering care. We do have a responsibility however to ensure that codes of practice are not only understood but valued and observed by all concerned.

What are the principles of good effective care? Are they put into practice and what needs to be done to ensure that they are? First of all, interviewing skills. The technique involved in detecting suicidal ideation during interviewing is indeed challenging and such skills need to be taught well. The sequence of questioning about suicidal ideas must not amount to an interrogation but should move sensitively and progressively on to what is a most distressing topic for the patient concerned. The understanding of the state of mind mentioned earlier is crucial: the ambivalence; the role of impulse and opportunity, perhaps reluctance to admit ideas of self-destruction, variability in degrees of distress, frequency of anger and even provocative behaviour apart from typical features of depression: all these may mislead the unwary. Once suicidal ideation has been detected it is then necessary to evaluate its precise meaning, intensity and the likelihood of it being acted out as well as the risk to others.

RISK FACTORS

It has long been a mainstay of suicide risk assessment to search for factors which have been shown to have a statistical relationship with suicide; thus the association of increasing age, male gender, social isolation, loss events, diagnostic categories such as depression, alcoholism, substance misuse, schizophrenia, intractable physical illness is taught as basic knowledge:

*High Risk Factors for Suicide:*
- Males > Females
- Older Age Group
- Divorced > Widowed > Single
- Living Alone
- Socially Isolated
- Unemployed/Retired
- Past Psychiatric History

- Family History of Affective Illness
- Previous Self-harm
- Recent Event: Bereavement/Separation/Loss of Job
- Poor Physical Health
- Evidence of Depressive Illness
- Abuse of Alcohol

Yet the problem of low specificity and sensitivity adds greatly to the uncertainty of the prediction process. Within these diagnostic groups further attempts have been made to identify sub-groups of particularly high risk but these still suffer from problems of low specificity and sensitivity.

Table 6
Diagnostic Groups: Suicide Risk

| Diagnosis | Risk Factors |
| --- | --- |
| Depression | Male, older, single/separated, socially isolated, previous deliberate self-harm, persistent insomnia, self-neglect, impaired memory, agitation. |
| Schizophrenia | Male, younger, previous deliberate self-harm, and depressive episodes with anorexia, weight loss; more serious illness, recurrent relapse. |
| Alcohol/Drug Addiction | Adverse life events, previous deliberate self harm, depressed mood, serious physical complications. |

Pokorny has commented that we who look after individuals work in a time frame consisting of minutes, hours or days in dealing with a suicidal crisis whereas the frame of months or years is used by clinical researchers. In spite of these limitations however traditional risk factors remain useful providing they are used appropriately, if only as a double-check on clinical decisions based on individual assessment and on more immediate issues. There remains much to be done in widening the nature of the data which are scrutinised for possible risk factors. In particular the way individuals relate to others, for example in a hospital ward or in a prison setting. The importance of terminal progressive alienation of suicidal individuals from those around them needs especially to be understood more fully.

### CLINICAL PROCEDURES

The hazards and uncertainties of managing suicidal risk in a hospital setting are illustrated in findings from a study based in Avon, UK which reviewed a consecutive series of unexpected deaths in people who were either psychiatric inpatients at the time they had died, or they had been discharged within the previous eight weeks. In twenty of the twenty-seven suicides the seriousness of the risk was not fully recognised and in only ten of them had it been considered necessary to take special precautions to prevent it. Eleven of the suicides had resumed living in the community in various ways before they died. A significant number were able to leave the ward without permission. Such findings reflected uncertainties and hazards in predicting suicide risk rather than deficiencies in quality of care. Misleading clinical improvement in the absence of resolution of situational difficulties as well as alienation from others seemed relevant in 80% of this series.

Table 7
Bristol Suicides: Possible Reasons Suicide was not Prevented

|  | *(n=27)* |
| --- | --- |
| Significant Clinical Improvement | 14 |
| *(problems remained unresolved in 12)* | |
| Alienation | 15 |
| Clinical Improvement +/- Alienation | 22 |

### MANAGEMENT

The way in which suicidal patients should be supervised has fuelled much debate. The well known danger times – soon after psychiatric admission, probably reflecting to some extent the remand situation in prison; times of staff change-over; or soon after discharge - should be well understood. The rigid clinical procedures used in Victorian asylums, whereby suicidal patients were subjected to the suicidal caution card practice and were signed for as responsibility for their management passed between various members of staff, evokes an unpleasant picture of care in the 19th century. It happened however to be quite good in preventing suicide, the patient effectively being under intensive surveillance: yet the overall cure rates were not high. The reaction against this was to assume that an open-door policy with few restrictions, but good communications between all members of staff was the best ward policy in caring for the suicidal patient. Yet this in turn failed to recognise the need for intensive care when the risk of suicide is high. The best approach is to aim at an alliance with the patient against suicidal ideas with clearly understood levels of supportive observation according to the degree of risk. In hospital practice the need to set limits upon challenging behaviour when it arises for reasons other than suicide risk often complicates things considerably. This is an area in which our clinical skills are tested to the full. We often are wrong in our judgement as to exactly what to expect, how much an individual can achieve, and what we could expect of that person in setting treatment strategies. Much of my research has been concerned with the way in which suicidal patients become progressively alienated from others. I believe this is liable to occur particularly when recurrent depression is encountered, and the individual fails to respond to our therapeutic overtures, or alternatively the individual is very challenging, perhaps aggressive towards us and we need to be vigilant about our own negative responses which may reinforce such terminal alienation and make it finally impossible for the individual to get any help at all.

It must be obvious by now that in my view there is a great deal that we, who work in institutions of various kinds, need to do in the cause of suicide prevention. Perhaps the most important of all is that we should refuse to adopt negative attitudes, institutionalised attitudes if you like, those which may prevent us from even trying to prevent suicide or which lead us to denigrate in all kinds of ways the persons who are at risk. Rigid demarcation of responsibility is one way in which we can become institutionalised. For example one who takes the trouble to anticipate the pending weekend with someone at risk, say a person who attends a clinic or a surgery late on a Friday afternoon when we are all keen to get away, one who rehearses the likely difficulties and plans of action if crisis occurs, where to get help, makes it clear that it is worthwhile trying. Such an approach can be far more effective than one which is based on encyclopaedic knowledge of risk factors yet which does not attempt to reach out to the individual concerned.

Innovation and enthusiasm are important. I turn again to Edwin Shneidman and I quote:

> The main point of work with lethally orientated persons
> - in the give and take of talk, the advice, the

interpretations, the listening - is to increase that individual's psychological sense of possible choices and the sense of being emotionally supported. Relatives, friends and colleagues should, after they are assessed to be on the lifeside of the individual's ambivalence, be closely involved in the total treatment process. Suicide prevention is not best done as a solo practice. A combination of consultation, ancillary therapies, and the use of all the interpersonal and community resources that one can involve is in general the best way of proceeding.

And in an attempt to decrease the conceptual constriction:

anything and almost everything possible to cater to the infantile idiosyncrasies, the dependency needs, the sense of pressure and futility, the feelings of hopelessness and helplessness that the individual is experiencing.

Before concluding, let me give as an example one innovation which we adopted in Avon. We call it the Green Card Study, which involved giving to first time drug-overdosers a little Green Card which invited the patient to come for help at an early stage should any difficulties occur:

### The Green Card

*This card explains how to get immediate help from the hospital if, in the future, you feel despairing, unable to cope, or have thoughts of harming yourself.*

*At any time of day, or night, a doctor in psychiatry is available to speak to you on the phone, or to see you in person at the hospital.*

*The doctor will discuss your problem with you and tell you how he/she can help. If you would like a break from home, to help put your problem in perspective, the doctor will arrange for you to stay in one of our wards overnight.*

The random sample of 50 per cent received this card and the result was a reduction not only in repetition of self-harm but also in the amount of seeking help from others such as general practitioners and specialists. In other word having a lifeline seemed to enable people to cope. Only a few needed to make contact and this they did usually by telephone.

Table 8
Deliberate Self-Harm: Secondary Prevention (The Bristol Green Card Study)

|  | No Repeat | Repeat | Total |
|---|---|---|---|
| Green Card | 87 | 6 | 93 |
| No Green Card | 82 | 17 | 99 |
| Total | 169 | 23 | 192 |

$X^2 = 5.226$ $df=1$ $p<0.05$

It must be obvious, in summary that I believe there is a great deal that we who work in institutions can do in the cause of suicide prevention. Above all we need to acknowledge that deceptively simple techniques such as listening can get people through what might seem irreversible crises. The Samaritans can teach us so much on how to do this. The greatest disservice we can do to any other, either by way of what we do, or do not do, is to confirm their despair.

Editor's Note
1. This figure is now 25 per cent.

# Four

# Prison suicide: What progress research?

*Alison Liebling*

Since I did it last time, I have thought about doing it again. I've even thought about overdosing. These people, right, they think, 'Oh, he's trying to commit suicide, he's daft; he don't know what he's doing'. But we think - I've done it - we know what it feels like to be hurt. They don't. All they're thinking is, 'He's daft'. They don't know what you're going through. They don't know what your mind's thinking. You can't talk to no-one in here, so you take it out on yourself, and that's why the majority of people commit suicide in prison, because they can't talk to no-one. (Prisoner)

### INTRODUCTION

This chapter looks briefly at some of the results from two long-term research projects carried out by the author (Liebling, 1992) and with a colleague (Liebling and Krarup, 1993) on suicides and suicide attempts in prison. It outlines some of the limitations of previous research, showing that important differences between types of prison suicide must be taken into account in order to understand the dynamics of such crises. Most important is the recognition of the limitations inherent in statistical approaches to the problem. Verbal accounts from prisoners must be included in any meaningful research endeavour.

### THE PROBLEM OF PRISON SUICIDE

The rate of prison suicide in England and Wales (and elsewhere in Europe, in the USA, Australia and Canada) has remained disproportionately high since its drastic increase in 1987. The Table below shows how the increase in prison suicide has been larger than any increase in the average daily population (ADP) in custody in any one year.

Table 1

Self-Inflicted Deaths in Prison in England and Wales 1985 - 1993

|      | Adult Male | Male Under 21 | Female | Total no | ADP* | Rate per 100,000** |
|------|------------|---------------|--------|----------|--------|---------------------|
| 1985 | 26 | 3 | 1 | 29 | 46,278 | 62.7 |
| 1986 | 18 | 3 |   | 21 | 46,889 | 44.8 |
| 1987 | 39 | 7 | - | 46 | 48,963 | 93.9 |
| 1988 | 28 | 9 | - | 37 | 49,949 | 74.0 |
| 1989 | 35 | 11 | 2 | 48 | 49,800 | 96.4 |
| 1990 | 39 | 10 | 1 | 50 | 47,936 | 104.3 |
| 1991 | 37 | 5 | - | 42 | 46,472 | 90.4 |
| 1992 | 32 | 7 | 2 | 41 | 44,628 | 91.9 |
| 1993 | 41 | 7 | - | 48 | 46,976 | 102.2 |

*\* ADP = Average Daily Population (includes police cells; different sources give slightly different figures; source: prison service annual reports)*
*\*\* Rate per 100,000 ADP*

The rate of prison suicide during 1984 - 1987 was 56 per 100,000 ADP (Dooley, 1990a: 41). The total figures can be misleading for two reasons. First, the problems inherent in measuring the rate of suicide in a non-static population are legion (see Liebling, 1992; O'Mahony, 1994). It is arguable that a satisfactory rate should take into account both the number of receptions entering custody in a year and the 'time-at-risk' (that is, the length of time spent in custody) of each prisoner. The rate should also be compared with the rate of the equivalent adjusted population in the community (see Winfree, 1985) - that is, a population adjusted to match the prison population in terms of age, sex, ethnic breakdown and social class. Such an exercise is extremely difficult and the relevant data are not available. Prison suicide rates can only be used as a guide to the size and nature of the problem. Some suicides are narrowly averted. This is more likely in the prison setting than in the community due to the closer surveillance of prisoners and the limited methods of suicide available. Others may still be misclassified, despite recent prison service efforts to include all self-inflicted deaths in their annual figures, whether or not they receive a suicide verdict at the inquest. It is possible that classification differs between unnatural deaths in prison (where an inquest must be held in front of a jury) and those which occur the community setting (where inquests in front of a jury are not necessary; see Liebling, 1992).

Secondly, there is no single profile of the suicidal prisoner. The Figure below shows three of the main and largely distinct groups of prisoners who have taken their own lives in custody in sufficient numbers between 1988 and 1992 to constitute such an identifiable group.

Figure 1
Three Types of Prison Suicide

|  | Proportion of total suicides | Average age | Important features |
|---|---|---|---|
| Psychiatrically Ill | 25-30% | 30+ | Infrequent previous self-injury; single; motivation = fear, loss of control, alienation, etc. |
| Life Sentence Prisoners | 10-15% | 30+ | Infrequent previous self-injury; often on remand; some well into sentence; motivation = guilt/no future. |
| Poor Copers | 50-60% | Under 26 | More impulsive, situation-specific; previous self-injury frequent; motivation = fear, helplessness, distress. |

A careful look at the details of each case (for more detail, see Liebling and Krarup, 1993; Prison Service, 1993) suggests that there are at least three (but probably more, including sex offenders, short sentence prisoners, remand prisoners, etc.) fairly distinct types of prison suicide, which if considered together, give a distorted picture of the nature of the 'prison suicide profile' appearing in most of our previous research (see especially Lloyd, 1990 for a review; also Burtch and Ericson, 1979; Dooley, 1990a).

It has been known for some time that one of the most significant differences between suicides in prison and those in the community is that only a third of those suicides occurring in custody can be shown to have been suffering from a psychiatric illness or disorder. In the community, this figure is closer to 90 per cent (see Liebling, 1992; Dooley, 1990a; Backett, 1988; Barraclough and Hughes, 1986). In the figure on p.43 (Figure 1), which has been compiled from prison service data made available from the Suicide Awareness Support Unit, it is shown that prisoners suffering from psychiatric illness constitute no more than a third of the total number of prison suicides in any one year. This is despite the high levels of psychiatric morbidity in the prison population as a whole (see Liebling, 1992; Dooley, 1990a; Gunn et al, 1991). They tend to be older than the average age of completed suicides. They may also differ in a number of other important respects, such as offence type and the significance of the situation in the onset of their suicidal action. Thus it can be argued that they constitute a distinct sub-group amongst prison suicides. Another distinct group requiring special consideration are life sentence prisoners - or those prisoners facing domestic homicide charges. West showed in 1965 that in the UK at least (but probably elsewhere, where the proportion of domestic homicides to stranger homicides is high) a third of all murders were followed by suicide (West, 1965). It is likely that many of these suicides will occur in custody. Again, this group differ in significant respects from other completed suicides, being slightly older than average and planning their suicides carefully, often taking their lives at later stages during custody. There is some evidence from the UK that these latter two groups may include an increasing number of prisoners facing charges for sexual violence.

Together, there two groups make up no more than 40 to 50 per cent of the total number of prison suicides in any one year. The presence of these two groups amongst the 'profiles' described in previous studies (see especially Lloyd, 1990; Topp, 1979; Hankoff, 1980; Danto, 1973, etc.) has been misleading, suggesting that prisoners charged with or convicted of violent offences and those serving longer than average sentences are more at risk of suicide than other prisoners. This may be true for certain groups, but as this paper will go on to show, it is not true for even a majority of prison suicides, which tend to occur disproportionately amongst the young, those with no psychiatric illness, and those charged with or convicted of common (acquisitive) crimes. This third but highly significant group can be described as the young prisoner (up to about age 26) with little or no psychiatric illness who cannot cope with the demands made by his or her environment.

These suicides (noted briefly in a very few other studies, such as Hatty and Walker, 1986), who constitute by far the largest group, may be impulsive, situationally-induced, and preventible. It is this group to whom the remainder of this chapter is dedicated.

## VULNERABILITY AND PRISON SUICIDE

Serious omissions, such as the tendency described above to see all prison suicides as alike, have been made in previous research. Other omissions include an over-reliance on statistical information, an almost exclusively medical model of suicide risk, the drive to predict suicide rather than a desire to understand it, and a failure to make the necessary connections between attempted suicide, self-injury and completed suicide. Each of these limitations will be briefly discussed below.

### The Statistical Fallacy

The clearest illustration of the dangers of a statistical approach to suicide is Dooley's recent finding that those self-inflicted deaths in prison not receiving suicide verdicts at inquests (but receiving other verdicts such as 'open', 'misadventure', 'accidental', 'lack of care' etc.) were significantly different from those receiving suicide verdicts (see Dooley, 1990b) over a fifteen year period. Unexpected groups such as the young, women, and those who had injured themelves before, were less likely to receive a verdict of suicide that other self-inflicted deaths in prison. This demonstrates that many of our previous studies and their profiles of 'the suicide risk' are seriously flawed, based as they are on suicides recorded as such by coroners. This argument can be extended to suicide attempts and self-injury, much of which remains unrecorded (see Liebling and Krarup, 1993; Home Office, 1990). Where such events are recorded, only selective and often poor quality information is included in the record.

### A MEDICAL MODEL OF SUICIDE RISK

The complex reasons for the medicalisation of suicide have been discussed elsewhere (see Liebling and Ward, 1994a; Liebling and Ward, 1994b; Jack, 1992). It is especially true of prison suicide that this drive to see suicide risk as a medical or psychiatric problem can be misleading (see Liebling, 1992). A 'pathology' model renders the behaviour meaningless (cp. Jack, 1992) and permits the use of negative labels for the prisoners' distress. The following brief extract from an interview with a 21 year old prisoner who had recently attempted suicide may illustrate this process:

Q: Have you ever seen a psychiatrist?
A: Yes, a couple of times.
Q: When was that?
A: Last time I tried to commit suicide.
Q: What did he/she say to you? Was your contact with the psychiatrist helpful?
A: He said I've got 'ASB'.
Q: 'ASB'? What is that?
A: 'Attention-Seeking Behaviour'.

That this 'diagnosis' was repeated so faithfully and seriously by the young prisoner during his interview was important. Other prisoners corrected information they assumed I might have found in their files during interviews, explaining that they had 'agreed with what the doctor had suggested', because 'I didn't know what else to say', or 'I didn't understand the questions', or 'I felt so stupid afterwards'. Perhaps the most frequent misunderstanding was the use of the term 'bored'. Many - especially young male - prisoners used this word as a shorthand for many different feelings which were difficult to describe. They did not readily use words like 'depression', 'distress' or 'pain', for many reasons (see Liebling, 1992; Gilligan, 1986) despite describing these sensations in many other ways at different moments during the interview. This use of the term 'bored' was often taken at face value and again used to judge the behaviour as ridiculous: 'He says he did it because he was bored!'. The exclamation mark illustrates an attitude from some professionals and some uniformed staff (see Morgan, this volume) which prisoners felt acutely. The difficulties and yet the significance of allowing sufficient time and encouragement to find the right words can be illustrated by the following brief extracts from interviews:

Q: Do you ever feel 'lethargic'?
A: (silence...) What does ' lethargic' mean?
Q: Well ... it means sort of not feeling interested in anything, bored, not feeling motivated to do anything, a bit down, lacking in energy...
A: (silence, whilst thinks) ...I think I have felt lethargic all my life! ... I like that - 'lethargic'..

This prisoner continued to come back to this word throughout the rest of the interview, with a delight that he had a new word which was meaningful to him, and which gave a satisfactory label to some of his feelings. A similar situation occurred with a young female prisoner, who had talked at length about her feelings towards the family she felt had let her down. She constantly used the word 'depressed'. She had expressed many times her frustration and anger at a series of disappointments and hurts throughout the interview, but she had not named these feelings:

Q: What is your most common feeling, most of the time?
A: (Silence...) ... I just feel depressed.
Q: ... You sometimes sound a little angry to me, too.
A: Angry? ...

She smiled as she used this word, perhaps for the first time. Later on during the interview, she commented that she thought she liked feeling angry. The new term gave her a sense of strength she had not acknowledged before. She discussed this at several stages towards the end of the interview.

The significance of the struggle to find 'the right' words is that without them, other words and other labels may be applied by professionals and others which can be destructive, negating and misleading. Once committed to prison files, the consequences of these labels can be most damaging. For whatever reason, and especially in the prison situation, there do not seem to be many medical or psychiatric labels available which bring with them positive or therapeutic consequences for the recipient (see Jack, 1992; also Sim, 1990).

### Predicting or Understanding Suicide?

Social science has historically been concerned with a desire to understand, to improve, and inevitably to some extent, to control. The adoption of scientific methodology and ideology has achieved for social science a partial respectability not always afforded to other academic disciplines. Debates continue about the applicability of statistical and scientific methodologies in social science research. Criminology and 'suicidology' have been variously influenced by such debates, and have also been subject to the pressures exerted by their founders, sponsors and 'customers' (see Denzin and Lincoln, 1994 for a review). The small but growing and increasingly interdisciplinary field of prison suicide has largely been caught in the trap of medico-scientific approaches to research. Most of our available studies have been carried out by prison doctors. Few studies have ventured further than the composite analysis of figures, the search for suicide risk profiles and the need to predict, preferably upon reception into custody, and in as short a time as possible, which prisoners are most likely to attempt suicide whilst in custody. This limited approach has dominated prison suicide research to date. This has been despite the failure of such prediction-profile approaches to reduce the number of suicides. It is built upon the (false) assumption that 'suicide risk' is a fixed characteristic of identifiable groups of prisoners. It does not allow for the complexity nor the transience of many suicidal crises.

It is my argument here that the need to *understand* suicide risk is *at least* as urgent as the need to predict risk in individuals and that in fact the urge to predict has hampered our search for solutions to the problem of prison suicide.

## A Continuum of Vulnerability to Suicide

Half of those prisoners who take their own lives in custody have attempted suicide or injured themselves before (see Liebling, 1992; Liebling and Krarup, 1993; Dooley, 1990a; Backett, 1987). There is no question that self-injury can be a declaration of bankruptcy, that even where such injuries are 'strategically' carried out - for example to secure a move from a wing into the prison health care centre to escape from intolerable pressures - such an act is carried out from a position already close to despair (Sparks, 1994). If such a last ditch effort to communicate and change a situation proves unsuccessful, the next step along this continuum is despair. Some would argue that the continuum begins with suicidal thought; overlapping and continuing along the pathway is self-injury, followed by suicide attempts and then suicide. Individuals can enter and leave the continuum at different points, but once upon it, the direction, and the risk, must be taken seriously. This process is illustrated by Eldrid's idea of a 'suicide ladder' (see Liebling, 1992), where prisoners can move from the expression of distress to the expression of despair, if no response is forthcoming.

It is important to note the proximity of the two aims of communication (of distress) and of escape (from despair). The lack of a response to the communication of distress makes this translation of hope into despair increasingly likely: 'What else was there to do?'.

Studies have found that those most likely to repeat suicide attempts are the young, those with conduct problems and those with few supportive and confiding relationships (Hawton, et al, 1982; Hawton and Goldacre, 1985). The traditional separation of populations into 'completed suicides' and 'parasuicides' has not addressed this relationship adequately. The research reported here found very little difference in either the types of problems reported or the feelings expressed (and therefore in the sorts of responses or solutions required) between prisoners who made near-lethal suicide attempts, and those whose injuries were less immediately life threatening. Looking at the common features of the many different degrees of self-destructive behaviour (and arguably including suicidal ideation, cp. Dexter, 1993) may be more instructive than the search for differences between two arbitrarily defined populations. Once more is known about these complex processes, and about movement along such pathways, a more informed investigation of the possible differences between 'survivors' and those who go on to take their own lives may be possible. It is likely that life situations as well as personality characteristics, coping abilities and prior experiences will be important in such studies.

RECENT PRISON SUICIDE RESEARCH

Between 1987 and 1992, two research projects were carried out in order to explore the nature and extent of suicide, suicide attempts and self-injury in prison. Both research projects have been described elsewhere and the findings reported in full (Liebling, 1992; Liebling and Krarup, 1993). Briefly, the research aimed to achieve a better understanding of prison suicide than had been possible in previous studies by talking systematically and at length to prisoners who had attempted suicide, to prisoners drawn randomly from the general populations of the establishments in which the research was conducted, and to staff. As this chapter has as its focus the particular issue of vulnerability to suicide amongst prisoners, the important matter of prison staff views and experiences will not be addressed here. Further detail can be found in Liebling, 1994b and future work on staff will be forthcoming.

The research projects looked at suicide attempts amongst young sentenced prisoners and amongst male prisoners of all ages, whether sentenced or on remand, and compared their descriptions of their lives and their experiences of custody with a random sample of prisoners who had not made suicide attempts. The important differences to emerge from the two groups can be summarised as follows: Although there were some important differences *of degree* in terms of the backgrounds and family lives of the suicide attempters, this group being more likely to have experienced repeated family breakdown, violence or abuse at home, repeated foster or care proceedings, truancy at school, etc., by far the most important differences were found in the descriptions of the vulnerable group of their experience of custody. The main features which distinguished the vulnerable group (suicide attempters) from the other prisoners are summarised below (for more detail see Liebling, 1992 and Liebling and Krarup, 1993).

---

### A Vulnerability Profile

### Criminal Justice History
more previous convictions
less than 3-6 months at liberty since last custody

### Background
no qualifications/trouble reading and writing
frequent truancy (for different reasons)
bullied at school
more frequent local authority care (and reasons)
unstable employment history
family/behaviour problems
previous psychiatric contact
major drink problems
experimentation with wider range of drugs
witnessed/experienced more severe parental violence
child sexual abuse
previous self-injury (often several)

### Current Sentence
prefers to share a cell
dislikes or avoids physical education/gym
no job in prison
inactive in cell
spends more time in cell
more likely to feel (increasingly) bored
cannot relieve boredom
has expectations and needs of staff
few friends inside

met only mates in prison
sticks to self
difficulties with other prisoners
disciplinary problems
spends more time in isolation/segregation
frequent/recent referrals to doctor/psychiatrist
reports current problems
previous self-injury in prison

### Family and Outside Support
fewer visits
writes fewer letters
a long time since last visit
misses family more
less contact from the probation service
finds thinking of outside difficult
no release plans

### Coping with Custody
wants to change self
not using the sentence/custody constructively
daydreams a lot
not hopeful about release
persistent problems sleeping
finds prison difficult
finds being locked up difficult
more frequent and severe feelings of hopelessness
more frequent and severe thoughts of suicide
thinks other prisoners' suicide attempts are more serious

What emerged from this study was that the prison population is disproportionately vulnerable in a general sense, due to the backgrounds and the life experiences of many prisoners (for more detail, see Liebling, 1992). This is important. It tells us something extremely significant about the groups we imprison. It has implications for any understanding of the operation of the criminal justice system and our understanding of the sorts of offending behaviour which leads to imprisonment. The research also demonstrated that the general prison population contains within it particularly vulnerable groups, whose experience of imprisonment is more traumatic than for other prisoners, and which is arguably more traumatic than criminal justice professionals intend. This is another point worthy of serious reflection. Prisoners we spoke to talked of the shock of custody, the eternal hope that a sentence will not be imposed (however unrealistic), the numbness and impersonality of their treatment by the courts, the tragic and sporadic efforts made to stay out of trouble against considerable odds, their own sense of failure when they are caught again, and then the experience of removal from a troubled world into an even more troubling one, where contacts are difficult, imaginations wild, and distraction not often forthcoming. Add to this, bullying, overcrowding, inactivity, a few bad visits, over-stretched staff and no future prospects, and it is hardly surprising that the prison suicide rate is on the increase. Each individual had a story to tell - which cannot be reflected in generalisations. The themes which did emerge were of disadvantage, deprivation and misery - often denied or masked with bravado, drugs, and crime.

Well, I lived at this place in Sheffield, with my three brothers and my mother and father ... it's a rough area of Sheffield ... me mum found somebody else and left when I was five, never seen her since. My dad had a good job working for a company ... he had to leave that to bring us up. So for ten years, my father was unemployed. We had to wear education clothing. We used to get the odd bit of stick at school. Then when I was about 15 my dad got remarried and I didn't like my step-mother from day one because she'd got a mentally handicapped son, who was me step-brother, and there was too much favouritism. Now it sounds silly, but we were all jealous. I weren't bothered because I was always out doing a paper round and that, so I'd always got money, and one day I were fed up with it, so I left home. I just packed me bags. My dad was in tears and asking me to stay, and why couldn't we start again, and my step-mother just piped up and said, 'why don't you let him go, if he wants to go?' and I felt like slapping her for that. It was me and me dad and I didn't want her interfering. From that point on, I was in the outside world and I met all the underworld. (Prisoner)

I used to get regular beatings. If anything went wrong it was my fault. I was the runt of the litter, it was always that way. I was the one that used to get into trouble the most, fight the most. I turned my parents and my family off when I was very young and I used to go and sit in the garden on me own like and let them get on with it. (Prisoner)

It was not always the suicide attempt group who had experienced the worst at particular stages either of their lives or of custody - it was the combination of each individual's history, experience and their current situation, including the current level of available support, which seemed to determine their ability to cope and persist. Background vulnerability, characterised by a history of depression, of self-injury, of persistent drug use and other destructive behaviour, left the prisoner with fewer resources with which to endure the experience of custody. Such prisoners were therefore more dependent upon 'external sustaining resources' such as activity, company and support, and were more susceptible to the 'pains of imprisonment' such as inactivity, isolation and feelings of powerlessness (cp. Sykes, 1958).

DOING PRISON SUICIDE RESEARCH

It has become clear during the process of carrying out the research outlined above that far more weight should be given to verbal and sociological accounts of life in prison than has been possible in many previous studies. The 'hierarchy of credibility' which automatically places written evidence or recorded information as inherently superior to prisoners' own accounts has no justification, according to the results presented here. When given the opportunity, prisoners can be fluent, honest, open, reflective and generous. Many commented at the end of interviews that they had never been presented with an opportunity to talk so openly (and for so long) before. Where they had tried, they had not been believed or listened to. They complained of not being taken seriously, or of being laughed at. Some were so expectant of rejection in their daily interactions that they were thought to have (or had developed) speech difficulties. Many of these difficulties (such as covering their mouths when speaking, mumbling or struggling to find words) disappeared once they were assured that this interaction was solely concerned with their own thoughts and feelings. As Canon Eric James commented at a Prison Chaplaincy conference in 1990: Many prisoners have never had to opportunity to be listened to or to be believed in all of their lives. No wonder that they despair.

# Five

# Research, policy and practice: What progress?

*David Neal*

INTRODUCTION

My contribution to this shared presentation is to talk about developments in *policy* and *practice* in the care of suicidal prisoners in England and Wales.

Alison Liebling and I have prepared our presentations independently, but I hope you will find many echoes of what she has said about research in what I am going to say about policy and practice. The research by the Institute of Criminology has been one of the key influences on our thinking over the last three to four years.

What I am going to say will be in six parts. I want to start by summarising the background to the problem - where we were three years ago - and then give a brief overview of how the suicide awareness programme has developed - what we've been doing to get us to where we are now. Then I shall summarise the *new national policy statement* on the care of the suicidal which we have just launched, picking out from the statement the key principles which are guiding our current approach. Fourthly, I will review some specific *changes in practice* which I believe have occurred since the last Conference. I will then attempt to stand back a little and ask as objectively as I can *what we have achieved* so far; and conclude by discussing some of the key *challenges* which lie ahead in the future.

BACKGROUND (1987-91)

Let me start with a bit of history. This was the situation we were in at the time of the last Conference in 1991. Those of you who work in the Prison Service need little reminding; but for others in the audience it may provide a useful context.

Firstly, there had been a sharp *increase in suicides* from 1987 onwards; I shall look at the figures in more detail later. As a result of this increase, there was enormous *political pressure* on the Prison Service to take action to reduce the number of suicides. And this pressure transmitted to Coroners' inquests into deaths in custody, which became more controversial and received greater media attention. There was particular concern about two groups: young prisoners and mentally disordered prisoners. Many of you will remember the sequences of suicides at Risley, Leeds and Brixton prisons on which much of the political attention was focused. But the repercussions were felt right across the Prison Service.

There were also acute *system pressures*. Our local prisons and remand centres were chronically overcrowded in the late 1980s, and also suffered from generally poor conditions and regime facilities. The industrial relations climate continued to be difficult. A variety of management and operational issues came to a head in April 1990 when the Prison Service experienced the worst disturbance in its history at Strangeways Prison, Manchester.

Against this crisis-ridden background, it is hardly surprising that there was widespread *staff concern* in relation to suicides. I believe that the staff of the Prison Service have had a very unfair press in recent years. Our staff are in general remarkably caring and persevering. They want their prisons to be safe, humane and well-ordered institutions. But their commitment has been undermined by a lack of confidence that better care could be provided given the conditions in which staff operated and the poor training and support they received. There was also a blame culture in the Prison Service. Staff feared being held responsible for deaths in custody. This created tensions between different groups of staff and resulted in overdefensive and frequently insensitive treatment of suicidal prisoners.

Many of you will be familiar with the report published in December 1990 by the Chief Inspector of Prisons, Judge Tumim. He criticised the Service for relying too much on medical assessment and treatment, and for neglecting the social and environmental factors which contributed to prisoners' distress. The report called for a less defensive approach and for a more positive emphasis on *quality of care* right across the prison regime.

These recommendations were in part informed by the *new research* into suicide and self-harm which was underway at the Institute of Criminology (see Liebling, 1992 and Liebling and & Krarup, 1992). Alison Liebling's post-graduate thesis became available to us in 1991 and provided strong academic support for a radically different approach to prison suicide.

So far, I have not mentioned Prison Service Headquarters: what used to be called the Prison Department of the Home Office in the days before we became an executive agency. What leadership were we providing at that time? The answer, I fear, is not a great deal. We had, of course, issued instructions on what we then termed 'suicide prevention.' But we had no programme for supporting the implementation of those instructions, and no established way of reviewing whether they were the right instructions. We also had a major problem of trust. The perception of prison staff was that our loyalty was to Government Ministers; our main concern was bad publicity; and that we did not really understand the nature of the problems they were dealing with.

I took on responsibility for suicide prevention policy within Prison Service Headquarters in 1989 but I confess that it was not until early in 1991 that it started to dawn on me how much work we had to do. Taking Judge Tumim's report as our starting point, we began to map out a programme for the future. Two things were very clear to me:

- it had to be a *long-term* programme to which we could give sustained commitment: there were no quick, ready-made solutions to a complex problem, and we needed to take time to find the right way forward and be patient in the face of continuing criticism;
- it had to be a *supportive* programme which recognised the feelings of anxiety and powerlessness in the field: a change of attitude could not be imposed, we had to *enable* it to happen by being more available, by taking the time to listen, by supporting and allowing staff to take risks to move forward.

In May 1991, shortly after the last conference, we formally established the Suicide Awareness Support Unit. It is not a large unit - there are just three members of staff - and clearly we are limited practically in how much we can do. But the unit's creation was a signal to Governors and staff that we were trying to address both the issues and their concerns seriously. We started to communicate with the field and I think succeeded quite quickly in raising the profile of suicide awareness policy.

ROLE OF SUICIDE AWARENESS TEAMS

The closer attention we were giving to the problem of suicide was soon matched by a growing local commitment, led by the Suicide Awareness Teams in each establishment. The role of these teams has developed significantly since they were first established in 1987, when they were called Suicide Prevention Management Groups. As Judge Tumim's report pointed out, the impact of these groups was initially fairly limited. In most cases, they met rarely, generated few ideas, and received little support from within the establishment. I suspect they also felt no ownership of the Prison Service's policy at that time.

Suicide Awareness Teams are now the lynch-pin of the new strategy. They have well recognised responsibilities for maintaining awareness; advising the Governor on the development of local policy; ensuring effective coordination within the establishment and with outside agencies; and monitoring procedures and incidents of self-harm. Most Suicide Awareness Teams now take their responsibilities extremely seriously. I would like to think that Headquarters' prompting and encouragement has played a part, but the main reason for change has been that staff themselves wanted to do more.

So the development of the suicide awareness programme has been a partnership between the centre and the field, not simply a top-down process.

DEVELOPMENT OF THE SUICIDE AWARENESS PROGRAMME

There have been five key aspects of the way we have developed the programme:

- *Support for local initiatives.* I think this was particularly important to start with because of the prevailing uncertainty about suicide and also an overdependence on centrally prescribed instructions. We wanted to give establishments more discretion. I think the need for support has now reduced because there is a more confident climate of innovation within the Prison Service generally. There is now so much going on we can hardly keep up with it.
- *Sharing research and good practice.* We publish a quarterly newsletter called 'Life Support' as a vehicle for sharing

57

information about new research, national policy developments and above all good practice in the field. I think that in a large, dispersed service there will always be a need to communicate information in this way. Though I should say that our experience has been that wherever possible face-to-face communication is much more effective in building trust and changing attitudes. We've tried to visit as many establishments as we can and also arrange seminars and forums, but of course you can never see everybody you would like to.

- *Partnership with Samaritans.* We funded the Samaritans to appoint a full-time Prison Liaison Officer for two years, Kathy Biggar. She and her team of volunteers have made an immense contribution not only in developing the role of the Samaritans in prisons, but also in supporting our programme as a whole. Initially there was a lot of mistrust between the two organizations. The Prison Service had a lot to learn about suicide. The Samaritans had a lot to learn about prisons. Misunderstanding has faded as we started to work together. We now recognize that the clear and simple principles of the Samaritan movement can be applied to the care of the suicidal in custody.
- *Review of Policy and Procedures.* This has been a gradual process as we have learned more about the nature of the problem and gathered ideas about the best way forward. We've sought to involve staff from the field as much as possible in the review. This has now resulted in a new policy statement; revised national procedures; and a guidance pack which pulls together a variety of good practice. The guidance is not prescriptive, it's there for Suicide Awareness Teams to draw upon in the light of local circumstances and priorities.
- *Review of Training.* Having identified a new policy direction we then looked at the training implications. A new video and training pack have been launched to support the implementation of the new policy.

I want to say a little more about the new procedures and training programme later when I look to the future. But first I want to spend some time looking at the new statement of policy which we issued in February of this year.

### New Policy Statement
Overall aim: The Prison Service has a duty to care for all prisoners. We aim particularly to identify, and provide special

care for prisoners in distress and despair and so reduce the risk of suicide and self-harm.

The purpose of the Suicide Awareness Unit is to:

- assist establishments to develop strategies of care which will reduce the incidence of suicide and self-harm;
- support establishments after the death of a prisoner and ensure that support is available to all those affected;
- increase understanding of the problems of suicide and self-harm inside and outside the prison service.

The statement has an overall aim, which is then broken down, distinguishing between primary care, special care and aftercare; and finally it introduces the concept of community responsibility for the care of prisoners. I am not going to go through the whole statement word for word but would like to touch on each part briefly.

First the overall aim of the policy. Notice that we do not see our task simply in terms of preventing suicide. Rather the aim is a positive one: the care of the suicidal, seen not in isolation but as an extension of our normal duty of care. If we do not hold on to this principle there is a danger that we justify treating prisoners in ways that are not caring in the name of suicide prevention. Moreover, an emphasis on prevention implies that suicide is a behaviour which we can control. I believe that is to misunderstand the nature of suicide, in which there is always an element of personal choice, and to put intolerable and unreasonable pressure on our staff.

We cannot guarantee to prevent suicide, but we are committed to doing all we can to reduce the risk of suicide attempts. This is in no way to lower our standards of care. In fact it involves setting higher standards to try to tackle the underlying causes of suicidal behaviour.

The concept of *primary care* embraces the wider, social dimension to prison suicide highlighted in Judge Tumim's report.

- the impact of the *environment* on prisoners: issues of safety and decency;
- the network of *relationships* inside and outside the prison community which help to reduce isolation and sustain hope; relationships between staff and prisoners; with family and other visitors; and relationships among prisoners themselves;
- and then a range of measures to help prisoners *cope with the problems of custody:* including reception and induction

programmes, counselling and group work, anti-bullying strategies, education, pre-release training and so on.

Primary care is essentially about providing a first line of support to the prisoner within the normal, day-to-day regime, and about dealing with the underlying stresses of imprisonment. We may not always be able to solve prisoners' problems. But we can try to contain them before they reach crisis point. Primary care is integral to our strategy because we cannot always be sure of knowing exactly when a prisoner may become acutely suicidal and of being able to mobilize crisis support. We cannot measure the number of *potential* suicides which are averted through early intervention by staff or others.

At the same time we do not intend to neglect the provision of *special care* for those at highest risk. Identifying the at-risk group is not straightforward, because as Alison Liebling has explained, it is not a single group with a single profile, and the degree of suicide risk may vary from time to time. Screening techniques are useful but they have their limitations. Our staff are having to develop a more sophisticated understanding of the range of possible factors identified by research, and continue to use their experience and judgement in assessing and re-assessing prisoners who cause concern.

Special care is fundamentally about treating distressed prisoners with dignity, as individuals, and providing appropriate support and supervision. It is no longer in our view mainly a matter of taking away the opportunity and the means of suicide. Very close supervision may be justified during acute periods, but we cannot ultimately prevent people from deciding their own destiny - and it may be counter-productive to try to do so. What we can do is attempt to sustain the prisoner through the crisis, enabling the prisoner to recover the will to live. The key to this is listening and understanding.

The third aspect of our duty of care is aftercare. Both for the prisoner who survives an act of self-harm and for all those - family, staff, other prisoners - who may be affected by incidents of self-harm or suicide. There are many very real needs here - emotional and practical needs - some of which we have neglected in the past. The Prison Service is now more conscious of what is involved in coping with the impact of suicide, or indeed any death in custody. I shall refer in a moment to specific changes in practice in this respect.

Finally, our policy statement speaks of the responsibility of the whole prison community. Suicide is everybody's business. No-one has a monopoly of expertise in being aware of and responding to human distress. Anyone who is involved with prisoners in some way has a part to play - and this very much includes prisoners themselves.

Communication, of course, is vital; but it is more than the exchange of information, it is about staff, prisoners, outside agencies and families working together to provide the most appropriate care for the individual - and also supporting each other in coping with stress and taking risks.

The concept of community responsibility has meant a switch in emphasis for the Prison Service away from our previous dependence on medical assessment and intervention. Whereas, in the past, suicide prevention was seen as something which happened in the hospital, we now place the residential unit at the centre of a multi-disciplinary approach, supported by a network of other staff and agencies.

Health care staff clearly play a vital role in meeting assessed psychiatric needs, and providing acute care when necessary. But we do not want to take the business of care away from other staff who also have skills and insights to contribute. For example, probation officers, psychologists, chaplains, teachers, instructors, above all prison officers. The relationships they establish may well be the key to enabling the prisoner both to get through a crisis *and* to cope more effectively in the long term.

I am sometimes asked where accountability lies under this model. This is a highly sensitive question because staff understandably feel on trial when they attend inquests. Under the new procedures we are currently introducing the burden of decision making and intervention is shared by staff acting as a team. The Governor is ultimately accountable for the care which the establishment provides. The sharing of responsibility extends to Prison Service Headquarters. As well as providing advice and guidance where required, we will support decisions staff have taken in good faith should these need to be explained at an inquest.

CHANGES IN PRACTICE

I have spent some time outlining our broad vision of the future, but some of you may want to know whether anything has yet changed in practice. I believe it has, and I find this is regularly confirmed to me by independent observers. What most people refer to is the emergence of a more sensitive attitude to the whole issue of suicide. Attitude change is, however, difficult to measure and we have undertaken little evaluation so far, so I shall confine myself to a selection of practical developments in three areas. I hope these will give you a tangible indication of the progress the Service has already made.

## USE OF UNFURNISHED AND PROTECTIVE ACCOMMODATION

The Prison Service has been rightly criticised in the past for resorting to the use of unfurnished and protective accommodation as the first line of defence against a suicide attempt. Such treatment is generally damaging to prisoners' mental health and undermines their relationships with staff. Our policy now is that it is only justified as a last line of defence for the most disturbed prisoner, and then only for the shortest possible period. The Directorate of Health Care monitors the use of such accommodation closely. Over the last three years, we have seen a reduction of around 70 per cent.

How has this been achieved? The starting point was to give staff permission to take risks. Staff regularly tell me that they loathed using the so-called strip cell and were only too pleased to be able to consider alternatives. Concerted efforts are now being made - especially by young offender establishments (eg Hindley, Deerbolt and Moorland) - to help vulnerable prisoners to survive on the residential unit, rather than overmedicalising their problems and isolating them from the regime. In the more acute cases, where a more sheltered location is appropriate, health care staff are seeking to nurse prisoners in wards wherever they can and involve them in therapeutic activities. Systems of care planning and review have been introduced, based on best practice in the National Health Service.

We have also seen the remarkable innovation at Ranby Prison, in which suicidal prisoners share a fully furnished care room with volunteer prisoners until the crisis is over. This scheme is now being introduced in many other prisons.

## BEFRIENDING AND SUPPORT SERVICES

This leads into befriending and support services. We have seen a huge increase in the involvement of volunteers, working alongside staff to provide an additional, confidential source of support to those at risk. All our establishments now have representatives of the local Samaritan branch on their Suicide Awareness Team. The work of the Samaritans includes not only visiting prisoners and taking calls on dedicated prison phone lines, but also staff training and support. More recently, the support network has extended to include prisoners themselves.

Drawing on an idea from the United States, Swansea Prison led the way in developing the principles of the 'Listeners' scheme. Carefully selected prisoners are trained by the Samaritans in befriending skills. They receive on-going support from staff liaison officers and the Samaritans - and one of the benefits of the scheme is that it makes much better use of the resources of Samaritan volunteers.

We now have at least 45 listener schemes, most of them established in the last year. Evaluations have been carried out at Swansea and at Styal Women's Prison, which indicate that befriending schemes have made a real difference to prisoners' lives. They may also have spin-off benefits such as reductions in assaults and improved race relations.

I would like to pay tribute to Kathy Biggar's work as the Samaritans' Prison Liaison Officer. (See further Chapter 12, this volume).

AFTERCARE

Thirdly, aftercare following suicides. Few people in the Prison Service would disagree that the way we responded in the past to the needs of staff, families and prisoners left a lot to be desired. I suspect we still do not always get it right. But equally, I am sure that the Service is now exercising greater care and sensitivity in this area. In relation to staff, the Prison Service now has its own Staff Care and Welfare Service with care teams in every establishment and a national support network of counsellors. It is standard practice to debrief staff after serious incidents and ensure they have the opportunity to talk about their feelings confidentially if they need to.

In relation to families, it is now normal practice for the establishment to offer on-going contact, support and information to bereaved relatives. We have also changed our policy to allow the disclosure of relevant documents prior to the inquest, with the Coroner's consent.

In relation to prisoners, there is I believe an increased awareness of the impact of suicide on the whole community. We regularly receive reports of the steps being taken to involve prisoners in the grieving process and give extra attention to those who may be at risk.

If I had time I would like to have said more about wider developments in the Service which are contributing to reducing the risk of suicide and self-harm. For example, improvements in family ties, induction programmes, personal officer schemes and anti-bullying strategies. I have also not done justice to the many relevant changes taking place in prison health care - in particular, the involvement of community psychiatric services and arrangements for keeping the mentally ill out of prison custody. There are colleagues of mine here from the Prison Health Care Service who will be better able than me to comment on health care practice during the Conference.

WHAT HAVE WE ACHIEVED?

We have, then, made real progress in some areas. But what, overall, can we say we have achieved? It has to be said that the figures are not encouraging. You can see from this table (Table 1, over) the sharp rise in suicides in 1987, since when they have levelled out at between 40 and 50 a year. In 1991 and 1992, the numbers fell slightly, but they rose again in 1993. There may be a connection with the level of the prison population, which has again been rising sharply since the middle of last year after falling at the beginning of the decade. But the crude conclusion is that the measures that we have taken, while they may have contained the problem, have not significantly reduced the number of deaths.

What are we to make of this? Let me make three brief points. First, I think some account has to be taken of the wider social context. Suicides by men under the age of 45 in England and Wales rose by 80 per cent in the 1980s, and the trend is still upwards. The Prison Service is of course dealing with many of the most vulnerable people in our society. Secondly, statistics never tell the whole story. I do believe that the level of awareness and concern, and the quality of care for the suicidal, are now significantly higher than three years ago. Many lives have been saved. Much has been done to improve the treatment of prisoners and provide hope for the future. The Service is more open with families and the media. We may not have solved the problem but we are coping with it. Our staff can and should take pride in that. But thirdly, no matter how we try to explain the figures, we are left with the nagging feeling that there must be more to be done.

Table 1
Self-Inflicted Deaths by Prisoners in England and Wales

| Year | Deaths | Average Prison Population (thousands) |
|------|--------|----------------------|
| 1983 | 27 | 43.5 |
| 1984 | 26 | 43.3 |
| 1985 | 27 | 46.2 |
| 1986 | 21 | 46.8 |
| 1987 | 46 | 48.4 |
| 1988 | 37 | 48.9 |
| 1989 | 48 | 48.5 |
| 1990 | 50 | 45.0 |
| 1991 | 42 | 44.8 |
| 1992 | 41 | 44.7 |
| 1993 | 47 | 44.6 |

I do believe we are on the right road, but I do not want to give the impression for one moment that we are satisfied with what we have achieved so far, or that there are not still significant problems which we need to address.

CHALLENGES FOR THE FUTURE

I therefore want to end this presentation by suggesting five key challenges for the future.

*Care for the individual*

Caring for the needs of the individual is a constant challenge for institutions, especially the total institution such as a prison with its vast range of necessary day-to-day tasks and procedures. Busy institutions are always vulnerable to allowing routine to take over, de-personalising and stripping inmates of dignity and control. The Prison Service is working hard to treat prisoners as individuals - it is one of our core values - but the operational pressures which work in the opposite direction can be formidable. One young offender establishment told me recently they had 80 prisoners on their At-Risk Register - over 10 per cent of their population. How do they ensure all their needs are met? Local prisons and remand centres, dealing with the constantly changing but highly vulnerable remand population - how can they deal with them as people? How do we minimize the stress of imprisonment when prisoners are having to be moved further from their families due to the pressure on places?

*Multi-disciplinary approach*

Part of the answer - but only part - may lie in improving communication through the multi-disciplinary approach. By ensuring more people are aware and involved, we expand the resources available to care for individual needs in the most appropriate way. The procedures are based on a form called the 'Self-harm At Risk Form.' It incorporates a 'support plan,' drawn up in consultation between the key staff involved in the prisoner's management, and a record of the action taken. The form stays open while the prisoner is kept under review.

We piloted the procedures at eight prisons last year. We were encouraged by the pilot evaluation but we also learned not to expect miracles. It will take time to develop the confidence and skills of staff, and to get the systems right. Ongoing management support will be a crucial factor. We will be continuing to evaluate the procedures and will be prepared to review them if necessary, taking account of the views of staff and prisoners.

*Staff training*

Staff training is vital. We have not frankly been able to give our staff the quantity or quality of training they are entitled to. We now have a much enhanced modular training package, based on research, which aims both to maintain general staff awareness and develop particular skills in assessing and supporting at-risk prisoners. I have been impressed by the enthusiasm and imagination of staff trainers using the package. The training programme deserves continuing support, but it must also compete with many other valid training needs.

*Attitudes to self-harm*

Fourthly, I think we need to acknowledge that there is still some work to be done on attitudes, particularly in relation to self-harm. There is a tendency among institutional staff to judge this behaviour too simplistically, frequently dismissing it as attention-seeking or manipulative, and under-estimating the genuine distress and suicidal feelings which may be present. This is a difficult issue because self-harm is a complex problem which staff find disturbing and frustrating. But it is one which needs to be tackled head on by managers and trainers. There are signs that this is happening. Paradoxically, I have been encouraged to see some establishments reporting higher self-harm figures because it suggests that incidents are being monitored more carefully. We have to be careful how these figures are interpreted because recording practice varies a good deal.

I also think there is scope for further research and guidance to staff on effective strategies for managing and counselling self-harmers.

*Maintaining awareness and commitment*

Finally, how do we maintain the momentum of the programme, avoiding both complacency on the one hand and excessive anxiety on the other? I address this point as much to senior management in Headquarters as to those of you in the field. We have, I believe, set out a clear and well understood direction for providing more professional standards of care. But will we be able to provide the long-term support needed to realise this vision? We are never going to eliminate suicides. How high a priority will the suicide awareness programme have against other initiatives where perhaps it is easier to measure progress? And finally, will we be able to hold on to our values and sustain hope in our prisons in the face of continuing setbacks and tragedies?

# Six

# Deaths of detained mental patients

*Sir Louis Blom-Cooper*

*On doit des égards aux vivants; on ne doit aux morts
que la vérité.* *
Voltaire, *Oeuvres*, 1758, Vol. I, p.15n. (*Première Lettre sur
Oedipe*)

Death is both irreversible and irrecusable; it is not optional, as
Americans are said to believe. Because human beings find it
difficult to accept their mortality, an infinite variety of complex
philosophical and religious beliefs have been constructed, many
of which have the sole function of preparing men and women for
the only certain event in their lives. These beliefs have the
incidental but important purpose of consoling the bereaved for
their loss. Most of us are unable confidently and sensibly to talk
of death, least of all sudden and unexpected death. Thus, around
the notion of death a whole series of institutional practices has
arisen, creating a sense of social balance, in which the realisation
of mortality is incorporated into the fabric of human experience.
The fact of death is rendered tolerable only so long as that sense
of balance is maintained.

Death in a closed institution - be it a prison or a hospital -
tends to disturb this sense of balance. The mere occurrence of the
death of a prisoner or a detained patient in a mental hospital,
occurring as it does out of public sight and mind, instinctively
excites the notion that the death was unnatural, if not also
violent. The death of the prisoner or detained patient is,
moreover, unsettling, not just to the prisoner's or patient's family

---

*To the living we owe respect; to the dead only truth.

68

and his or her community, but also to the medical and nursing staff, as well as the management of the closed institution, who may justifiably claim to have provided the optimum care and treatment for the patient in life. As a consequence there is an understandable public arousal of the most deep seated fears and anxieties about how death came about. And it is not just the immediate circumstances surrounding the death that is troubling, but all that went before, in terms of the care and treatment of the deceased while in the institution.

The only sensible response to the disturbance of the social balance is for the relevant prison or hospital authorities notionally to treat every death as suspicious. The approach by the authorities is not just a question of doing everything to avoid accusation of improper treatment, and formal allegations to an appropriate complaints body, but because instances of death in closed institutions merit particular attention due to the perceived, if not actual, heightened risk of assault on patients by fellow patients, or unhappily on occasion, by staff. There are also issues about the clinical judgement of medical staff, the establishment of Care Plans and their proper implementation, as well as procedural requirements to safeguard the rights and interests of patients who need protection from these persons as well as from themselves. To begin from a point of suspicion leads to the proposition that procedures must be permanently in place to investigate the death of a patient.

To anticipate my conclusion: whenever a death of a detained mental patient occurs in hospital, management must instantly set up an internal inquiry whose report should invariably be made available to the next of kin of the deceased. What form the inquiry should take will depend on the circumstances leading up to, and surrounding the death of the deceased patient. Where the patient has been the victim of an unlawful homicide, there is a clear line of action; the police must be informed and the case will be investigated within the system of criminal justice. That does not preclude the hospital from conducting a parallel inquiry, although, for obvious reasons, the internal inquiry may have to be postponed once a person has been charged and until the criminal process has run its forensic course.

In all other cases of death of a detained patient, hospital management should proceed forthwith, with a sense of urgency, with its own internal inquiry. There should be no need to postpone the internal inquiry pending an inquest, if only because such an inquiry may readily facilitate the supply of information by the hospital to the coroner. There should be no delay in ascertaining all the circumstances leading up to the patient's death and, importantly in cases of unexpected death, in promoting the welfare and counselling services for relatives and staff alike.

What, you may say, is the purpose of duplicating (at least potentially) the role and function of the coroner's inquest? I proceed to address the reasons for wanting to invoke an overlapping, if not exactly a parallel, inquisition into the death of a detained patient. I turn then to the coroner and his function.

### THE DUTY TO REPORT THE DEATH OF A PATIENT

Before the coming into force of the Mental Health Act 1959 the law required all deaths of patients in hospitals for the mentally disordered (whether or not they were compulsorily detained there) to be reported to a coroner. The position was reviewed by the Royal Commission on Mental Illness and Mental Deficiency (The Percy Commission) which reported in 1957. The Percy Commission made a recommendation in the following terms:

> At present the death of any temporary or certified patient, any patient detained under Sections 20 or 21A of the Lunacy Act 1890 and any patient in a mental deficiency hospital or certified institution or under guardianship, has to be reported to the coroner. We do not consider this necessary. The practice in relation to patients who die in psychiatric hospitals in future should be the same as for patients dying in other hospitals or at home, there should be an obligation to report the death to the coroner only in circumstances requiring the holding of an inquest or enquiry, i.e., where there are suspicious circumstances or when the death is sudden and the cause unknown.

The recommendation was accepted, and implemented in the Mental Health Act 1959. The Act repealed all the provisions which had made it mandatory for the deaths of any patient in hospital for the mentally disordered to be reported to a coroner. Since that date, the deaths of psychiatric patients, whether or not they are compulsorily detained, have been reported to coroners only when there were such circumstances as would require the notification of any other death. The matter was fully re-considered in 1971 by the Committee on Death Certification and Coroners (The Brodrick Committee).

Partly in consequence of this change in the 1959 law, the number of deaths of patients in psychiatric hospitals reported to coroners fell dramatically from approximately 10,000 in the year before the Act came into operation, to about 1,000 in the next decade. The Brodrick Committee pressed for the return to the pre-1959 position, insofar as there was an absolute duty to report the deaths of compulsorily detained patients. It said, à propos the Percy Committee's view:

We appreciate, and indeed sympathise with, the thinking which we believe lay behind this recommendation, but we were somewhat disappointed not to find in the Commission's Report any indication that had been given to the desirability of making a distinction between the deaths of patients who were or who were not compulsorily detained. We admit that this distinction can sometimes be an artificial one - because 'voluntary' patients may, and often do, share the same conditions as patients who are not legally free to walk out of a hospital and because, in practical terms, so called 'voluntary' patients may have no prospect of leaving. Moreover, there is a considerable measure of freedom afforded to certified patients. But, in the last resort, the two categories of patient are in totally different positions and we suggest that it would be fitting for the law to recognise this fact. We believe that society has a greater moral responsibility for those who have been confined under its own rules. As regards patients in psychiatric hospitals the 'rules' are contained in Parts IV and V of the Mental Health Act 1959. Part IV relates to detention on the recommendation of doctors and Part V provides the authority by which criminal courts and the Home Secretary may make orders and directions authorising the detention of a patient. We were informed that in 1969 approximately 7 per cent of all patients in psychiatric hospitals were detained under one or other of these provisions. We have concluded that it would be both sensible and practicable to make a distinction (so far as concerns the reporting of deaths to coroners) between the compulsorily detained and voluntary patients. We recommend, therefore, that it should be a requirement of the law that the death of compulsorily detained psychiatric patient should be reported to the coroner and the obligation to make such a report should be placed on the person in administrative charge of the hospital in which the patient was detained.

This civil libertarian approach was commendable, but it remained unheeded. The Mental Health Act 1983 was silent on the issue.

In other comparable areas of social policy the law has developed differentially. The death of a prisoner in custody in a prison or young offender institution must be reported by the Governor of the penal establishment forthwith to the coroner. By contrast, where a child accommodated in a children's home dies, the death need not be reported to the coroner, but must be notified by the responsible authority, as soon as possible, to a variety of other persons and authorities; (see Children's Homes Regulations 1991, Regulation 91). Should mental hospitals follow the course of the penal system or that of child welfare? The question is, not what should be automatically reported to the coroner, but what response should be forthcoming from management to a death on its hands. And should management be susceptible to extended regulation or supervision?

An alternative agency to whom a death of detained patients can be reported exists at present. The Mental Health Act Commission two years ago reminded all hospital trusts, health authorities and mental nursing homes of a standing request, expressed ever since the Commission was established under the Mental Health Act 1983, that it should be informed of the death of any detained patient as soon as possible after it has occurred, and that it also be advised at the earliest opportunity of the date and venue of any coroner's inquest. Between 1991 and 1993 the Committee was notified of 391 deaths and recorded information on 143 inquests. Deaths not followed by an inquest were reported to be those of patients having died from expected natural causes or physical disorders clearly established by the post mortem report. Of those reviewed at inquests, 95 (66 per cent) were of sudden, unexpected deaths, of which 72 (76 per cent of sudden deaths) were the result of self-harm, and a further 9 (92 per cent of sudden deaths) occurred during an episode of severe mental disturbance where the cause of death was attributable to a number of different factors, in which pre-existing physical conditions, medication, control and restraint, physical over-activity and emotional arousal may have played a significant part, but where medication - particular a cocktail of neuroleptic drugs - appeared to play an important part.

In its Fifth Biennial Report 1991-1993, laid before Parliament by the Secretary of State for Health on 1st December, the Commission said that it was aware of the possibility that its figures might reflect an under-reporting by hospitals of deaths. The Commission is undertaking a more detailed analysis of the data in order to establish whether deaths of detained patients occur more frequently than could reasonably be expected. Such information might identify trends which could assist providers of mental health care services to ensure the reduction in the number of untoward incidents and deaths of detained patients to an irreducible minimum. It is, however, too easy to infer an unacceptable level of deaths from crude numbers. Thus a cluster of suicides of patients (or recent former patients) at the Edith Morgan Centre at Torbay Hospital between June 1988 and June 1989 caused local concern about the style of the service and about the management of the Centre. Professor Gethin Morgan, Professor of Psychiatry at Bristol University, was invited by the Regional Medical Officer to conduct a review of the cases of suicide; in particular he was asked to look at the assessment and management of suicide risk. In his report, Professor Morgan doubted whether the run of suicides, viewed statistically, was significantly different from other services in the country. He did, however, make a number of constructive suggestions about how the Centre might develop better policies and training on suicide prevention. He also pointed out the fragmentation and communication problems between community and in-patient services, the lack of good clinical management for the in-patient services, the importance of developing long term facilities for younger patients with persistent behavioural difficulties, and the need for better statistical monitoring of *some activity*. Professor Morgan's report has formed a part of a recent independent review of the mental health services of South Devon Healthcare Trust, whose report is to be published in April 1994.

The Commission's more detailed analysis of deaths of detained patients will be available later this year, when it should be revealed whether or not deaths are relatively infrequent or are matters of nationwide concern. It will be possible also to gauge the frequency with which sudden deaths are not followed by a coroners inquest. Before considering further the role and function of the Commission in relation to the death of detained patients, a fleeting glance at the coroner's role is necessary.

The coroner's duty is to hold an inquest if he has reasonable cause to suspect that the body within his district is that of a person who died 'in prison'. Since there is no statutory definition of prison, it has been argued that it means something other than the establishments under prison legislation, and covers any place where a person is restrained in his/her liberty, or is in 'prison-like custody'. Jervis on the Office and Duties of Coroners (11th edition, 1993) suggests (5-58, page 75) that the narrower interpretation is the correct one.

There is official acknowledgement that the legislative intent is that the public needs to be reassured that those who are set apart from society as a whole, do not die from improper treatment. Although it has no statutory force, guidance is given in a Home Office circular 109/1982 of December 1982 which seeks to equate deaths of detained patients and of prisoners. The relevant parts of the circular reads as follows:

> Guidance was given in Home Office circulars 35/1969 and 23/1981, as to the Secretary of State's view that it was desirable for an inquest to be held with a jury, in all cases of deaths occurring in any form of legal custody, even though the death may have occurred in hospital or elsewhere and even though it may have been due to natural causes

## CORONERS JURISDICTION

It is not always appreciated that a coroner's inquest is an inquiry with a very limited objective. It is limited to ascertaining who the deceased was; how, when and where the deceased came by his or her death. There is a further specific limitation that the coroner's verdict must not be framed in such a way as to appear to determine any question of criminal liability on the part of a named person, or of civil liability. While the courts have in recent years accepted that the coroner's court may add a rider of 'lack of care' to the verdict as to the cause of death, it must not intrude upon the concept of civil negligence. The rider cannot be used to indicate a breach of duty by anyone. It can relate only to the physical or mental condition of the deceased which caused the death, in the circumstances immediately surrounding the death. 'Care' in this context means physical attention, or 'care' in the narrow sense of the word. It does not encompass the more abstract sense of the legal duty of care.

The conclusion is concerned with an absence of care. Death resulting from inappropriate treatment by medication or rough handling by nursing staff may be an accident, a misadventure or unlawful homicide, but it is not lack of care. To constitute 'lack of care' there must be a clear causal connection between the lack of physical care and the death. Put another way, there must be a distinct act or omission closely and directly associated with the death as its cause, or as one of its causes. Thus, it is not 'lack of care' if the missing care would only have ameliorated the pre-existing condition but its absence did not aggravate it.

In conducting the fact-finding exercise as to the cause of death, the coroner may be involved in considering a chain of causation of almost infinite length. The coroner will have to break in somewhere to keep his limited inquiry into the cause of death within tolerable bounds. No such limitation need be imposed by an inquiring body that is concerned to investigate the care and treatment given to a patient who died. Even if the coroner records a finding of 'lack of care', that may not suffice to allay the families' worries about the case.

If the legal limitations upon the jurisdiction of the coroner's remit often frustrate the families of deceased patients, the procedures of the coroner do little or nothing to assuage the worries of families that *authority* appears too often to be covering up deficiencies in the care and treatment of patients who die in hospital. The inability of families, deprived of publicly funded legal representation, to participate in coroner's inquests, merely fuels the frustration. It is little wonder therefore that much perturbation is expressed about the role and functions of coroners. Since there is little prospect of immediate reform of the coroner system, it is less than helpful to seek incremental change through test cases in the courts. Rather, we should look at the alternative - appropriate, unrestricted inquiries by hospital authorities under the eagle eye of the Mental Health Act Commission.

The Mental Health Act Commission has a duty to investigate 'any complaint made by a person in respect of a matter that occurred while he was detained under the Act and which he [the detained person] considers has not been satisfactorily dealt with by the managers of the hospital' (Section 120(1)(b)(i) Mental Health Act 1983). Strictly interpreted, this long stop investigatory power is not available in the case of a deceased patient. A living relative of the deceased does not qualify, but the

Commission has on occasion ignored the statutory limitation, on the footing that the complaint may often include matters on which an informal complaint existed prior to the patient's decease. The section in the Act clearly needs to be amended.

A recent example will suffice. A young man died in a district hospital last year having been admitted suffering from long term schizophrenic illness, exacerbated more recently by the development of polydypsia (morbid or abnormal thirst). The inquest recorded a 'lack of care', in that there had been deficiencies in the manner of the care provided on the night the deceased died. The Health Authority's own internal inquiry acknowledged that. Its report said that in respect of managers 'there had been a number of areas of concern ... Appropriate action had been instigated'. An additional complaint alleged that there had not been a varied and therapeutic care plan. On that, the Health Authority's report said that a 'care plan had been continually adapted and updated to take into account his changing circumstances (and) that the care plan in operation throughout his stay was appropriate in balancing the inevitable risks associated with providing the patient with the quality of life which both he and all around him sought to secure'.

The young man's mother was dissatisfied with the inquiry and invoked the investigatory power of the Commission. In addition to the complaint about the absence of any care plan, she complained a) that her son's continuing care was not of a sufficient standard to prevent the events which killed her son; and b) that failure of adequate communication between the relevant medical staff and the patient's parents about specific aspects of their son's clinical condition and management had contributed to his death.

The Commission found that the initial care plan with regard to excessive drinking was appropriate, but that more effective monitoring of the intake of fluid might have been instituted, and greater efforts should have been made to reduce the patient's cigarette smoking, a factor in potentiating water intoxication. The Commission was critical of the failure of senior medical staff to warn nurses of the potential risks of excessive drinking, leading to water intoxication. The Commission said it was 'gravely concerned by the apparent lack of medical supervision and involvement to ensure instructions were implemented'. The Commission found that the Care Plan was not effectively implemented; nor was it appropriately modified to reflect the patient's increasingly serious clinical condition. This led to the inadequacy of information given to staff on the evening of the patient's death, and their failure to intervene. In consequence the nursing staff had not fully appreciated the seriousness of the patient's condition. The Commission stated that following an acute episode it should be expected that medical staff would personally discuss the situation with the patient's parents. That was the hospital's intention, but it failed to materialise. The Commission ended its 17 page report with recommendations. The report was sent to the mother of the deceased, with copies to the Health Authority and the Department of Health.

CONCLUSION

This example of a comprehensive inquiry is both edifying and educative. The deep-seated fears, justifiable or not, exhibited by the deceased detained patients' family, cannot hope to be allayed by the process of the coroner's inquest, however expertly and aptly fulfilled. Accordingly, any expectation that the inquest will satisfy the need for public inquiry into the death of a detained patient is unrealistic and un-realisable. At best it will fulfil the limited purpose of determining judicially the cause (or causes) of death. It may not determine, or even assist the processes of civil and criminal law liabilities. Likewise it cannot be a substitute for official, if extra judicial, inquiry. Every death prompts inquiry.

The death from natural causes will instantly be revealed, requiring no further action, either by way of a report to the coroner or by further hospital inquiry.

The relatives of the deceased should immediately be informed of that conclusion, supplying the medical report of the doctor certifying death. Death which is sudden and unexpected requires more detailed inquiry. The nature and extent of that inquiry will depend on the circumstances. All inquiries about the death of a detained patient must be reported to the Mental Health Act Commission which will monitor all inquiries, including attendance by Commissioners at inquests, which by definition will be conducted where there are suspicious circumstances or when the death is sudden and the cause unknown. The recommendation of the Percy Commission in 1957, not to require mandatory reporting to the coroner of deaths of detained patients, was right; in the light of recent developments in the unofficial inquiry system, so also was Parliament in 1959 and 1983.

# Part Two:

# Special Issues

# Seven

# Australian deaths in custody: The impact of the Royal Commission into Aboriginal Deaths in Custody

*David McDonald*

INTRODUCTION

John Peter Pat died of closed head injuries in the juvenile cell of the police station lock-up in Roebourne [Western Australia] on the night of 28 September 1983. He was almost seventeen years old. Earlier that night he had been arrested during an incident involving several police officers and an Aboriginal police Aide. All officers were off duty at the time. The incident of which I speak was a fight outside the Victoria Hotel in Roebourne. The participants in the fight were several Aboriginal youths and several police officers. Of the five Aboriginal men arrested, John Pat was the only juvenile. During the fight he suffered a closed head injury which rapidly caused his death.

After his arrest, Pat was placed in one of the two police vans which attended the hotel and he and the other Aboriginal men who were arrested were taken to the police station. They were then unloaded from the vans. There, in the station yard, Pat and at least two other prisoners were assaulted to varying degrees by some of the police officers.

Pat was placed in an unconscious or semi-conscious state in the juvenile cell and left there until he was found dead during a cell check.

Following the death there was a police investigation conducted at a very high level. This was somewhat ineffectual. An Inquest was commenced in Roebourne about a month after the death, at the conclusion of which four police officers and a police aide stood trial on a charge of manslaughter. They stood trial in the Supreme Court in Karratha and all were acquitted (Johnston 1991:1-2).

The Report of the Inquiry into the Death of John Peter Pat, completed in early 1991, was the last of the individual case reports to be published presenting the findings of the Australian Royal Commission into Aboriginal Deaths in Custody (RCIADIC). The Royal Commission had investigated the 99 deaths of Australia's indigenous people - Aboriginal people and Torres Strait Islanders - who had died in the custody of police, prisons or juvenile justice authorities throughout Australia during the period 1 January 1980 to 31 May 1989. The Royal Commission is said to have been the most expensive in Australian history (Prasser 1992:5) but could well be seen as being 100 separate Royal Commissions: one into each of the 99 deaths and one into the common underlying issues (Cowlishaw 1991:110).

In Australia, along with a number of other countries with legal systems derived from that of Britain, a Royal Commission is appointed by a government to undertake an independent inquiry into the matters specified in its Letters Patent. Its investigatory powers are wide but it does not have power to punish a person for any wrongdoing identified. Rather, a Royal Commission concludes its work by presenting its report to the government or governments which appointed it. As discussed towards the end of this chapter, subsequent action is the prerogative of the government.

The death of sixteen-year-old John Pat was instrumental in the development of a groundswell of demand for action to address Aboriginal deaths in custody. The Australian Aboriginal community and its supporters called for a Royal Commission to be appointed. As it eventuated, the Royal Commission was established in 1987 under the legislation of the Australian Commonwealth Government and that of the six states and the Northern Territory of Australia where Aboriginal deaths in custody had occurred since 1980. It presented its final National Report in May 1991 (RCIADIC 1991).

The purpose of this paper is to summarise and discuss the central findings of the Royal Commission and its impact. Following these introductory remarks, the paper outlines the findings concerned specifically with the Aboriginal deaths in custody investigated by the Royal Commission, and provides an indication of the wide scope of the Royal Commission's investigations into the underlying issues which contribute to Aboriginal deaths in custody. The epidemiology of Australian deaths in custody is reviewed, and the paper concludes with a discussion of the varied responses to the Royal Commission's report.

THE SIGNIFICANCE OF CUSTODIAL DEATHS

In recent times, Australia has experienced some 60 to 70 deaths in custody, from all causes, each year. This number is quite small compared with other categories of death that receive considerable public attention, including deaths from the Sudden Infant Death Syndrome (308 in 1992), motor vehicle crashes (2,066) and suicide (2,294).[1] Although the number of deaths is relatively small, deaths in custody have received a substantial degree of government, media and public attention in recent years. The Royal Commission into Aboriginal Deaths in Custody is said to have cost almost $30 million in direct Commonwealth expenditures alone. The Commonwealth Government's response to the Royal Commission has included the commitment of hundreds of millions of dollars to be spent over the next few years. These funds are to be supplemented by expenditures by the State and Territory governments. It could be argued that the 60-odd deaths do not warrant this level of attention, considering that resources available for addressing public health concerns in the community are so limited.

Why, then, do custodial deaths attract so much attention from community groups and so much government funding? I suggest that the answer lies in three areas. First, people who are in custody - in our prisons, police lockups, juvenile detention centres and other forms of custody - are by definition 'in the hands of the state'. Their liberty, and consequently their capacity to care for themselves, has been severely restricted as a result of decisions by the courts or by individual custodians acting as agents of the state. This means that the state, and its agents, have specific responsibilities – a duty of care – regarding the people in their custody. The significance of this responsibility is highlighted by the fact that a proportion of these deaths are preventable: that approximately half of them are self-inflicted underscores this point.

Secondly, the deaths frequently occur in places to which members of the public do not have ready access: prisons and police cells. Typically, family and friends are not present. This means that people must rely on the word of the custodians as to the cause and manner of death (at least until the inquest is completed). Where deep distrust exists between the community and the custodial authorities, this fact is an inevitable source of tension.

The third rationale for placing a great deal of attention on deaths in custody, and their prevention, is that in doing so we are addressing issues of concern to our society generally about the ways in which it uses custodial sanctions. In focusing on individual custodial deaths we concern ourselves with the number of people in custody, the reasons for their being in custody and the ways in which they are handled within the custodial settings. In other words, attention becomes focused on the use of custody overall and the well-being of people in custody. With over 15,500 people in prison in Australia, up to 1,000 in police custody and over 700 in juvenile detention centres, the extent of the duty of care that the community and custodians exercise is substantial.

## THE ROYAL COMMISSION INTO ABORIGINAL DEATHS IN CUSTODY

The Letters Patent (or terms of reference) under which the Royal Commission operated gave the Commission responsibility for investigating both the 99 deaths in custody and, importantly, the broader issues which aid understanding of those deaths. The Royal Commission was authorised to investigate:

> The deaths in Australia since 1 January 1980 of Aboriginals and Torres Strait Islanders whilst in police custody, in prison or in any other place of detention, but not including such a death occurring in a hospital, mental institution, infirmary or medical treatment centre unless injuries suffered whilst in police custody, in prison or in any place of detention caused or contributed to that death (RCIADIC 1991, vol. 5:158).

The Letters Patent were subsequently amended to broaden the scope of the inquiry:

> for the purpose of reporting on any underlying issues associated with those deaths, you [the Commissioners] are authorised to take account of social, cultural and legal factors which, in your judgement, appear to have a bearing on those deaths (RCIADIC 1991, vol. 5:158).

The first Royal Commissioner appointed was Commissioner J. H. Muirhead (appointed 16 October 1987). Three additional Commissioners were appointed on 6 May 1988 when it became apparent that the number of deaths to be investigated was far higher than originally believed; their responsibility was to report to Commissioner Muirhead. The appointees were Commissioners E. F. Johnston, J. H. Wootten and L. F. Wyvill. On 27 October 1987 Commissioner D. J. O'Dea was appointed and on 27 April 1989 Commissioner Muirhead resigned and Commissioner Johnston took over as the senior (national) Commissioner. The last change was the appointment of Commissioner P. L. Dodson on 28 June 1989. The final date for Commissioner Johnston to present his National Report was set at 26 April 1991; it was tabled by the Commonwealth Minister for Aboriginal and Torres Strait Islander Affairs in the Parliament of Australia on 9 May 1991.

FINDINGS REGARDING THE DEATHS

The Royal Commission found that 99 Aboriginal people died in Australia in the nine-and-a-half years period (1 January 1980 and 31 May 1989) covered by its inquiries. The deaths occurred in each of Australia's six states and the Northern Territory. Included within the 99 cases were 11 females and 88 males. They were relatively young people, having a mean age of 32 years and a median age of only 29 years. The youngest was a 14-year-old girl who died in a self-ignited fire in a Queensland juvenile welfare centre's detention room, and the oldest a 62-year-old man who died in a Western Australian police cell from a brain haemorrhage caused by a blow to the head. The distribution, by state and custodial authority, is shown in Table 1.

As is commonplace within the Aboriginal community, the vast majority of the deceased were unemployed prior to their last detention - 83 of the 99 cases were classified this way. Of the 69 people who were considered to have a usual occupation, 40 were labourers and an additional eight were pensioners. Their education levels were generally low, again reflecting the position of the Aboriginal population as a whole, with eight people having received no formal schooling, 32 having received elementary education and an additional 50 having received some secondary education. More than half the cases (59) were living in cities or country towns shortly prior to their final period of incarceration, with a further 21 people having lived in discreet, formal

Table 1
Aboriginal Deaths in Custody, Custodial Authority, State and
Territory, 1980-1989*

| State | Police | Prison | Juvenile centre | Total |
|-------|--------|--------|-----------------|-------|
| NSW | 9 | 5 | 1 | 15 |
| Vic. | 3 | - | - | 3 |
| Qld | 19 | 7 | 1 | 27 |
| WA | 19 | 13 | - | 32 |
| SA | 7 | 4 | 1 | 12 |
| Tas. | 1 | - | - | 1 |
| NT | 5 | 4 | - | 9 |
| ACT | - | - | - | - |
| Australia | 63 | 33 | 3 | 99 |

* *1 January 1980 to 31 May 1989*

Aboriginal communities. Again reflecting the experiences of the
Australian Aboriginal population, more than half of the deceased
had been separated from their natural families as children as a
result of interventions by government agencies, church mission
organisations or others. The tragic history of Australia's attempts
at the forced assimilation of its indigenous people has yet to be
fully told within mainstream society. It is well known, however,
to Aboriginal people (see, for example, Edwards & Read 1989).

With regard to the reasons for the final period of detention,
public drunkenness dominated: in 35 cases the most serious
offence leading to the final period of custody was public
drunkenness, either as an offence or on the basis of protective
custody in those states and territories where public drunkenness
had been decriminalised. In only 21 of the 99 cases were people in
custody as a result of a serious offence against the person (e.g.
homicide, assault or sexual offences) and, indeed, in two cases
the Aboriginal people who died in custody were found to have
been unlawfully detained.

Deaths occurred among people held in police custody, in
prison and in juvenile detention centres. Some two-thirds of the
cases (63 deaths) occurred in police custody: these were in almost
all cases of people being held for very short periods, in the main
for drunkenness or other minor offences. Thirty-three people
died in prison custody, that is, they had either been sentenced to
prison or were remanded in prison, by a court, pending the

Table 2
Aboriginal Deaths in Custody, Manner of Death, 1980-1989*

| Cause | Number |
|---|---|
| Natural causes | 37 |
| Hanging | 30 |
| Head injuries | 12 |
| Gunshot wounds | 4 |
| Other external trauma | 7 |
| Alcohol and/or other drugs | 9 |
| Total | 99 |

*\* 1 January 1980 to 31 May 1989*

outcome of a trial. In an additional three cases, the deceased were young people being held in juvenile detention centres.

It is noteworthy that, in only 39 of the 99 cases, the deceased were actually serving a sentence for an offence. In an additional 48 cases the people had either not yet been brought before a court or were remanded in custody awaiting trial or the outcome of a trial; in eight cases the people were held under protective custody owing to public drunkenness and special circumstances determined the custodial status of an additional four cases.

Turning now to the patterns of the deaths themselves, it was observed that deaths occurred in each of the nine and a half years reviewed by the Royal Commission. Although the mean annual number of deaths was 10.4, one of the outstanding observations is that in 1987 twenty Aboriginal deaths occurred (16 of these were in police custody and four in prison). This relatively high incidence continued the following year, 1988, with 14 cases. This substantial increase in custodial deaths in 1987 was instrumental in the appointment of the Royal Commission.

The Royal Commission investigated very closely the cause and manner of death. Thirty-eight of the deaths were found by the Royal Commissioners to have been self-inflicted, 30 of them by hanging. The manner of death is summarised in Table 2.

The most frequent cause of death was the category 'natural causes', that is, deaths from diseases rather than external events, at 37 cases. The Commissioners found that, in many of these cases, the deaths occurred as a result of poor quality of care, either on the part of custodians or health professionals. The illnesses represented in the 'natural causes' deaths broadly reflect the generally poor state of health of Australia's Aboriginal people

(Thomson 1991). Nineteen of these deaths were from heart disease, seven from respiratory illnesses, three from epilepsy, two from stroke, two from hypoglycaemia, and one each from acute pancreatitis, meningitis, haemorrhage caused by a ruptured ovarian cyst and haemorrhage within the lungs, these last two illnesses being associated with advanced liver disease.

Twelve deaths were from head injury, four from gunshot, seven from other forms of external trauma (e.g. stabbing), five from the acute effects of alcohol and four from the acute effects of other drugs.

RESPONSIBILITY FOR THE DEATHS

The inquiries into the 99 deaths were (in the main) exceedingly thorough even though, in some cases, the events being investigated took place a decade before the Royal Commission's inquiries were initiated. A widespread expectation existed within both the Aboriginal and non-Aboriginal communities that the Royal Commission would find that, in at least a number of cases, the deaths had occurred as a result of culpable behaviour on the part of custodial officers and the result would be the bringing of serious charges against them. This expectation was not met. The National Commissioner, Elliott Johnston, expressed the overall finding in the following terms:

> The conclusions reached in this report will not accord with the expectations of those who anticipated that findings of foul play would be inevitable and frequent. That is not the conclusion which Commissioners reached. As reported in the individual case reports which have been released, Commissioners did not find that the deaths were the product of deliberate violence or brutality by police or prison officers.
>
> But Commissioners did find that, generally, there appeared to be little appreciation of and less dedication to the duty of care owed by custodial authorities and their officers to persons in custody. We found many system defects in relation to care, many failures to exercise proper care and in general a poor standard of care. In some cases the defects and failures were causally related to the deaths, in some cases they were not and in others it was open to debate... It can certainly be said that in many cases death was contributed to by system failures or absence of due care (RCIADIC 1991, vol. 1:3).

As discussed below, this finding was not acceptable to many Aboriginal people who considered that the Royal Commission was yet another example of the dominant society failing to take proper account of the oppression experienced by Aboriginal people in Australia. Nevertheless, a conclusion like this has resulted in a focus on the system defects and institutionalised racism which contributed so much to the deaths, rather than the scapegoating of individual custodial officers. With the passage of time since the Royal Commission's findings were announced, leading members of the Aboriginal community are increasingly demanding that more attention be placed on these system issues.

FINDINGS REGARDING THE ADEQUACY OF PREVIOUS INVESTIGATIONS

The Royal Commissioners looked closely at the adequacy, or otherwise, of the previous investigations which were conducted into the 99 deaths. In the main, the Royal Commission was highly critical of the quality of those investigations, particularly those conducted earlier in the decade. Although post-mortem examinations were conducted in all cases, inquests were not held in 12 of the cases. In the 87 cases where inquests were conducted, the coroner was assisted by a lawyer in only 26 cases and the families of the deceased were legally represented in only 69 cases.

The deficiencies in these post-death investigations meant that the interests of the families of the deceased, and of the broader community, were not well served in many cases, the Commission concluded. Too often, the investigations by police officers were perfunctory. In some cases, officers who were implicated in the events surrounding a death were also involved in the post-death investigations! Too often, the Commission found, the investigations carried out by police officers and presented to the inquest, and the focus of the inquest itself, were far too narrowly conceived. In the main, the emphasis in the inquests was on determining just how the death occurred and whether or not any person was legally culpable for that death. Particularly earlier in the decade, coroners generally failed to look closely at the circumstances of the death with the aim of producing recommendations as to how similar deaths could be avoided in the future. The Royal Commission was critical of the very limited capacity of coroners, in most states and territories, to conduct any kind of independent investigation of the circumstances of the deaths: they depended, in the main, on investigations conducted by police officers. For this reason, the Commission's report includes recommendations aiming to strengthen the investigative power of coroners and to ensure that police officers who are assisting coroners are well trained in their work and able to operate with a high degree of independence from the police services from which they are drawn.

The Commission was also highly critical, in many cases, of the lack of respect shown to the families of the deceased and the final report of the inquiry included a number of recommendations aimed at ensuring that the families of people who die in custody are kept appraised of actions being taken consequent upon the deaths and, furthermore, to ensure that the families' interests are adequately represented, by legal counsel, during the course of the inquest.

### FINDINGS REGARDING UNDERLYING ISSUES

A central finding of the Royal Commission was that the high level of deaths in custody of indigenous people is a direct result of their disproportionate representation in the custodial population. Aboriginal people comprise only one percent of the Australian adult population but make up 14 per cent of the national prison population and 29 per cent of the people held in police lockups (McDonald, Walker & Howlett 1994). The custodial death rates of Aboriginal people in the 1980-1989 period were similar to those of non-Aboriginal people when the custodial populations are used as the denominators in the calculation of the rates (Thomson & McDonald 1993). This conclusion led the Commissioners to identify the multiple causes of the over-representation of Aboriginal people in custody, essentially their extremely disadvantaged position on most social indicators. They stressed that it is this disadvantage (relative to the non-Aboriginal population) that demands attention, along with criminal justice system improvements that are directly related to minimising the incidence of custodial deaths.

One of the great strengths of the Royal Commission was the breadth of its focus. Its final National Report covers the following areas:

- The deaths investigated by the Royal Commission
- The disproportionate number of Aboriginal people in custody
- The underlying issues which explain the disproportionate number of Aboriginal people in custody
- Reducing the numbers in custody

- Reducing the risks of death in custody
- The underlying issues: Directions for change
- Towards reconciliation.

It paid a great deal of attention to the underlying social, cultural, historical and legal issues which, in the words of its terms of reference, appear to have a bearing on the deaths. An indication of the scope may be given by listing the chapter titles of the final National Report which are concerned with underlying issues:

- The legacy of history
- Aboriginal society today
- Relations with the non-Aboriginal community
- The criminal justice system: relations with police
- Young Aboriginal people and the juvenile justice system
- Aboriginal health
- The harmful use of alcohol and other drugs
- Education
- Employment, unemployment and poverty
- Housing and infrastructure
- Land needs
- Self-determination
- International obligations
- Reconciliation.

Detailed recommendations in each of these areas are to be found in the National Report and in the Regional Reports which were also prepared by the Commissioners.

AUSTRALIAN DEATHS IN CUSTODY 1980-1992: AN OVERVIEW

To place the Aboriginal deaths in custody discussed above into the broader context of Australian custodial deaths, I turn now to an overview of such death during the period 1980 to 1992. During the seven years 1980 to 1986, Australia experienced on average 44 deaths in police and prison custody each year, with the number each year fluctuating little. The total more than doubled in 1987 to 94 deaths. The percentage increase was similar for both Aboriginal and non-Aboriginal detainees, and for both prison and police custody. The numbers in each of these groupings fell by approximately one-third the following year (1988) and have remained fairly constant since then, except for a recent pleasing fall in Aboriginal deaths in police lockups. Details covering the 1980-1992 period are in Table 3 and Figure 1.[2]

Table 3
Year of Death, Custodial Authority and Aboriginality, 1980-1992

| Year | Police | | | Prison | | | Total | | |
|------|--------|-----|-------|--------|-----|-------|-------|-----|-------|
|      | A | N-A | Total | A | N-A | Total | A | N-A | Total |
| 1980 | 5 | 7 | 12 | 5 | 25 | 30 | 10 | 32 | 42 |
| 1981 | 3 | 12 | 15 | 1 | 27 | 28 | 4 | 39 | 43 |
| 1982 | 4 | 15 | 19 | 4 | 21 | 25 | 8 | 36 | 44 |
| 1983 | 6 | 10 | 16 | 5 | 26 | 31 | 11 | 36 | 47 |
| 1984 | 3 | 12 | 15 | 4 | 27 | 31 | 7 | 39 | 46 |
| 1985 | 6 | 16 | 22 | 4 | 22 | 26 | 10 | 38 | 48 |
| 1986 | 8 | 13 | 21 | 1 | 16 | 17 | 9 | 29 | 38 |
| 1987 | 15 | 26 | 41 | 5 | 48 | 53 | 20 | 74 | 94 |
| 1988 | 7 | 14 | 21 | 6 | 36 | 42 | 13 | 50 | 63 |
| 1989 | 10 | 11 | 21 | 3 | 37 | 40 | 13 | 48 | 61 |
| 1990 | 2 | 20 | 22 | 6 | 25 | 31 | 8 | 45 | 53 |
| 1991 | 3 | 19 | 22 | 8 | 31 | 39 | 11 | 50 | 61 |
| 1992 | 5 | 21 | 26 | 2 | 34 | 36 | 7 | 55 | 62 |
| Total | 77 | 196 | 273 | 54 | 375 | 429 | 131 | 571 | 702 |

*Note:* A=Aboriginal, N-A=Non-Aboriginal

**FIGURE 1**
*Year of Death and Aboriginality, 1980-1992*

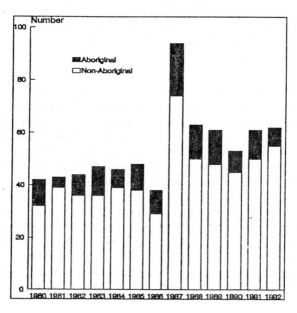

Table 4
Deaths in Custody 1992: Jurisdiction

| Year | Police | | | Prison | | | Total | | |
|------|---|-----|-------|---|-----|-------|---|-----|-------|
|      | A | N-A | Total | A | N-A | Total | A | N-A | Total |
| NSW  | 3 | 11  | 14    | 1 | 12  | 13    | 4 | 23  | 27 |
| Vic. | 1 | 6   | 7     | - | 3   | 3     | 1 | 9   | 10 |
| Qld  | 1 | 2   | 3     | 1 | 9   | 10    | 2 | 11  | 13 |
| WA   | - | -   | -     | - | 3   | 3     | - | 3   | 3 |
| SA   | - | 1   | 1     | - | 4   | 4     | - | 5   | 5 |
| Tas. | - | 1   | 1     | - | 2   | 2     | - | 3   | 3 |
| NT   | - | -   | -     | - | 1   | 1     | - | 1   | 1 |
| ACT  | - | -   | -     | - | -   | -     | - | -   | - |
| Aust.| 5 | 21  | 26    | 2 | 34  | 36    | 7 | 55  | 62 |

**Note**: *A=Aboriginal, N-A=Non-Aboriginal*

1992 is the latest calendar year for which data have been published (McDonald & Howlett 1993, the primary source of the information provided in this section). Table 4, above, shows that 36 of the 62 deaths in 1992 were of people in prison custody with the balance (26) in police custody. Seven Aboriginal deaths occurred, five in police custody (including three in police lockups and two in other forms of police custody) and two in prison.

Most of the deaths were of males, with five females dying in custody during the year. The ages of the deceased detainees ranged from 14 to 77 years, with a mean of 30 and a median of 29.5. Tragically, seven of the deaths were of people aged between 14 and 19 years of age; these all occurred in police or prison custody.

As is usually the case, both in Australia and overseas, remandees were heavily over-represented. Ten of the 36 prison custody deaths were of people on remand; this proportion (28 per cent) should be compared with the proportion of remandees in the national prison population, just 12 per cent.

Turning to the cause and manner of death, it is noted that, nationally, half of the deaths (31 cases) were self-inflicted. Two-thirds (22) of these were by hanging. An additional 11 were caused by gunshot (either inflicted by custodial officers or self-inflicted); nine were attributed to 'natural causes', i.e. illnesses; three to head injury; seven to other external trauma (e.g. assaults and motor vehicle pursuit crashes); eight to alcohol or other drugs; and one each to choking in association with alcohol (inhalation of vomit) and asphyxiation by means of a plastic bag

Table 5
Deaths in Custody 1992: Manner of Death

| Year | Police | | | Prison | | | Total | | |
|---|---|---|---|---|---|---|---|---|---|
| | A | N-A | Total | A | N-A | Total | A | N-A | Total |
| Hanging | 1 | 3 | 4 | 1 | 17 | 18 | 2 | 20 | 22 |
| Natural causes | 1 | 1 | 2 | 1 | 6 | 7 | 2 | 7 | 9 |
| Gunshot | - | 9 | 9 | - | 2 | 2 | - | 11 | 11 |
| Head injury | - | 3 | 3 | - | - | - | - | 3 | 3 |
| Other external trauma | 1 | 2 | 3 | - | 4 | 4 | 1 | 6 | 7 |
| Drugs/alcohol | 2 | 2 | 2 | - | 4 | 4 | 2 | 6 | 8 |
| Other | - | 1 | 1 | - | 1 | 1 | - | 2 | 2 |
| Total | 5 | 21 | 26 | 2 | 34 | 36 | 7 | 55 | 62 |

*Note*: A=Aboriginal, N-A=Non-Aboriginal

placed over the head. Table 5 has details.

The Australian Institute of Criminology publishes six-monthly monographs presenting statistics and analyses of trends in Australian custodial deaths. These are available free on request to the Institute, as part of the Commonwealth Government's response to the recommendations of the Royal Commission into Aboriginal Deaths in Custody.

### RESPONSES TO THE ROYAL COMMISSION'S REPORT

Perhaps predictably, governments and the Aboriginal community have responded in very different ways to the Royal Commission's final National Report. For governments, the response has been one of accepting the broad thrust of the Commission's findings and agreeing to support almost all of its recommendations. The commitments which they have made are far-reaching:

> We therefore fully accept the Royal Commission's insistence that the problem be tackled simultaneously at two levels - an improvement to the position of Aboriginal and Torres Strait Islander people in relation to the criminal justice system, and a strengthened commitment to correct the fundamental factors which bring Aboriginal and Torres Strait Islander people into contact with that system (Aboriginal Deaths in Custody: Overview of the Response by Governments 1992:1).

*and*

[we recognize] the single most important theme to emerge from the Royal Commission is the need to put behind us a history of dispossession, dependency and efforts at forced assimilation and move decisively into a new era of Aboriginal and Torres Strait Islander empowerment and self-determination (op. cit.:3).

These words were accompanied by a commitment of additional funding, by the Commonwealth Government, amounting to A$400 million over five years. The funding was allocated to programs in such areas as alcohol and other drug abuse, support for Aboriginal community-controlled legal services, land acquisition and development, business development, employment programs, etc. It does not cover matters directly concerning the operation of the criminal justice system (especially policing and alternatives to custody) as these are the constitutional responsibility of the Australian states and territories.

The Aboriginal community sees these responses in a different light. Its members have argued that the official government responses to the recommendations of the Royal Commission are, too frequently, a brushing away of the problems. This view is illustrated in the response of the Government of New South Wales, Australia's most populous state and the one with the largest Aboriginal (but not Torres Strait Islander) population, to the Royal Commission's recommendation that '[a]ll police services should adopt and apply the principle of arrest being the sanction of last resort in dealing with offenders'. Its official, written response was a curt '[T]his is the case in New South Wales'. Furthermore, in responding to the recommendation that 'Governments which have not already done so should legislate to enforce the principle that imprisonment should be utilised only as a sanction of last resort', that Government responded: 'Implemented. Section 80AB of the Justices Act 1978 and s. 33(2) of the Children (Criminal Proceedings) Act 1987 currently provide for the principle of imprisonment as a sanction of last resort' (Aboriginal Deaths in Custody: Response by Governments, vol. 1, 1992:308; 332-3). The sad irony is that in New South Wales, the proportion of people taken into police custody who were Aboriginal rose by 13 per cent between 1988 and 1992 (compared with a national average increase of only one per cent) and the rate of imprisonment of Aboriginal people in that state rose by 44 per cent over the same period (McDonald, Walker & Howlett 1994).

Aboriginal people are also dissatisfied with the specific findings of the Royal Commission concerning the deaths and the responses of governments to those findings. Writing on behalf of the National Committee to Defend Black Rights (NCDBR: an Aboriginal organization actively concerned with the continuing problem of Aboriginal deaths in custody), Paxman (1993:154) emphasised the fact that:

> The NCDBR and the Aboriginal community believe that the Royal Commission's findings failed to bring to justice those responsible for the deaths. Questions remain about the deaths of John Pat, Eddie Murray, Kingsley Dixon, Robert Walker, Barbara Yarrie, Bruce Leslie, and dozens of others.

They argue that, in some cases, the Commission erred in failing to find that individual police and prison officers had directly caused some of the deaths investigated. They are also concerned that governments have failed to prosecute the officers who were found by the Royal Commission to have contributed to the deaths in some manner (e.g. through failure to exercise sufficiently their duty of care towards those in their custody), or who sought to conceal facts from the Royal Commission, e.g. through falsifying official records or perjuring themselves before the Commission.

These perceptions leave members of the families of those who died in custody, along with many of their supporters, feeling that the Royal Commission was a gross waste of resources and, indeed, became a 'white-wash' for the wrongdoings of individual custodians and the failure of governments to enforce adequate standards of care of prisoners. At least one of the Royal Commissioners has responded to these claims by pointing to the differing standards of proof required by a Royal Commission, on the one hand, and a court, on the other. He argued that the Royal Commission needed to leave it to the governments which received the Commission's report to decide if prosecutions of custodial officers before the courts were warranted (Wootten 1991). The legal correctness of this position provides little comfort to the Aboriginal people who feel betrayed by the Royal Commission process.

CONCLUSION

It is unlikely that deaths in custody will ever be totally eliminated. The many people who see the deaths of Australia's indigenous people in custody as the continuation of two centuries of oppression and, indeed, of genocide, will remain sceptical about the impact of the Royal Commission into Aboriginal Deaths in Custody. For some audiences, the information derived through the Australian Institute of Criminology's program of monitoring custodial deaths is seen as important in evaluating the impact of the implementation of the recommendations of the Royal Commission into Aboriginal Deaths in Custody. Although (as discussed above) one of the great strengths of the Royal Commission was that its recommendations cover a very wide scope, many people are still looking to statistics on the number of custodial deaths, particularly Aboriginal and Torres Strait Islander custodial deaths, as key indicators of the impact of the work flowing from the Royal Commission's recommendations. Current indications are that, nationally, the number of Aboriginal deaths in custody across Australia each year, over the period since the Royal Commission concluded its work, is very similar to the number that occurred during the January 1980 to May 1989 period covered by the Letters Patent under which the Royal Commission operated (McDonald, Walker & Howlett (1994). The main change observed is a marked reduction in the incidence of Aboriginal deaths in police lockups, accompanied by a slight increase in deaths in other forms of custody.

Many Australians, and members of the international community, are looking for more action, and more effective action, in all the areas addressed by the Royal Commission's recommendations, including the empowerment of Aboriginal and Torres Strait Islander people, economic development, education, health, housing and infrastructure, women's issues, youth issues, law and justice, etc. In public policy terms, however, even if substantial advances are made in these areas but the number of custodial deaths (particularly the deaths of Aboriginal and Torres Strait Islander people in custody) does not fall substantially, legitimate questions can be raised about the appropriateness of the Royal Commission's recommendations and/or the effectiveness of their implementation.

The international community, particularly influential groups such as Amnesty International (e.g. Amnesty International 1993), have focused directly on the number of custodial deaths and on the over-representation of Aboriginal and Torres Strait

Islander people in custody as key indicators of the level of human rights within Australia. Having available timely and comprehensive information about the custodial populations and the levels and patterns of custodial deaths will continue to be an important tool for evaluating Australia's progress in this area and for enhancing the level of accountability of the people in government and community agencies who are responsible for actions aimed at reducing the over-representation of indigenous people in custody and minimising the number of deaths in custody.

**A note on sources**
Some of the material in this paper was presented to a public seminar convened by the Institute of Criminology, The University of Sydney, Sydney, 29 September 1993. It also includes edited extracts from D. McDonald & K. Whimp, 'Australia's Royal Commission into Aboriginal Deaths in Custody: Law and Justice Issues', in K. Hazlehurst (ed.), Indigenous People and the Application of the Criminal Law, in press.

Further information on the matters touched upon in this paper may be obtained from:

* National Deaths in Custody Monitoring and Research Unit, Australian Institute of Criminology, GPO Box 2944, Canberra, ACT, 2601, Australia.
* Manager, Royal Commission Government Monitoring Unit, Aboriginal and Torres Strait Islander Commission, PO Box 289, Woden, ACT, 2606, Australia.

**References**
1   These figures refer to deaths registered in 1992, the most recent year for which causes of death data are available. Source: Australian Bureau of Statistics 1993.
2   Clearly there are sources of error and omission in this data series, as the 1980-1987 data were collected retrospectively; different custodial agencies (the sources of the data) would have applied different inclusion criteria; the inclusion criteria could have changed over time; etc. Nevertheless, these data are the best available and are far more complete than those of most other countries.

# Eight

# The prevention of deaths in police custody: A review of police practice within the Metropolitan Police

*Chief Inspector Brian Wade*
*& Police Sergeant Paul Etheridge*

INTRODUCTION

In March, 1992 following an inquest into the death of a person in hospital, having been transferred there by ambulance from police custody, the coroner, having recorded a verdict of 'Accidental Death', announced in open court that he would make the following recommendations:

1.  A clear set of guidelines should be given to every police station outlining definitive methods of evaluating altered states of consciousness.
2.  An altered state of consciousness thought due to alcohol, together with any form of head injury, no matter how trivial, should necessitate the attendance of the Forensic Medical Examiner, or the person being sent to hospital.

A review was undertaken of those cases which had resulted in a death in custody in order to establish a means by which officers could identify vulnerable persons in their custody, how the medical care of those persons could be improved and ultimately the incidence of death reduced. Whilst this chapter deals primarily with the problems associated with the custody of persons who are detained for being drunk, the review did not ignore those persons who have suicidal tendencies or who are mentally ill.

Figure 1
Metropolitan Police District
Deaths in Police Custody or Care 1983/84-1993/4

| | $^{83}/_{84}$ | $^{84}/_{85}$ | $^{85}/_{86}$ | $^{86}/_{87}$ | $^{87}/_{88}$ | $^{88}/_{89}$ | $^{89}/_{90}$ | $^{90}/_{91}$ | $^{91}/_{92}$ | $^{92}/_{93}$ | Total |
|---|---|---|---|---|---|---|---|---|---|---|---|
| Total Deaths | 18 | 15 | 14 | 15 | 28 | 30 | 37 | 20 | 21 | 18 | 216 |
| Alcohol featured | 12 | 12 | 12 | 10 | 13 | 15 | 16 | 10 | 7 | 10 | 117 |
| Suicide | 3 | - | - | 1 | 1 | 1 | 2 | 1 | 2 | 2 | 13 |
| Natural Causes | 3 | 2 | 3 | 4 | 4 | 7 | 4 | 1 | 1 | 2 | 31 |

Total Number of Arrests for 1991 = 419,624

PROBLEM IDENTIFICATION

Figure 1 shows the primary cause of death in police custody within the Metropolitan Police. The figures relating to alcohol are taken from the synopsis of incidents contained within the Commissioners Annual Reports[1], whilst those for suicide and natural causes are based on inquest verdicts also taken from the same source. The combination of alcohol and or drugs and illness/ injury, the most serious being the undetected fracture of the skull figured highly in the review. The review identified common problem areas. The first arose before the person was even in police custody - namely the drunken person collapsed in the street, to which the Ambulance service and Police service are called. It was recognised that, on occasions persons who were ostensibly drunk were given into police care.

This is perfectly understandable and correct when not wishing to fill busy casualty wards with such persons, but not so understandable when the person has other possible injuries. This was a general problem and not one associated with all the cases resulting in death.

As previously mentioned a small percentage of Coroner's inquests had resulted in adverse comments. It was recognised that any verdict which has a rider 'aggravated by lack of care' could ultimately result in the Commissioner of Police being sued for negligence. As there is a general inclination to commence civil claims, the standards of care employed by any service and the instructions given to its employees assume greater importance. The instructions given to police officers responsible for overseeing the custody and care of a person whilst in police detention were either at variance or open to a wide interpretation. They failed to take into consideration the potential rapid medical deterioration of a person or the need for constant supervision of a person with suicidal tendencies who await the arrival of either an ambulance or Forensic Medical Examiner (FME). The culture within the police service of "letting drunks sleep it off" has developed over many years and so has bad practice in the care of such persons. It was recognised that some officers were making only cursory checks on the fitness of the detained person through the cell wickets without physically checking and rousing the person. Officers would accept, through ignorance, that certain responses were indicative of 'sleeping it off' where in reality the person was, in once instance slipping into coma. Other officers were making quasi-medical examinations which were beyond their ability and duty and which were used as a basis for deciding whether to call a FME, Ambulance or neither.

It was identified that some officers, whether on the street or in the police station, were not recognising obvious indicators of illness or injury. For example the passerby who calls police to the collapsed drunk would inform the officer they saw the person fall and hit their head. This fact failed to raise any alarm bells in the mind of the officer, nor was it brought to the attention of the custody officer. Tablets found on a detained person, who had also consumed alcohol, were wrongly identified by the police officer and no questions were asked as to whether the person had taken any. Such communication failures in not asking the person direct questions, as an early opportunity to assess their health or a failure to listen to a person whilst in custody or on release who is indicating suicidal tendencies had dire consequences.

## PROBLEM SOLUTION

These therefore were the main problem areas which generated a

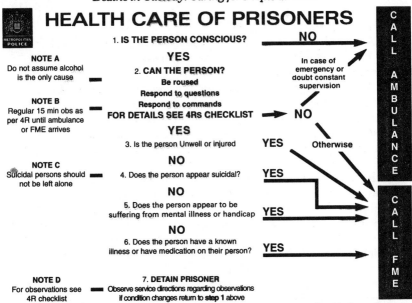

Copyright Metropolitan Police

S03 Graphics G565

working party being formed to find solutions. It was important that the composition of such a group was drawn from various disciplines both within the Metropolitan Police Service and outside. Apart from police officers the group consisted of Occupational Health advisors, a Forensic Scientist with responsibility for FME training, a First Aid trainer and one of Her Majesty's Coroners. Where necessary other organisations were invited to attend meetings and give advice on specific areas. For example a representative from the London Ambulance Service assisted in the drafting of new guidelines for police officers when dealing with collapsed drunks in the street where ambulance crews were also in attendance. A Mental Health Nurse who tutors at the Maudsley Hospital advised on the aspects concerning mentally ill persons in police custody.

The first area to be addressed was the need for officers to be aware of 'medical' problems and to take a positive response to such when identified. The chart at Figure 2 was designed to fulfil that function. Making officers follow a strict path and clearly stating that it is not acceptable not to physically rouse the drunken person was the first step. The 4 'R's' chart at Figure 3 gives officers clear instruction as to what is expected when rousing a drunken person. The chart removes the decision whether to call a doctor or an ambulance. More importantly the

# Health care of prisoners
# HRs Observation check list

**METROPOLITAN POLICE**

any prisoner fails to meet any of the following
iteria, an F.M.E or Ambulance MUST be called

**hen assessing the level of rousability consider:-**

ousability · **can they be woken?**

**into the cell.
ll their name.
ake gently.**

esponse to questions - **can they give appropriate
nswers to questions such as:**

**ats your name?
here do you live?
here do you think you are?**

esponse to commands - **can they respond
propriately to commands such as:-**

**en your eyes!
t one arm now the other arm!**

emember **to take into account the possibility or presence
other illnesses, injury or mental condition.
erson who is drowsy and smells of alcohol may also have
following:**

**betes
ilepsy
ad injury
ug intoxication or overdose
oke**

## IN DOUBT CALL AN AMBULANCE

person to whom an ambulance has been called or who is identified as suicidal and is awaiting medical assessment should not be left alone. It is intended that this chart will be issued in laminated card form to all officers supported by a large wall chart version within each custody suite.

Discussions turned to addressing first aid training and the provision of medical equipment within the custody suite. It was recognised early on within the group that we did not want police officers to have to make a medical diagnosis. Officers faced with a problem should clearly be able to perform emergency resuscitation and should have the necessary equipment to hand to assist them. In this respect two pieces of equipment, the V.Vac, a hand powered suction unit for clearing airways of vomit and the Ambu Spur Resuscitator, a manual disposable resuscitator were identified to fill that need.

The use of video monitoring of detained persons in the cell was another area which featured in discussions. This particular option raised objections not only from a civil liberties point of view but in respect of the fact it involved another person having to view a set of monitors and their span of attention. It was this potential human weakness to such a system above all else that resulted in this idea not being progressed further. Cost estimates for the provision of the V.Vac and Ambu Spur to cover all the custody suites within the Metropolitan Police District are in the region of £10,000.

Training of staff, not only in the use of equipment, but also on the whole issue presented a major problem which has not been satisfactorily addressed. It is estimated that in excess of 2,000 Sergeants would require training in addition to a potential total of 10-15,000 police constables. This represents a long term training program of at least a half day's training per officer plus the opportunity costs that represents. Whilst the working party revised the current instructions to cover the areas discussed, it was recognised that they could not replace the training requirement.

### FUTURE IMPLICATIONS FOR THE POLICE SERVICE

In 1984 the Commissioners Report[2] referring to deaths in custody where alcohol or drugs were a contributory factor stated:

> In all these cases, supervision by qualified medical staff would have greatly reduced the risk of fatality. This level of care cannot be provided by police and the Force

continues to support the need for the provision of approved centres within the Metropolitan Police District where people suspected of drunkenness can be taken to receive appropriate medical care, instead of being detained in police cells.

10 years on we still await such a facility in London. The provision of Forensic Nurses is a long term option for the future but only in respect of large custody suites commonly termed 'Bridewells'. The requirement for a suicide awareness programme in light of the conference is an area for further investigation.

It is recognised that the police service will continue to receive into custody those members of society who are vulnerable and require an enhanced level of care. The review and working party have begun a process of raising awareness, training and provision of equipment as part of a continuing program to prevent deaths in police custody.

**Notes**

1. Appendix tables 'Death in police custody or otherwise with the police' as contained with Reports of the Commissioner of the Police of the Metropolis for the Years 1988 - 1993 published by Her Majesty's Stationary Office.

2. Report of the Commissioner of the Police of the Metropolis 1984 page 74, published by Her Majesty's Stationary Office.

# Nine

# Deaths in custody: The situation in the Netherlands 1980 until today

*Irene Sagel-Grande*

INTRODUCTION

In the Netherlands there exists no national legal regulation about police-cells until now. But, of course, the police know very well how to keep arrested people correctly. Nevertheless the situation in Dutch police-cells is not at all as it should be. For many years the newspapers and not only the "gutter-press" informed the public about shocking situations and incidents in police-cells, which now and then, but not only exceptionally, caused the death of someone arrested. How many people die in police-cells yearly is not known, as these cases are not registered as such. One can guess that there are some tens per year in the whole country. The regular newspaper comments led by and by to action of the responsible institutions.

## THE AMSTERDAM SUPERVISING COMMISSION

In 1985 Hans Kok, an arrested squatter, died in a police-cell in Amsterdam. His death led to a lot of protest-actions of his friends and people with the same political insights. These actions were supported by the media and forced the Minister of Justice and the Lord Mayor of Amsterdam to give rise to intensive investigations. These resulted mainly in the statement, that neither the chief of the police nor the judicial and administrative authorities really know about what is going on in the police-cells. In consequence of these results the Minister of Justice only revised the guidelines about how ill arrested people must be kept in custody. Further he declared that special regulations would be prepared, but after this, nothing happened.

Better than more regulations is regular and objective supervision by independent persons. That model was already put to practice in the Netherlands in 1953 for prisoners in the regular prisons. In all prisons there exist supervising commissions and monthly changing commissions for direct interventions.

In Amsterdam, where the first and most independent commission for people's complaints about the way policemen are doing their jobs was developed, one decided that one should do more. After the death of Hans Kok in Amsterdam the Lord Mayor introduced a supervising commission for the police-cells of his city.[1] Until now Amsterdam stayed the only town with such a commission in the Netherlands.

The Amsterdam commission has 3-7 members, its secretary is a civil servant of the town. The task of the commission is to supervise the way the detained are treated and whether the regulations concerning the treatment of the arrested persons are put to practice correctly. The members of the commission regularly contact the different police branches and regularly visit the police-cells, most of which are in a bad condition. The members of the commission are allowed to visit all places where arrested persons are kept at any time. They can further ask for all information they think to be necessary. The commission publishes a report yearly and advises the Lord Mayor regularly. Reading the reports about the years 1990, 1991 and 1992 one can state that the commission is visiting most those cells that are in the worst condition. The work of this commission is of great help in improving the situation of the detained and reducing the chance of death in police-cells.

## REGISTRATION OF DEATHS IN POLICE CELLS

The Dutch National Ombudsman advised the Minister of Justice and the Minister for the Home Department already some years ago to introduce a national registration for deaths and attempted suicides in police-cells. In April of 1993 he repeated this demand very strictly[2]: "If the police are arresting people and keeping them in a police-cell, the police are highly responsible for the health and the safety of these people". The chance of suicide in a police-cell is relatively large. Research results[3] gave evidence to the fact that suicide is most likely to occur during the very first period of detention. As the situation in police-cells is mostly worse than in prison cells the probability of relatively more deaths in police-cells must be taken into account. Therefore it is very important to get to know how many persons really die in police-cells every year before one can develop adequate measures of prevention.

On the first of November 1993 the so-called police-ministers (Interior and Justice) sent a regulation concerning the registration of deaths and attempted suicides in police-cells in a circular-letter to all police-chiefs. A translation of the questionnaire belonging to it can be found at the end of this paper.[4] The national registration soon will make obvious whether the cases of deaths in police-cells that become publicly known really are, as often is affirmed, only the tip of an iceberg.[5]

### RECENT RESEARCH

The police itself initiated research to get more information about the quality of the arrest in Dutch police-cells and about the facts that influence the quality of the arrest-situation for the detained. The research was done at Leiden University by the Department of Clinical, Health and Personality Psychology and the Department of Social and Organisational Psychology.[6] I have to restrict myself to the main results that certainly will influence the future practice in the Netherlands:

Arrested people are looked after best where special persons with an adequate education are employed that only have the task to care for them, where there is a certain number of relatively new cells (that means a certain concentration of good cells at several police-stations), so that special rooms (a lawyer's room, a doctor's room, a searching-room, a bathroom, an extra cell for juveniles, an observation room, a room to spend day-time) are available and can be used efficiently, where a certain routine in handling arrested persons can develop that brings forth practical knowledge about the different kinds of detained persons (drug-addicts, alcoholics, mentally disordered people, juveniles, foreigners etc.) and where what is going on in the cells is registered regularly. Not only deaths and suicide-attempts should be registered but also vandalism, incendiarism and bodily injuries of detained and people who care for the arrested persons.[7] Further clear regulations about the rights of the detained in the police-cells should be worked out.[8] The arrested people should be informed about the course of things in the cell-block, everybody in his or her own language. Last but not least the conclusion of the scientists is that there should be introduced a supervising commission, styled after the Amsterdam model, everywhere where police-cells are made use of.

CONCLUDING REMARK

Overviewing the recent developments one can state that the present situation concerning deaths in police custody in the Netherlands opens a positive perspective for the future.

**Notes**

1. *Regeling inzake een commissie van toezicht voor de Amsterdamse Politiecelen van 10.6.1988.*
2. NRC/HB1. (Niewe Rotterdamse Courant/Handelsblad) of 14.4.1993, p.2.
3. W. Bernasco, A.J.F.M. Kerkhof, B. van der Linden, 'Suicidaal gedrag van gedetineerden in Nederland', *Tijdschrift voor Criminologie* 1988 p.61-76.
4. In connection with the coming in to force of the new Dutch Police law and the taking over of the registration-regulation into the Decree Regional Police, some details of little importance might become revised.
5. I. van den Brule, 'Sterfgevallen in handen van Justitie en politie', *Crimineel Jaarboek* 1987/1988, Coornhert-Liga.
6. E. Blaauw, A. Kerkhof, R. Vermunt, 'Zorg voor Arrestanten in Politiecellen', Serie: Psychologische Studies, DSWO Press, Rijksuniversiteit Leiden, 1993.
7. Ibid. p.189.
8. Ibid. p.193.

MODEL-QUESTIONNAIRE ON CASES OF DEATH AND ATTEMPTED SUICIDE

(Annex to the circular letter from the first of November 1993, number EA 93/U 3068)

At .................. (date) in the police station
.................................... (name of street)
at ................................ (place name)
of the corps ....................................

the following event took place:
[ ]      a detained person died (continue with question I)
[ ]      a detained person attempted suicide or was seriously wounded (continue with question II)
I      The cause of death was:
      [ ] natural death (continue with question 1)
      [ ] suicide (continue with question III)
II      The attempt consisted in
      [ ] hanging
      [ ] burning
      [ ] wounding with a sharp object
      [ ] taking medicine
      [ ] otherwise, namely ................................
      ....................................................
      (continue with question III)
III      Give a short description of the modus operandi.
      ....................................................
      ....................................................
      (continue with question 1)

Questions in relation to the person concerned

1. When was the person detained?
   Date: ........................
   Time: ........................

2. The reason for detention was:
      [ ] questioning
      [ ] provisional apprehension
      [ ] pre-trial confinement (confinement pending further investigation)
      [ ] confinement of alien(s)
      [ ] subsidiary detention
      [ ] assistance

3. If the person was detained by reason of a punishable offence this offence was the following:
      ....................................................

4. The person's demeanour at detention consisted in
      [ ] active cooperation
      [ ] passive cooperation (irresponsive)
      [ ] no cooperation
      [ ] resistance, using force

5. Was the person responsive?
     [ ] yes
     [ ] no

6. Was the person informed about the course of things in the cell-complex or the police station before detention?
     [ ] yes (continue with question 7)
     [ ] no (continue with question 8)

7. The person was informed about the course of things in the cell-complex or police station in the following manner:
     ........................................................
     ........................................................
     ........................................................

8. Why was the person not informed about the course of things in the cell-complex or in the police station?
     ........................................................
     ........................................................

9. Had the person been detained previously?
     [ ] yes (continue with question 10)
     [ ] no (continue with question 11)

10. If the person had been detained previously was this in connection with
     [ ] questioning
     [ ] provisional apprehension
     [ ] pre-trial confinement (confinement pending further investigation)
     [ ] confinement of alien(s)
     [ ] subsidiary detention
     [ ] assistance

11. Immediately before he was detained in the room where the event took place the person was
     [ ] searched (clothes)
     [ ] searched (body)
     [ ] searched (otherwise, namely ........................
        ........................................................
     [ ] not searched

Questions concerning the room/surroundings of the event

12. The event took place in
     [ ] a cell
     [ ] a cell for drunk people
     [ ] a room for short detention
     [ ] a room for questioning
     [ ] another room, namely ...............................

13. In this room there was a camera:
     [ ] yes (if the camera was switched on continue with question 14)
    (if the camera was not on continue with question 15)
     [ ] no (continue with question 15)

14. The camera was on for the following reason:

........................................................
........................................................
........................................................

15. The following furniture and objects were in the aforesaid room:

........................................................
........................................................
........................................................
........................................................

Questions regarding medical care

16. Did the person ask for a doctor?
      [ ] yes
      [ ] no

17. Did the person ask for medicine?
      [ ] yes
      [ ] no

18. Was a doctor called for?
      [ ] yes (continue with question 19)
      [ ] no (continue with question 25)

19. The doctor was called at ....... (time)

20. The (medical) reason for calling for a doctor was the following:

........................................................
........................................................
........................................................
........................................................

21. Did the doctor come?
      [ ] yes (continue with question 22)
      [ ] no (continue with question 25)

22. The doctor came at ....... (time)

23. Did the doctor give some advice?
      [ ] yes (continue with question 24)
      [ ] no (continue with question 25)

24. The doctor gave the following advice:

........................................................
........................................................
........................................................
........................................................

25. Was a medicine administered to the person concerned?
      [ ] yes

[ ] no

26. Was the person observed?
      [ ] yes (continue with question 27)
      [ ] no (continue with question 28)

27. The frequency of the observation was:
      [ ] every quarter of an hour
      [ ] three times in six hours
      [ ] as advised by the doctor, every ............(period)
      [ ] otherwise, namely
      ....................................................

28. Is a functionary in the police station or the cell-complex appointed to be responsible for the (medical) care of the detained?
      [ ] yes, (definition of function) ......................
      [ ] no

Questions concerning registration

29. Do you keep a register for the care of the detained?
      [ ] yes (continue with question 30)
      [ ] no (continue with question 31)

30. The following data are kept in the register of the cell-complex:
      [ ] personalia
      [ ] medical data
      [ ] time of        [ ]  detention
                          [ ]  meals
                          [ ]  airing
                          [ ]  visits
                          [ ]  baths
                          [ ]  visit of doctor
                          [ ]  visit of lawyer
                          [ ]  other data, namely ...............................
                                ....................................................
                                ....................................................

31. Further the following data are of importance:
      ....................................................
      ....................................................
      ....................................................
      ....................................................
      ....................................................
      ....................................................

To be sent to: Home Office, etc. etc.

# Ten

# HIV epidemiology in prisons: Anonymous voluntary HIV surveillance with risk factor elicitation

*Sheila M Gore, A Graham Bird and Sheila M Burns*

SUMMARY

The background to anonymous voluntary HIV surveillance (via saliva samples) with linked risk factor elicitation by self-completion questionnaire, as pioneered in the Scottish Prison Service, is reviewed. The major findings are: a sixth of inmates are injectors and nearly half the adult injector-inmates had, at some time, injected inside. These data underpinned the Scottish Prison Service's decision to introduce a drug reduction programme to HMP Saughton in 1992. Prisoners' high prevalence of sexual as well as injecting HIV risk behaviours makes prisons a suitable location to offer HIV/AIDS education and for inmates to check out their HIV status by uptake of confidential, personal HIV tests during incarceration. Some prisons in the east of Scotland have established inmates' trust sufficiently that HIV test requests average 16 per 1000 admissions annually.

Drug injecting in a Scottish jail, HMP Glenochil, during January to June 1993 is known to have transmitted HIV infection to more than 10 inmates. Urgently needed is a public health protocol that can be implemented when HIV transmission occurs in a prison, and which not only guarantees prisoners the right to medical confidentiality but also ensures that accurate epidemiological information is collected. Good practice in the aftermath of Glenochil's infections should be disseminated widely and, as importantly, forewarning given to avoid repetition of unsuccessful aspects. HIV infection was also transmitted (sexually) in an English prison in early 1994. These seroconversions are tragic and unnecessary confirmation – given the available evidence on prisoners' HIV risk behaviours – of inmates' need for greater access to harm reduction measures (condoms, disinfectant, drug reduction programmes).

A new design for the monitoring of temporal changes in HIV risk behaviours during incarceration and for surveillance of HIV seroconversions in prison is described. Safeguards in the new protocol include: locked salivette-safes and questionnaire-safes (keys held outwith the establishment); batch testing of saliva samples (100 or more) to guarantee against deductive disclosure; involvement by two laboratories (for receiving and testing of samples) to ensure ignorance at the testing laboratory of the concealed code by which a prisoner's initial and discharge samples are paired and linked to his risk factor questionnaire (which is self-completed at discharge); revelation of concealed codes to statistical centre in batches, and only after prisoner discharge, as additional security against deductive disclosure.

Other aspects of HIV epidemiology in prisons - CD4 counts for immunostaging of prevalent HIV infections and how to assess whether HIV progression is affected by incarceration - are briefly discussed. Careful research to evaluate needle exchange in prisons needs to take into account the interests of officers and other inmates as well as of injectors.

## INTRODUCTION

Anonymous voluntary HIV surveillance (via saliva samples) with linked risk factor elicitation by self-completion questionnaire was pioneered in the Scottish Prison Service. The first studies were cross-sectional (that is: of all inmates) and took place over one or two surveillance days at HMP Saughton in Edinburgh (August 1991[1]; repeated October 1992[2]) and at HMYOI Polmont (October 1992 (3)). A team of 15-25 external HIV-knowledgable volunteers conducted the surveillance studies, that is: they assisted inmates, as necessary, with completion of questionnaires (see Figures 1 and 2, at end of chapter) and in obtaining salivary samples.

In April 1993, three months' anonymous voluntary HIV surveillance by a research team of two nurses began of receptions into three London male prisons (Belmarsh, Pentonville and Wormwood Scrubs). Surveillance during busy, stressful reception periods is protracted, more costly and encountered greater difficulties than the above cross-sectional approach, which has worked very well (volunteer rates of 76% and 99%) when establishments were on recreation for the surveillance day(s). By contrast, the volunteer rate was 50% on repeat cross-sectional surveillance at HMP Saughton[2] when the prison was not on recreation; and participation rate was 54% of 1150 eligible London receptions.[4] At HMP Saughton, HIV surveillance studies were set in the context of a health-day; at HMYOI Polmont, a film 'The Butterfly Garden' about HIV infected prisoners was showing in an anteroom to the HIV surveillance area.

Advantages of the cross-sectional approach are that advance information can be given to inmates and officers about:

1.  the rationale for HIV surveillance in prison establishments and how prisons' HIV surveillance: (i) fits into a national strategy of surveillance (see Figure 3: other sentinel groups for HIV surveillance are pregnant women, attenders at sexually transmitted disease clinics, hospital inpatients, injecting drug users, travellers and university students) and (ii) allows better planning of healthcare and harm reduction for prisoners;

2.  the safeguards by which the external research team guarantees prisoners' anonymity, making it impossible for reported risk factors or HIV salivary result to be linked back to an individual prisoner, and the presence throughout of prisoner scrutineers to ensure that the study is conducted as intended;

3.  the arrangements to inform prisoners subsequently about the findings from the surveillance and the intention to publish them; and

4.  the separate arrangements that the prison medical service has established to provide HIV counselling and confidential personal tests for prisoners who wish to ascertain their HIV status.

Provision within the prison for inmates to access confidential HIV counselling and testing is an ethical pre-requisite to surveillance. Previous anonymous voluntary HIV surveillance studies with risk factor elicitation in establishments of the Scottish Prison Service have resulted in heightened HIV awareness among inmates and have been associated with increased requests to the prison medical service for confidential, counselled personal HIV tests.[2, 5] Over 90 requests - an unexpectedly high number - were made during HIV surveillance at HMYOI Polmont[3] and remarkably were met by the establishment within one week with hurriedly arranged assistance from outside HIV counsellors. Future studies, as now proposed, should plan in advance how to cope quickly and professionally with so many requests. That so many young men sought a personal test at a time of heightened HIV awareness, and when the requests could be made easily, underlines how prisons can be used effectively by inmates to check their HIV status[2, 3, 5] – some are markedly more successful in this role than others.[6]

Prisoners and young offenders are an important sentinel group for HIV surveillance because (see Figure 4) injecting drug users are imprisoned frequently – for theft and other crimes besides drugs-related offences. Also, prisons are a reflection of the communities they serve. Remand and short-stay prisoners, who are mostly young, sexually active, heterosexual males (see Figures 1 & 2), soon return to those communities. Importantly, HIV epidemiology in prisons allows better planning of harm reduction and healthcare for prisoners; and an advantage of prison (and university[7]) studies is that volunteer rate and bias (see, for example, Figure 1: lower volunteer rate by remand than convicted prisoners on repeat HIV surveillance at HMP Saughton in 1992) can be assessed by comparing age, place of residence and length of sentence (year of study) of participants versus all inmates (students).

PRECIS OF FINDINGS

Anonymous voluntary HIV surveillance with risk factor elicitation in establishments of the Scottish Prison Service has shown that injecting drug use (by 17 fold), multiplicity of female partners (by 12 fold), and homosexuality (by 4 fold) are more frequent in prisoners and young offenders than in males of the same age in the general population. Seventeen per cent of adult male prisoners in Saughton and of young offenders in Polmont had at some time injected non-medically prescribed drugs, with half of the adult and a quarter of the young offender injectors having injected whilst inside. Young offenders' prevalence of injecting drug use varied geographically: 28 per cent (33/120) of young offenders from Glasgow had injected drugs compared to 9 per cent (7/81) of those from Edinburgh and Fife. A high level of heterosexual activity was reported with 36 per cent of nearly 400 young offenders claiming to have had 6 or more female sexual partners in the year before imprisonment, as did 14 per cent of 85 Saughton prisoners aged 26-35 years in 1992. In adults and young offenders alike, HIV test uptake was higher by Edinburgh residents.[1,3] The prison studies also revealed a deficit in HIV test uptake by adult prisoners from Fife[1], thus highlighting regional variation in community HIV education and services. There was a doubling in HIV test uptake by non-injector heterosexual males who took part in 1991 and 1992 HIV surveillance at HMP Saughton. Accordingly, HIV test requests by non-injector heterosexuals in Scotland for the years 1989 to 1992 were subsequently reviewed, and corroborated the prison observations. Test requests are reported to the Scottish Centre for Infection and Environmental Health: for non-injector heterosexuals, they increased dramatically from just over 4000 in 1989 and more than 5000 in 1990 to over 8000 in 1991 and in 1992. During 1989-1992 in Scotland, HIV prevalence was 148 out of 27591 voluntary test requests by heterosexuals, or 5 in 1000.[8]

At HMP Saughton in 1991, HIV prevalence was only one quarter higher at 4.5 per cent than was known to the prison's medical officers. All 17 men who were HIV antibody positive on saliva testing were injectors, who had previously been HIV sero-tested. HIV prevalence was 25 per cent among injector-inmates. On 28 October 1992, no youth was HIV infected at Polmont, Scotland's largest young offenders' institution, but a high prevalence of HIV risk behaviours (see Figures 1 and 2) emphasised the importance of HIV surveillance for prison populations and 'the vulnerability of such populations to rapidly emerging HIV infection'. Sadly, within 6 months, that forewarning came true in an outbreak of HIV and Hepatitis B (HBV) transmission among injectors in HMP Glenochil.[9]

GLENOCHIL SEROCONVERSIONS FOR HEPATITIS B AND HIV

Arrangements were speedily made to offer counselling and confidential, non-nominal HIV blood testing, for which purpose a team of outside HIV counsellors, under the auspices of the

Scottish Centre for Infection and Environmental Health, was brought into HMP Glenochil. Of 378 then inmates, 227 (60%) accepted HIV counselling and 162 (43%) proceeded to have an HIV blood test; reasons for not proceeding will have included the absence of behavioural risk factors for HIV infection. Volunteer bias was not assessed, for example: by age-group, place of residence or prison wing. HIV transmissions are now known to have occurred in HMP Glenochil between February and May 1993. But the proportions who seroconverted: of injector inmates, or of injector-inmates who had injected in Glenochil between January and June 1993, OR of injector-inmates who shared needles or works[10] in Glenochil between January and June 1993 OR of HIV-exposed injectors are unknown. The reasons are fourfold:

1. the HIV transmission period was only identified by the confidential inquiry and serology of those who were found to be HIV infected;
2. there was modest uptake of confidential HIV blood tests by the then inmates;
3. moreover, information is incomplete on then inmates' HIV risk behaviours; and
4. molecular epidemiological information is, as yet, incomplete about likely source of infection (the presumed infector having died within one year of the outbreak).

A public health protocol that can be implemented when HIV transmission occurs in a jail[11] has been outlined: it guarantees prisoners' right to medical confidentiality while ensuring that accurate epidemiological information is collected. When HIV seroconversion occurs in a prison, other inmates must be told at the earliest opportunity that this has happened and that the extent of transmission is not yet known. Prisoners should have access to confidential counselling facilities from outside the prison, in addition to the prison's HIV trained staff-counsellors. An amnesty should be declared for prisoners to surrender needles; condoms should be made available; and the prison should set up a drug reduction programme if transmission was by needle sharing. For public health purposes which entail the dissemination of findings, prisoners should be asked to volunteer a saliva sample for anonymous HIV/HEP B testing and to complete a linked behavioural risk factor questionnaire. To maximise compliance inmates must be fully and frankly informed about how anonymity is secured, and should understand that good epidemiology, which is essential to inform present planning and future policy, requires their co-operation. Against the backdrop of anonymous surveillance (because it promotes requests for personal tests), there is need to facilitate prisoners' determination of personal HIV/HEP B status with maximum confidentiality and without disclosure of names if prisoners prefer it (see above: access to outside HIV counsellors). Prisons' need for such a public health protocol was not specifically envisaged in the 1993 WHO Guidelines on HIV Infection and AIDS in Prisons.[12] Nevertheless, it accords with the principles of confidentiality, comparability and independence of research which the guidelines endorse.

ANONYMOUS HIV SURVEILLANCE AT HMP&YOI GLENOCHIL<br>AND AT HMP BARLINNIE IN 1994

The planned anonymous voluntary HIV surveillance with risk factor elicitation at HMP&YOI Glenochil in July 1994 is set firmly in the context of our previous studies at HMP Saughton and HMYOI Polmont, and of proposed 1994 surveillance in Scotland's largest male prison, HMP Barlinnie, in Glasgow. By inclusion of three extra questions, however, we shall seek to establish whether an inmate of HMP Glenochil was incarcerated in Glenochil in the period January to June 1993; and took a blood test for HIV in Glenochil during that period; and whether current inmates, whether of HMP Glenochil or HMP Barlinnie, had injected in Glenochil during January to June 1993. We propose that the 'Glenochil annex of questions' be included for all future HIV surveillance studies in any adult male prison in Scotland; and that an explanation is given to prisoners of the reason for this: namely that injecting in Glenochil during the defined period is known to have transmitted HIV infection and so constitutes a specific HIV behavioural risk factor in the Scottish prison population.

The choice of Barlinnie as the second establishment in which to conduct HIV surveillance in 1994 is based not solely on its being Scotland's largest prison but for several other reasons. Firstly, the 1992 Polmont study had indicated a very much higher prevalence of injecting drug use by Glasgow youths; and in November 1993 there was a public inquiry into a representative four Glasgow deaths in young drug users.[13, 14, 15] Secondly, west of Scotland inmates were implicated in HIV transmissions in Glenochil. Thirdly, in 1990-91, there was a 7-

fold lower uptake during incarceration of confidential named HIV tests by male inmates in local prisons in the south and west of Scotland - including Barlinnie - than in the north and east.[6] Fourthly, healthcare and other initiatives on HIV/AIDS education by the South-West Prison Directorate of the Scottish Prison Service made it opportune to offer anonymous voluntary HIV surveillance with risk factor elicitation as part of those initiatives in 1994. Finally, HMP Barlinnie completes HIV surveillance with risk factor elicitation from east to west in major establishments of the Scottish Prison Service which are located in Scotland's central belt.

To achieve maximum compliance with anonymous voluntary HIV salivary testing linked to self-completion questionnaire, a protocol detailing actions by the establishment, research team and inmates is given in the Appendix. This protocol is based on the successful and now well-accepted methodology initiated at HMP Saughton in August 1991.

References to other methodologies are included in the additional reading. These feature: without consent, anonymized HIV testing of residues from obligatory blood samples (as in USA); anonymous voluntary HIV serosurveillance with minimal (as in British Columbia where prison nurses were responsible for obtaining blood samples) or more extensive risk factor elicitation (as in Sweden and France where research personnel conducted the studies); prisoner interviews or self-completion questionnaires in which questions about HIV status as well as about risk factors and HIV test uptake are posed; anonymous, voluntary HIV surveillance (using saliva samples) with risk factor elicitation in convenience quota samples of ex-prisoners; questions about terms of imprisonment posed to injecting drug users who participate in anonymous, voluntary HIV surveillance and complete a linked risk-factor questionnaire (as in the UK).

PILOT SURVEILLANCE OF HIV SEROCONVERSIONS AND TEMPORAL CHANGE IN RISK BEHAVIOURS (INCLUDING DURING INCARCERATION) WHICH ARE SELF-REPORTED AT DISCHARGE.

The 1993 HIV transmissions in Glenochil and the higher proportion of injectors among young inmates from Glasgow, as documented by the Polmont surveillance, point to HMP Glenochil & Barlinnie as suitable establishments in Scotland at which to pilot anonymous voluntary surveillance of HIV seroconversion and associated risk behaviours. This new design would require the pairing of initial with discharge saliva sample and linkage to a risk factor questionnaire, which was self-completed at discharge. Such surveillance could monitor temporal changes in HIV risk behaviours, including inside the establishment; and HIV seroconversions, if any, during incarceration. The former is particularly relevant because of the introduction, for example at HMP Glenochil in autumn 1993, of a rehabilitation programme for injecting drug users and, since December 1993, the provision of Milton tablets for disinfection to all prisoners in Scotland. The new discharge questionnaire would ask about prisoners' utilization of such new facilities to reduce HIV risk.

Only close attention to details (see Design) can ensure maximum compliance with provision of admission (or cross-sectional) and discharge salivary samples, their pairing, self-completion of linked discharge questionnaire, and batch HIV testing of saliva samples (minimum batch size for testing: 100 samples). Careful safeguards against deductive disclosure of the identity of volunteer inmates, transferred and ex-prisoners are built into the protocol. Equally important, however, is to track the volunteer rate at admission (or cross-sectionally) and at discharge on a temporal basis, and a simple scheme using tokens has been devised for doing so.

Many of Barlinnie's over 8000 admissions per annum are a prelude to prisoners' transfer to other establishments. Although admission and discharge samples could sensibly be paired from HMP Barlinnie (with or without special consideration being given to the transfers just described), at HMP Glenochil the waiting time to pair-formation would be unduly long - sentences are for over four years - unless the initial samples were cross-sectional, that is: obtained from current inmates. The new design is described for the pairing of admission and discharge samples. Adaptation to cope with the initial samples being cross-sectional is straightforward. Note that pilot surveillance of HIV seroconversions is a more difficult objective than surveillance of HIV prevalence. We suggest that it should not be attempted in establishments which have not taken part successfully in cross-sectional HIV surveillance.

ESSENTIAL FEATURES OF NEW DESIGN

The essential features of the new design are described in outline for HMP XXX. We assume that the initial saliva sample is requested at admission. Details would need to be fine-tuned in

122

consultation with the Governor and medical & nursing officers of any establishment concerned.

*In the establishment*

From an agreed start date, all new receptions to HMP XXX will be asked on the day after reception by a medical/nursing officer: voluntarily to provide for anonymous HIV testing a saliva sample by chewing on a cotton wool swab. The prisoner replaces the swab in the salivette from which it came; and selects at random (from a bag containing 50 or more) a grey wax sealed label-triple. He then puts his salivette together with the A-label (A for Admission) from his label-triple into a polythene bag, which he closes securely (e.g. by placing a rubber band around it) and which is then deposited by him in a locked salivette-safe. Keys to salivette-safe are held by Laboratory X (see below). If the inmate wishes not to provide a saliva sample, then he still selects at random a grey wax sealed label-triple but the A-label is fixed to a cardboard token which is deposited in the salivette-safe instead - to indicate that a prisoner has declined to provide an admission saliva sample. In this way, a grey wax sealed label-pair remains irrespective of whether the prisoner agreed to give a saliva sample or not. (No demographic or sentencing information is linked to the initial saliva sample or to the non-participant token.) The prisoner's number is then written in the A-label location before the remaining wax sealed grey label-pair is filed in the medical wing of the prison - in order of prisoner number for ease of retrieval.

On the day before a prisoner is due to be discharged, whose admission date was later than the start of the seroincidence surveillance study, he is escorted to the medical wing where the medical/nursing officer retrieves the man's label-pair from the grey sealed-label admission file. Otherwise, if the prisoner entered the establishment prior to the start of seroincidence surveillance, he is asked to select at random a blue wax sealed label-pair from a bag containing 50 or more such blue sealed label-pairs.

At this point, any prisoner about to be discharged should be in possession of a wax sealed label-pair: grey if he was invited to provide an admission sample, blue otherwise. If, in error, the prisoner was not invited to provide an admission sample - but did enter the establishment after the start of surveillance - then no grey wax sealed label-pair will have been located; or, if there had been a grey wax sealed label-pair for this man but it has been misplaced, the prisoner will be without a label-pair. Such prisoners, for whom there should have been a grey wax sealed label-pair but none has been located, are asked to select at random a red wax sealed label-pair from a bag containing 50 or more such red label-pairs. The colour coding - grey or blue or red – distinguishes the above three possibilities.

Prisoners who hold a grey label-pair are asked to satisfy themselves that the seals are intact. If they are not intact, a yellow breach-of-study-procedure token is placed in the locked salivette-safe with the prisoner's D-label on it and one in the locked questionnaire-safe with the prisoner's Q-label attached. The prisoner's further participation is not requested because his anonymity may have been breached.

All remaining prisoners about to be discharged now possess an intact wax sealed label-pair. They are then asked to volunteer a discharge saliva sample to be tested anonymously for HIV antibodies and to self-complete an HIV risk factor questionnaire which includes questions about risk behaviours during incarceration in HMP XXX and other prisons as well as before this sentence began. Prisoners must be afforded privacy while answering the questionnaire.

The prisoner may choose to complete some, all or none of the questionnaire; and/or he may decline to provide a discharge saliva sample. Men who volunteer a discharge saliva sample are asked to enclose the D-label (D for Discharge) of their sealed label-pair with their salivette in an individual cellophane bag, which is then secured carefully and deposited in the locked salivette-safe. Those who decline to provide a discharge saliva sample affix their D-label to a cardboard token instead, and it is deposited in the locked salivette-safe as a means of counting about-to-be-discharged non-participants. Prisoners are asked to affix the Q-label to the foot of their questionnaire - whether they have answered it completely, selectively or not at all; to fold the questionnaire into an envelope provided and to deposit the enveloped questionnaire in a locked questionnaire-safe, the key to which is held by a prison visitor. Typically, the questionnaire-safe will be emptied after 100 or more discharges from HMP XXX, so that non-participation rate and the quality of completion of questionnaires can reported to the establishment on a regular basis. The prevalence of HIV risk behaviours will be reported to HMP XXX per 300 or more consecutive discharges, but care will be taken to avoid deductive disclosure.

The HIV antibody test results at admission and discharge will eventually be compared for those who, having volunteered both admission and discharge samples, tested HIV antibody positive at discharge; and any seroconversions will be related to HIV risk behaviours which were self-reported on the linked discharge questionnaire. Recall that inmates who may have declined to give an admission sample hold grey label-pairs which are identical in appearance to those held by men who did provide an admission saliva sample, and so the subset of men who volunteer both admission and discharge saliva samples is not identifiable within the establishment.

The number of discharged prisoners who, for whatever reason, were not escorted to the medical wing to take part in discharge HIV surveillance needs to be computed, and recorded, by appropriate comparison of attendance tallies kept on the medical wing against discharges. Additionally, a check should be made on whether grey wax-sealed label pairs remain on file for the men who were discharged yesterday. If so, the corresponding pairs are removed from the file and the D- and Q-labels are fixed to orange tokens, which are deposited in the locked salivette and questionnaire safes respectively to denote that the prisoner whose labels these are has indeed been discharged but escort failure accounts for his non-participation.

The next paragraphs (see also Figure 5) describe the procedures for weekly transport of saliva samples from HMP XXX to Laboratory X, where the salivette-safe is opened and samples are logged-in, serial-numbered and spun; but they are tested at Laboratory Y. HIV antibody positive results are reported by Laboratory Y to the Statistical Centre. Permitted linkage by the statistical centre, via Laboratory X, of the admission and discharge antibody results for an individual ex-prisoner who tests HIV antibody positive on discharge is described below, together with the permitted information flow from Laboratory X to the statistical centre concerning discharged prisoners who did not volunteer a saliva sample at discharge. The permitted information is: discharge label colour and concealed number together with, if applicable, grey admission saliva serial number/admission non-participant status. This information allows the statistical centre to record the man's admission and discharge saliva result/non-participation alongside his discharge questionnaire data.

*At Laboratory X*

(Which receives salivettes/tokens, serially numbers the received salivettes and makes a computer log of the received & serial numbered salivettes & tokens).

Of three locked salivette-safes, there is always one in use at HMP XXX, one at Laboratory X for processing, and one not in use but en route between Laboratory X and HMP XXX. The locked salivette-safe is opened on receipt at Laboratory X, the tokens and salivettes are removed and a computer log is made of them as follows - one line of data for each token or salivette: batch code, date of receipt, salivette or token, colour of wax seal, concealed code (A or D), 6-digit serial number which is assigned to salivettes at Laboratory X (A or D @@@/@@@) consisting of batch code and serial count of saliva specimens per admission (A) or discharge (D) batch. If the wax seal is not intact on receipt at Laboratory X, saliva specimen is discarded untested; nor is any subsequent sample from this man passed to Laboratory Y for testing.

The three digit serial number counts how many A (for admission sample) or D (for discharge sample) salivettes have been logged in at Laboratory X but have not so far been passed to Laboratory Y for HIV antibody testing. At the end of the processing in Laboratory X of all salivettes/tokens for any particular study week, a check is made on whether the serial number of admission salivas awaiting HIV antibody testing exceeds 100. If so, the accumulated A-serial labelled salivas are sent to Laboratory Y for HIV antibody testing, the A-counter is reset to 000 for the next study week, and the A batch-code increases by 1. If not, the A-counter registers the last used A-serial label, from which labelling will continue for at least one other study week. Likewise, a check is made on whether the serial number of discharge salivas awaiting HIV antibody testing exceeds 100. If so, the accumulated D-serial labelled salivas are sent to Laboratory Y for HIV antibody testing, the D-counter is reset to 000, and the D batch-code increases by 1; otherwise the D-counter registers the last used D-serial label, from which labelling will continue for another study week.

Spun saliva samples are forwarded from Laboratory X to Laboratory Y in admission sample batches of at least 100; or in discharge sample batches of at least 100. Each batch receives an A or D batch code in sequence. Whenever Laboratory X sends an A or D batch of 100 or more serial-labelled samples to Laboratory Y for HIV antibody testing, Laboratory X also sends the following volunteer rate report to the statistical centre:

Batch type (A or D) and dates (first study week, last study week): #yellow breach-of-study-procedure tokens & #orange breach-of-escort tokens (discharge batches only).

Volunteer summary: #non-participation tokens {N}; #salivettes {S}; volunteer rate {S/(S+N)}.

Laboratory X has a further reporting responsibility. Whenever a D batch of 100 or more serial number-labelled discharge saliva samples is sent for HIV antibody testing to Laboratory Y, a discharged non-participant list is forwarded to the statistical centre pertaining to the study weeks for which the D batch of samples has just been issued for testing. For the relevant study weeks, the following details are given on the discharged non-participant list for any prisoner discharged during those study weeks who declined, or was not given the opportunity (orange tokens), to provide a discharge saliva sample and whose D-label was therefore affixed to a cardboard token on receipt at Laboratory X.[1]

On receipt of the above information the statistical centre registers the unavailability (code 8) of a discharge saliva sample; discharge label colour is cross-checked with the code already entered (based on matching colour of the ex-prisoner's Q-label); and in the 'Admission Sample' data-field is encoded whether an admission saliva was provided and, if so, its serial number (at least until HIV antibody test results for the A-batch to which the admission saliva belongs have been received, when HIV antibody test result will be entered).

## At Laboratory Y

Receipt of an A or D batch of 100 or more serially labelled samples constitutes permission for Laboratory Y to perform HIV antibody testing on the received batch of saliva samples. The serial-label of any sample (i) which is confirmed on Western blot as HIV antibody positive or (ii) for which there was insufficient saliva for testing is reported by Laboratory Y to the statistical centre.

## At Statistical Centre

Questionnaires are received from HMP XXX's locked questionnaire-safe at regular intervals. The key to the questionnaire-safe should be held by a prison visitor who supervises the monthly posting of questionnaires and tokens from the used safe to the statistical centre. During data processing of questionnaires wax-seals will be removed to reveal the prisoner's randomly selected concealed 5-digit number, by which the questionnaire data-file will be indexed together with colour of wax-seal (1 for grey, 2 for blue, 3 for red) and the latest date (i.e. study week) to which the questionnaire could pertain. Whenever a discharged non-participant list is received at the statistical centre from Laboratory X the questionnaire data-file is updated accordingly from the information received.

On completion of A batch testing at Laboratory Y, the statistical centre is informed by Laboratory Y of:

1. the A batch code, the study weeks it corresponds to, and number of samples in the batch of 100 or more admission saliva samples received HIV antibody testing;
2. the A serial numbers of those with insufficient saliva for testing; and
3. the A serial numbers of those which were Western blot-confirmed HIV antibody positive.

The statistical centre prepares an admission HIV prevalence report to complement the volunteer rate report previously received from Laboratory X when this A batch was forwarded to Laboratory Y for HIV antibody testing. No attempt is made by the statistical centre to ascertain from Laboratory X the concealed 5-digit numbers pertaining to HIV antibody positive inmates, because they may be incarcerated still at HMP XXX.

On completion of D batch testing at Laboratory Y, the statistical centre is informed by Laboratory Y of:

1. the D batch code, the study weeks it corresponds to, and number of samples in a batch of 100 or more discharge saliva samples received HIV antibody testing;
2. the D serial numbers of those with insufficient saliva for testing; and
3. the D serial numbers of those which were Western blot-confirmed HIV antibody positive.

The statistical centre then requests from Laboratory X the concealed 5-digit number and wax-seal colour pertaining to each D serial number in list ( ii) or (iii) above, so that the ex-prisoner's discharge saliva result can be entered on the questionnaire data-file, which is, of course, indexed by the requested data - concealed 5-digit number and colour. Also requested for these discharged individuals is the corresponding A serial-number of their admission saliva sample or the fact that an admission saliva sample was declined. A check is then made at the statistical centre to discover if the admission sample provided by those who tested HIV antibody positive on discharge was already HIV antibody positive at admission. If not, and a linkable (i.e. grey discharge seal) admission sample was provided, the ex-prisoner is counted as having seroconverted in HMP XXX. (The check is made simply by searching for the A serial-numbers provided by Laboratory X among those already notified by Laboratory Y as having tested HIV antibody positive - assuming, of course, that the A serial-numbers belong to an already HIV tested A-batch. If not, the foregoing check is repeated after the relevant A batch has been HIV tested). The questionnaire data-file is thus updated with the paired information concerning the admission sample for discharged prisoners whose discharge saliva sample was (ii) insufficient or (iii) HIV antibody positive.

Regular analyses - per 300 completed discharge questionnaires - should be made at the statistical centre of the prevalence of HIV risk behaviours, including during incarceration. Less frequently - per 600 paired discharge questionnaires and saliva tests - those risk behaviours will be analysed in relation to HIV prevalence at discharge. HMP XXX and current inmates will be notified immediately in the event that an HIV seroconversion during incarceration is discovered.

### DISCUSSION

Several limitations of the new design for monitoring HIV seroconversion and risk behaviours during incarceration are acknowledged before the discussion broadens to other aspects of HIV epidemiology in prisons. First, the seroconversion design will be limited in its function as an aid to timely prisoner notification about HIV exposure and associated risk behaviours unless: i) the discharge questionnaire asks about recent risk behaviours in prison as well as over the term of this imprisonment; ii) the calendar period to accumulate 300 discharges for analysis of risk behaviours is brief - for example, less than three months - so that the surveillance information is still directly relevant to a high proportion of current inmates who were imprisoned during the relevant calendar period; and iii) the admission-to-discharge interval is short for any ex-prisoner whose discharge (but not admission) saliva sample tested HIV antibody positive - so that current and ex-prisoners may be given reasonably precise information about the calendar period when, if they had engaged in specific HIV risk behaviours, they may have been exposed to an HIV infected individual who was seroconverting. Secondly, if the new design succeeds in identifying calendar periods when seroconversion(s) occurred during incarceration, there are dangers of deductive disclosure concerning the identity of the seroconverter(s) by the individual, by other inmates or by the prison authorities because detailed surveillance information has been revealed about calendar period of seroconversion and HIV risk behaviours of the infected ex-prisoner(s). The research team must determine the extent of disclosure that will be permitted in the event of seroconversions being recognised by surveillance; and must advise prisoners of these procedures in advance - for example, when inmates' voluntary participation in surveillance is invited. Thirdly, it may be inefficient to propose the new design for prisons in which previous cross-sectional surveillance has revealed neither a high prevalence of HIV infection nor of HIV risk behaviours. Fourthly, the more detailed are the questions about prisoners' utilization of HIV harm reduction measures, the greater is the value of the surveillance for informing prison policy but also the risk is higher of deducing from their answers the identity of individual ex-prisoners, to whom this risk of deductive disclosure may be unacceptable - because of later re-offences and re-admission - and so volunteer rate would be compromised. Surveillance of HIV seroconversions and risk behaviours during incarceration will be reliable as a guide to the effectiveness of the prison's harm reduction measures only if there is a consistently high volunteer rate and no evidence of volunteer bias - in terms of prison demography (see Figure 1) - in self-completion of discharge questionnaires. A fifth limitation is that if the prison authorities act punitively on surveillance information, for example by increased searches of cells and accommodation for injecting equipment or of visitors for drugs, then prisoners' co-operation is likely to be withdrawn or answers fabricated, which is even worse because harder to detect.

Cross-sectional surveillance of HIV prevalence in establishments of the Scottish Prison Service has so far disclosed prevalences which were only modestly (or not at all) higher than were known about by the prison's medical service, and this was reassuring for inmates and officers alike. We suggest, however, that in establishments where the undisclosed HIV prevalence is shown to be greater than the known HIV prevalence and where the estimated number of undisclosed HIV infections exceeds 20, then voluntary anonymous immunostaging of the undisclosed HIV infections should be attempted by inviting all, or sections of, inmates to volunteer a blood sample to be tested anonymously for HIV antibodies and, if positive, for the number of CD4 cells to be evaluated. CD4 cell count measures HIV disease progression and so current CD4 cell count could be compared between known (to the prison medical service) HIV infected inmates, those whose infection is undisclosed to the prison's medical service, and individuals who are themselves unaware of their HIV infection and who may (or may not) have seroconverted more recently.

Prisons have a duty of care as well as custody. One aspect of their duty of care is provision of a standard of healthcare which equals that outside. A study of whether periods of incarceration in HMP Saughton have affected the HIV progression of Edinburgh's HIV infected male injectors has been planned along the following lines. Typically, HIV infected drug users have multiple short periods of incarceration. These can be considered as time-dependent covariates (just as pregnancies are, for example, in female patients), the influence of which on HIV progression can be evaluated in a cohort of HIV infected injecting drug users for whom these periods of incarceration have been identified by confidential access to their prison records. Access must be by a medical researcher and arranged in such a way that the prison authorities cannot deduce which prison records have been accessed, and hence which inmates or ex-prisoners are known to be HIV infected. In this way the medical confidentiality of HIV infected injectors is safeguarded and the data are acquired to check whether periods of imprisonment have a measurable effect on HIV progression.

Harm reduction for prisoners could include one-for-one needle exchange within the prison.[12] Research studies to evaluate such schemes have not so far been initiated in the UK, but may be under way elsewhere. We have argued that research designs must take into account the interests of officers and other inmates as well as injectors.[16]

## Anonymised HIV surveillance in HM Prison, Saughton

Thank you for your help in this study which will enable us to plan better HIV care in prisons. We do not need to know your name nor any other form of identification when you complete this questionnaire. It goes to the Medical Research Council for analysis. No results will be reported which relate to fewer than 50 prisoners.

Please tick (✓) the box beside the answer that applies to you

|  |  |  | % (%I*) | [% all available inmates] |
|---|---|---|---|---|
| 1 | How old are you? | | | |
| | under 26 years | 87 | 38 ( 47) | |
| | 26-30 years | 56 | 24 ( 26) | 35% |
| | 31-35 years | 30 | 13 ( 13) | 23% |
| | 36-40 years | 23 | | 15% |
| | over 40 | 33 | 24 ( 13) | 28% |

2 Where did you live before coming in to Saughton prison?

| | | |
|---|---|---|
| NW Edinburgh (eg Muirhouse) | 21 | |
| NE Edinburgh (eg Leith) | 18 | 40% (40%) |
| SE Edinburgh (eg Craigmillar) | 30 | (68%) |
| SW Edinburgh (eg Dalry) | 23 | |

| | | % (%I*) | [% all available inmates] |
|---|---|---|---|
| Dundee | 30 | 13 ( 3) | 10% |
| Fife | 32 | 14 ( 8) | 12% |
| Glasgow | 30 | 13 ( 21) | |
| elsewhere | 75 | 33 ( 81) | 37% |

| 3 | How long is your present sentence? | | % (%I*) | [% all available inmates] |
|---|---|---|---|---|
| | REMAND PRISONER | 21 | 9 ( 10) | 20% |
| | less than 3 months | 9 | 21 ( 29) | 19% |
| | between 3 and 6 months | 38 | | |
| | between 7 and 12 months | 22 | 30 ( 37) | 24% |
| | between 1 and 3 years | 45 | | |
| | more than 3 years | 89 | 40 ( 24) | 38% |

NK = 5

| 4 | When did your present sentence begin? | | % (%I*) |
|---|---|---|---|
| | REMAND PRISONER | 21 | 9 ( 11) |
| | in 1992 | 109 | 49 ( 57) |
| | in 1991 | 18 | 8 ( 11) |
| | in 1990 or 1989 or 1988 or 1987 | 32 | 34 ( 20) |
| | in 1986 or 1985 or 1984 or 1983 | 25 | |
| | before 1983 | 19 | |

NK = 5

| 5 | How many times have you been inside before this sentence? | | % (%I*) |
|---|---|---|---|
| | never | 71 | 31 ( 5) |
| | once | 32 | 14 ( 8) |
| | 2 or 3 or 4 times | 42 | 18 ( 29) |
| | 5 or more times | 83 | 36 ( 58) |

NK = 1

| 6 | Have you been in a borstal or young offenders' institution? | | % (%I*) |
|---|---|---|---|
| | yes | 121 | 53 ( 66) |
| | no | 107 | 47 ( 34) |

NK = 1

| 7 | Have you ever been charged with a drugs-related offence? | | % (%I*) |
|---|---|---|---|
| | yes | 60 | 26 ( 74) |
| | no | 168 | 74 ( 26) |

NK = 1

| 8 | How much time have you done inside since January 1983 | | % (%I*) |
|---|---|---|---|
| | less than 6 months | 47 | 21 ( 8) |
| | between 7 and 12 months | 18 | 24 ( 21) |
| | between 1 and 3 years | 37 | |
| | more than 3 years | 123 | 55 ( 71) |

NK = 4

| 9 | In which year did you first inject (non medically prescribed drugs)? | | % (%I*) |
|---|---|---|---|
| | NEVER INJECTED | 186 | 81 (NA) |
| | 1979 or earlier | | |
| | 1980-1982 | | 7 ( 42) |
| | 1983-1985 | 10 | 9 ( 53) |
| | 1986-1988 | 10 | |
| | 1989 or later | 2 | 1 ( 5) |

NK = 5

| 10 | In which year did you last inject? | |
|---|---|---|
| | NEVER INJECTED | 186 |
| | 1979 or earlier | 4 |
| | 1980-1982 | 2 |
| | 1983-1985 | 2 |
| | 1986-1988 | 0 |
| | 1989 or later | 23 |

NK = 6

| 11 | Have you ever injected while inside? | | % (%I*) |
|---|---|---|---|
| | yes | 16 | 7 ( 40) |
| | no | 211 | 93 ( 60) |

NK = 2

| 12 | Have you ever taken the blood test for HIV? | | % (%I*) |
|---|---|---|---|
| | yes | 84 | 37 ( 84) |
| | no | 140 | 63 ( 16) |

NK = 5

| 13 | Have you had an acute attack of hepatitis or yellow jaundice? | | % (%I*) |
|---|---|---|---|
| | yes | 24 | 11 ( 37) |
| | no | 202 | 89 ( 63) |

NK = 3

| 14 | In the last year before this sentence, how many women did you have sex with? | | % (%I*) |
|---|---|---|---|
| | none | 22 | 10 ( 8) |
| | 1 | 68 | 30 ( 22) |
| | 2 - 5 | 106 | 46 ( 54) |
| | 6 - 10 | 22 | 14 ( 16) |
| | 11 or more | 9 | |

NK = 2

| 15 | In the last year before this sentence, how many men did you have sex with? | | % (%I*) |
|---|---|---|---|
| | none | 219 | 97 ( 92) |
| | 1 | 5 | |
| | 2 - 5 | 2 | |
| | 6 - 10 | 0 | 13 ( 8) |
| | 11 or more | 0 | |

NK = 3

| 16 | Have you accepted money for sex? | | % (%I*) |
|---|---|---|---|
| | yes | 3 | 1 |
| | no | 225 | |

NK = 1

| 17 | Have you paid money for sex? | | % (%I*) |
|---|---|---|---|
| | yes | 12 | 5 ( 5) |
| | no | 213 | 95 ( 95) |

NK = 4

| 18 | Have you ever had anal sex in prison? | | % (%I*) |
|---|---|---|---|
| | yes | 1 | |
| | no | 227 | |

NK = 1

Thank you for answering this confidential questionnaire.

Please fix sealed label here.

MRC

We do not need to know your name nor any other form of identification when you complete this questionnaire. It goes to the Medical Research Council for analysis. No results will be reported which relate to fewer than 50 percents.

Please tick (✓) the box beside the answer that applies to you

**1  How old are you?**
| | N | % (%*) |
|---|---|---|
| under 18 years | 83 | 21 ( 13) |
| 18 to 19 years | 181 | 45 ( 50) |
| 20 or 21 years | 137 | 34 ( 37) |

**2  Where did you live before coming in to Polmont Y.O. Institution?**
| | N | |
|---|---|---|
| HW Edinburgh (eg Muirhouse) | 10 | |
| NE Edinburgh (eg Leith) | 15 | 15% (7%) |
| SE Edinburgh (eg Craigmillar) | 18 | |
| SW Edinburgh (eg Dalry) | 16 | |
| NK1 | | |
| Dundee | | 6 ( 3) |
| Fife | 27 | |
| Glasgow | 123 | 49 ( 49) |
| elsewhere | 196 | 49 ( 41) |

**3  How long is your present sentence?**  NK = 1
| | PRISONERS | REMAND | |
|---|---|---|---|
| less than 3 months | 22 | 44 | 11 ( 6) |
| between 3 and 6 months | | 81 | 20 ( 19) |
| between 7 and 12 months | | 68 | 17 ( 21) |
| between 1 and 3 years | | 148 | 37 ( 31) |
| more than 3 years | | 40 | 10 ( 16) |
| | | | 5 ( 7) |

**4  When did your present sentence begin?**  NK = 4
| | PRISONERS | REMAND | |
|---|---|---|---|
| in 1992 | 22 | 303 | 5 ( 8) |
| in 1991 | 68 | | 76 ( 71) |
| in 1990 or 1989 or 1988 or 1987 | 7 | | 17 ( 20) |
| in 1986 or 1985 or 1984 or 1983 | | | 2 ( 2) |

**5  How many times have you been inside before this sentence?**
| | N | |
|---|---|---|
| never | 142 | 35 ( 16) |
| once | 79 | 20 ( 25) |
| 2 or 3 to 4 times | 114 | 28 ( 35) |
| 5 or more times | 67 | 17 ( 24) |

**7  Have you ever been charged with a drugs related offence?**  NK = 3
| | N | |
|---|---|---|
| yes | 141 | 16 ( 55) |
| no | 258 | 64 ( 45) |

**8  How much time have you done inside since January 1983**  NK = 19 (5%)
| | N | |
|---|---|---|
| less than 6 months | 158 | 41 ( 28) |
| between 7 and 12 months | 94 | 24 ( 17) |
| between 1 and 3 years | 96 | 25 ( 38) |
| more than 3 years | 37 | 10 ( 17) |

---

NK = 6
| NEVER INJECTED | | |
|---|---|---|
| 1979 or earlier | 130 | 51 ( 68) |
| 1980-1982 | 0 | |
| 1983-1985 | 2 | 1 ( 3) |
| 1986-1988 | 16 | 16 ( 23) |
| 1989 or later | 50 | 11 ( 74) |

**10  In which year did you last inject?**  NK = 7
| NEVER INJECTED | | |
|---|---|---|
| 1979 or earlier | 130 | 1 ( 0) |
| 1980-1982 | 0 | |
| 1983-1985 | 0 | |
| 1986-1988 | 4 | |
| 1989 or later | 63 | |

**11  Have you ever injected while inside?**  NK = 5
| | N | |
|---|---|---|
| yes | 17 | 4 ( 25) |
| no | 382 | 96 ( 75) |

**12  Have you ever taken the blood test for HIV?**  NK = 10 (2%)
| | N | |
|---|---|---|
| yes | 12 | 8 ( 27) |
| no | 362 | 92 ( 71) |

**13  Have you ever had an acute attack of hepatitis or yellow jaundice?**  NK = 11 (3%)
| | N | |
|---|---|---|
| yes | 16 | 4 ( 12) |
| no | 375 | 96 ( 88) |

**14  In the last year before this sentence, how many women did you have sex with?**  NK = 7
| | N | |
|---|---|---|
| none | 10 | 3 ( 0) |
| 1 | 64 | 16 ( 15) |
| 2 - 5 | 181 | 46 ( 38) |
| 6 - 10 | 85 | 21 ( 37) |
| 11 or more | 57 | 14 ( 10) |

**15  In the last year before this sentence, how many men did you have sex with?**  NK = 9
| | N | |
|---|---|---|
| none | 376 | 95 ( 95) |
| 1 | 54 | 1 ( 1) |
| 2 - 5 | 9 | |
| 6 - 10 | 4 | 5 ( 5) |
| 11 or more | 2 | |

(9/10 gave same answer to questions 14 & 15; 1/9 was injecting drug user)

**16  Have you ever accepted money for sex?**  NK = 2
| | N | |
|---|---|---|
| yes | 5 | 1 ( 5) |
| no | 397 | 99 ( 95) |

**17  Have you ever paid money for sex?**  NK = 3
| | N | |
|---|---|---|
| yes | 3 | |
| no | 393 | |

**18  Have you ever had anal sex in prison?**  NK = 1
| | N | |
|---|---|---|
| yes | 3 | |
| no | 400 | |

Thank you for answering this confidential questionnaire.

Please fix sealed label here.

MRC
Medical Research Council
Biostatistics Unit
Cambridge

**FIGURE 2**

FIGURE 3

# nonymous voluntary HIV rveillance with risk-factor elicitation in risons

**Why prisons?**

- Injecting drug users are imprisoned for theft and other crimes besides drugs-related offences.
- Prisons are a reflection of the communities they serve. Remand and short-stay prisoners - mostly young, sexually active, heterosexual males - soon return to those communities.
- Advantage of prison studies: volunteer rate and bias can be assessed by comparing age, place of residence and length of sentence of participants versus all inmates.
- HIV epidemiology in prisons allows better planning for the health care of prisoners.

**Which prisons and when?**

- HM Prison Saughton in Edinburgh is local prison for Lothian region and its environs: 1st study - Aug 91.
- HM Y.O.I. Polmont is Scotland's largest young offenders' institution, & serves the whole of Scotland: 1st study - Oct 92.
- Receptions into London male prisons: 1st study - began Apr 93. (Thames regions have highest HIV prevalence in England)
- HM Prison Holloway, the largest UK establishment for female prisoners, comes next.

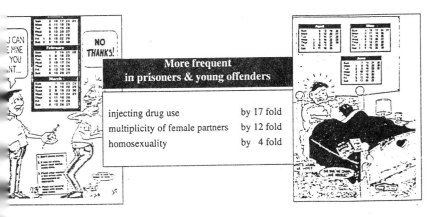

**More frequent in prisoners & young offenders**

| | |
|---|---|
| injecting drug use | by 17 fold |
| multiplicity of female partners | by 12 fold |
| homosexuality | by 4 fold |

RE 4

**Paired design: anonymity features ~ between laboratory transfer of renumbered saliva specimens (for HIV testing) and restricted information flow from laboratories to statistical centre (SC)**

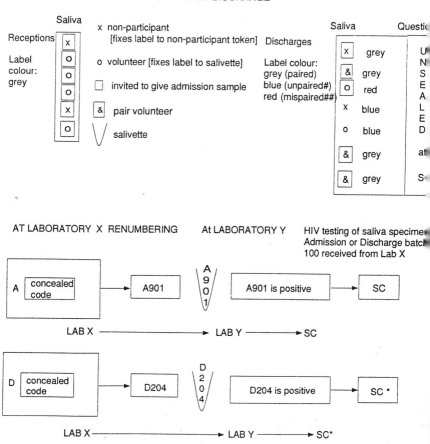

IN THE PRISON AT RECEPTION AND AT DISCHARGE

*Link between concealed codes and A/D serial number is held securely within LAB X and never divulg to LAB Y. SC asks LAB X for label colour, concealed code and admission result for D204. LAB X reports to SC that admission code was A901. SC knows that this admission sample was positive.

\# unpaired ~ because prisoner entered the establishment prior to the start of seroincidence surveillar
\#\# mispaired ~ because of failure to locate prisoner's remaining grey label-pair

FIGURE 5

**Notes**

1. Bird AG, Gore SM, Jolliffe DW, Burns SM. 'Anonymous HIV Surveillance in Saughton Prison, Edinburgh'. *AIDS* 1992; 6: 725 - 733. The required details from the computer log are: discharge batch code, colour of token, colour of prisoner's discharge wax-seal, IF grey discharge wax-seal, did the inmate provide an admission saliva? (code 1 for no, 2 for yes), If inmate provided admission saliva, serial number assigned to it at Laboratory X: A@@@/@@@.

2. Bird AG, Gore SM, Jolliffe DW, Burns SM. 'Second Anonymous HIV Surveillance in Saughton Prison, Edinburgh: Prisoners Give a Lead to Other Heterosexuals on Being HIV Tested'. *AIDS* 1993; 7: 1277 - 1279.

3. Bird AG, Gore SM, Burns SM, Duggie JG. 'Study of Infection with HIV and Related Risk Factors in Young Offenders' Institution'. *British Medical Journal* 1993; 307: 228 - 231.

4. Noone A, Gore SM, Curran L. 'Pilot Survey of HIV and Hepatitis B Infections in Men Received into Three London Prisons'. *Communicable Disease Report* 1994 (submitted).

5. Gore SM, Jolliffe DW, Bird AG. 'Prisoners' Uptake of Confidential, Named HIV Testing. *Lancet* 1992; 339: 149 -1492.

6. Gore SM, Basson J, Bird AG, Goldberg DJ. 'Uptake of Confidential, Named HIV Testing in Scottish Prisons'. *Lancet* 1993; 340: 907 - 908.

7. Raab GM, Burns SM, Scott G, Cudmore S, Ross A, Gore SM, O'Brien F, Shaw T. 'HIV Prevalence and Risk Factors in University Students'. *AIDS* 1994 (submitted).

8. Allardice G, Goldberg DJ, Raab GM, Gore SM. 'HIV Testing in Scotland: Who, Where, When, Why and With What Result?' *Lancet* 1994 (in preparation).

9. Christie B. 'HIV Outbreak Investigated in Scottish Jail'. *British Medical Journal* 1993; 307: 151.

10. Turnbull P, Stimson GV. 'Drug Use in Prison'. *British Medical Journal* 1994; 308: 1716.

11. Gore SM, Bird AG. No escape: 'HIV Transmissio ı in Jail. Prisons Need Protocols for HIV Outbreaks'. *Britisɬ Medical Journal* 1993; 307: 147 - 148.

12. *Global Programme on AIDS. WHO Guidelines on HIV Infection and AIDS In Prisons.* World Health Organization: Geneva, March 1993.

13. Gaba M. 'Glasgow Inquires into Drug Fatalities'. *British Medical Journal* 1993; 307: 822.

14. House of Commons Scottish Affairs Committee. *Drug Abuse in Scotland.* HMSO: Edinburgh & London, 1994.

15. Christie B. 'Report Recommends Drug Agency for Scotland'. *British Medical Journal* 1994; 308: 1318 - 1319.
16. Gore SM, Bird AG. 'Transmission of HIV in Prison'. *British Medical Journal* 1993; 307: 681.

**Additional Reading**
17. Taylor A, Goldberg D, Frisher M, Emslie J. 'Transmission of HIV in Prison'. *British Medical Journal* 1993; 307: 623.
18. Emslie J, MacGregor J, Wrench J, Gruer L, Follett EAC, Cameron S, Clements GB. 'Transmission of HIV in Prison'. *British Medical Journal* 1993; 307: 622-623.
19. Ross M, Grossman AB, Murdoch S, Bundy R, Golding J, Purchase S, Munyard T, Scott M, Bridger A. *Prison: Shield from Threat, or Threat to Survival?*
20. Kall KI, Olin RG. 'HIV Status and Changes in Risk Behaviour Amongst Intravenous Drug Users in Stockholm 1987-88'. *AIDS* 1990; 4: 153-157.
21. Turnbull PJ, Dolan KA, Stimson GV. *Prison, HIV and AIDS: Risks and Experiences in Custodial Care.* AVERT: Horsham, 1991.
22. Vlahov D, Brewer TF, Castro KG et al. 'Prevalence of Antibody to HIV-1 among Entrants to US Correctional Facilities'. *JAMA* 1991; 265: 1129 - 1132.
23. Power KG, Markova I, Rowlands A, McKee KJ, Anslow PJ, Kilfedder C. 'Sexual Behaviour in Scottish Prisons'. *British Medical Journal* 1991; 302: 1507 - 1508.
24. Kennedy DH, Nair G, Elliott L, Ditton J. 'Drug Misuse and Sharing of Needles in Scottish Prisons'. *British Medical Journal* 1991; 302: 1507.
25. Rotily M, Galinier P, Obadia Y, Moatti JP, Toubiana P, Vernay-Vaisse C. 'HIV Testing, HIV Infection and Associated Risk Factors Among Inmates in South-Eastern French Prisons'. *AIDS* 1994 (in press).
26. Bath GE, Davies AG, Dominy NJ, Peters A, Raab GM. 'Imprisonment and HIV Prevalence'. *Lancet* 1993; 342: 1368.

APPENDIX: CROSS-SECTIONAL SURVEILLANCE
OF HIV PREVALENCE & RISK BEHAVIOURS

To achieve maximum compliance with anonymous HIV salivary testing linked to self-completion questionnaire, actions are required as follows:

ACTIONS: THE ESTABLISHMENT

(1) Permission of the Governor for the establishment to be on recreation on the HIV surveillance day(s) - more than one day may be necessary (unless two surveillance areas can be assigned and a double team of external volunteers enlisted).

(2) Governor, prison medical and nursing officers to determine the surveillance days in consultation with research team leaders, so that the research team has at least 6 weeks notice of the surveillance date. To be taken into consideration:

2.i) avoidance of visitors' days,

2.ii) whether to provide some backdrop to HIV surveillance - such as health day or showing of 'The Butterfly Garden' - which enhances interest in surveillance without creating undue delays;

2.iii) in the week prior to HIV surveillance, arrangements made for research team leader to explain to inmates, for example hall by hall: i) how the study will be conducted, when, by whom, why, and the importance of previous similar studies; and ii) the safeguards of anonymity which have been built in. Prisoners should have an opportunity to ask questions, and will also be told about the appointment of prisoner scrutineers. An explanation will also be given for the inclusion in this, and in all future prison studies in Scotland, of questions relating to incarceration and injecting in Glenochil Prison between January and June 1993;

2.iv) arrangements made to ensure that duty officers also have advance information about the purpose, location and modus operandi of anonymous voluntary HIV surveillance with risk factor elicitation by self-completion questionnaire;

2.v) availability of a large area with separate entry and exit (gymnasium, chapel, visiting hall have been used previously) in which to locate the HIV surveillance;

2.vi) an efficient scheme for escorting inmates in groups of up to 20 to and from the surveillance area. (Efficient organization by the establishment of these escort duties - at 15 to 20 minute intervals - allows surveillance of 60 to 80 inmates per hour and hence of 6 times that number per surveillance day. Having a deputy governor visibly responsible for these arrangements underlines their importance to all concerned;

2.vii) availability of 20 individual small tables with 2 facing chairs per table arranged along the side-walls of the surveillance area with tables sufficiently spaced for privacy; also 4 tables, one per quadrant, centrally located in the surveillance hall with a semi-circle of 6 chairs in proximity to each table;

2.viii) provision of fruit/crisps/chocolate or tea & biscuits as prisoners exit from surveillance area (delays in throughput of prisoners occur when tea & biscuits, which need to be consumed on site, are provided rather than a refreshment that may be taken back to hall);

2.ix) domestic arrangements (e.g. soup and sandwich lunch) for the team of external volunteers who conduct the HIV surveillance;

2.x) simple, confidential system to be agreed with prison's medical and nursing officers whereby inmates who wish HIV counselling and a confidential personal HIV blood test can communicate their request without other inmates or officers being aware of their having done so. (The system in HMYOI Polmont was that external team members noted down on paper slips the prison number of any inmate who requested a personal test and who had agreed that his number could be given to a named senior HIV-trained nursing officer - on the understanding the inmate would receive (and did) HIV counselling within the next week);

2.xi) decision by prison medical and nursing officers about whether, and how best, to involve outside HIV counsellors in meeting a possibly very much increased number of inmates' requests for confidential personal HIV tests as a consequence of surveillance-heightened HIV awareness:

2.xii) availability of private consultancy rooms - apart from the anonymous HIV surveillance area - for requested confidential HIV counselling and venepuncture.

(3) Permission of the Governor for research team leader to obtain from the establishment's computing officer the tally (for the surveillance day) of all available (for surveillance) prisoners. Deduction has to be made of those who were at court, on home leave, hospitalised outside of the prison, or otherwise outwith the establishment. In addition, the age-group, start year and length of sentence and area of residence distributions for all inmates (and for those unavailable for surveillance) are required from the

computing officer so that volunteer bias can be assessed. This requirement is discussed with the Governor and his computing officer at the research team's preliminary visit to the establishment; and a dummy run for a pre-surveillance day's inmates is agreed upon for practice. Also requested from the prison's medical officer on the surveillance day are the number, demography and injector status of known HIV infected inmates; this information is provided non-nominally; it allows comparison of surveillance-estimated versus disclosed HIV prevalence and of volunteer rate between known HIV infected inmates and others.

### ACTIONS: THE RESEARCH TEAM

(4) Funding for the proposed HIV surveillance to cover the cost of salivettes, the testing of saliva samples at a Regional Virus Laboratory, provision of sealed label pairs and questionnaires, together with travel expenses for five return journeys by the research team leaders to the establishment.

(5) A team of HIV-knowledgeable external volunteers is assembled and briefed by the research leaders as follows: to emphasise to prisoners that the only risk behaviours of which the research team has knowledge are those self-reported on completed questionnaires. There is clear the disjunction between anonymous HIV salivary surveillance for epidemiological purposes and personal HIV counselling and testing by which an individual prisoner may choose to establish his HIV status. Moreover, inmates are assured in pre-briefing and again when they come to the surveillance area that they may choose to answer some, all or none of the questions, but that we hope they will choose to answer all.

(6) Ethical approval for HIV surveillance will be sought from the locally organized research ethics committee of the Health Board in whose jurisdiction lies the laboratory where salivary HIV testing is done and also from the geographically appropriate Prison Service Directorate.

(7) The findings from anonymous voluntary HIV surveillance studies with risk factor elicitation will be disseminated to current inmates and officers of the establishment concerned by the research team - in summary page format and/or as a talk - prior to publication. Typically, full results are available within two months of the surveillance date; publication takes several months thereafter.

ACTIONS: INMATES

(8) Determination of prisoner scrutineers in a manner which meets with the Governor's and inmates' approval.

(9) On entry to the HIV surveillance area, each inmate who participates takes a seat at one of the four central locations. There he will find a clip-board with questionnaire attached and a biro. The team leader explains to a group of five men that questions 1 to 8 - demographic and about present and past sentences - are answered as they sit together; thereafter, each man is given a salivette (see Figure 5) and an explanation of how to give a saliva sample, asked to select randomly an envelope (from a bag of 50 such envelopes) in which he will find two black sealed labels (one of which he will attach to his completed questionnaire and the other around the top of his salivette) and invited to go to one of the individual tables at the perimeter of the surveillance area, there to complete the second part of the questionnaire in privacy and, while doing so, to chew on the cotton wool swab. He later replaces the chewed cotton wool swab in the salivette, closes it and attaches one of the label pair to it. The other label is fixed to the bottom of his completed questionnaire, which is then folded into the envelope from which the label-pair came. The same unknown number is concealed under the label-pair seals; the salivette seals are removed in the laboratory, the questionnaire seals at the statistical centre. Any saliva sample remains untested for which the questionnaire seal or its own was not intact on receipt - this contingency has not so far arisen in over 1000 pairs.

The team leader's explanation reminds the prisoners that a man may choose to answer some, none or all of the questions and he may give a saliva sample or decide not to; however, it is hoped that he will opt to answer all questions and to give a saliva sample. Other members of the external team are peripherally located in the HIV surveillance area to be available to give assistance with completion of the second part of the questionnaire if requested or with obtaining the saliva sample.

On leaving the surveillance area, the prisoner deposits his questionnaire in one clear container, his salivette in another and receives some refreshment to counter the cotton wool swab. The salivette container is emptied only after a minimum of 100 salivettes has been deposited; typically this happens only at lunchtime and again at the end of the afternoon to speed the laboratory's work.

# Eleven—Part 1

# Befriending in prison

*Kathy Biggar*

*Man's real need, his most terrible need, is for someone to listen to him not as a patient (or a prisoner) but as a human soul.*                          **(Lake 1986)**

Ensuring that a prisoner's need to be listened to 'as a human soul' when he or she is isolated, despairing and at risk of suicide is everybody's responsibility and in the prison setting staff, prisoners and visitors are all continually offering a listening ear to those in distress.

Befriending support is now recognised as a vital part of the Prison Service's Suicide Awareness Strategy in England and Wales. It is also accepted that prison staff, other professionals, family and friends are sometimes too close to the prisoners to help or are unable to at the time support is most needed. Consequently the role of the volunteer befriender is being steadily developed and it is now the policy of the Prison Service to work in partnership with the Samaritans, in the care and support of the suicidal in custody, which involves both Samaritan and prisoner volunteers.

The Samaritans is a nation-wide charity founded in 1953 which exists to provide confidential, emotional support to any person, irrespective of race, creed, age or status who is suicidal or despairing and to increase public awareness of suicide and suicidal feelings.

The Samaritan service is provided 24 hours a day, 365 days a year by 23,000 carefully selected and trained volunteers working from 200 branches throughout the UK, Eire, Isle of Man and Channel Islands.

The Samaritans are essentially a crisis organisation

befriending people who call on our emergency telephone lines, visit the Samaritan Centre or write. Where appropriate we undertake longer term befriending, we also encourage our callers to accept continuing help from other professional and voluntary agencies. We respond to third party referrals from concerned professionals, family members or friends and discretely offer befriending to the person causing concern.

The Samaritans is a member of Befrienders International, the worldwide organisation of those groups dedicated to developing volunteer action to prevent suicide. There are over 100 affiliated centres in 25 other countries.

It has taken nearly 15 years to reach the stage where Samaritan befriending should now be available to all prisoners in distress in England and Wales.

I was one of many Samaritans involved at national level, supported by many Samaritan branches locally who in the early 1980s were becoming increasingly concerned about the suicidal and despairing in our society, who were really unable or unlikely to make contact with the Samaritans. People on remand or serving a sentence in custody were not only amongst those most likely to commit suicide, they were also behind bars and unable to contact us even if they wanted to. Some Samaritan branches try to make contact at a local level with minimal success, at a national level our request to open discussions about the support we could offer to suicidal prisoners were kindly but firmly refused.

Encouragement eventually came in 1986 when we were approached by the then Director of Prison Medical Services, who was reviewing the Prison Service in England and Wales' approach to caring for the suicidal, and discussions about Samaritan support for prisoners and staff took place. Further encouraged by the Director's recommendation to involve the Samaritans in his report of that year, the partnership began to develop. Experience at local level where branches were beginning to offer support and our special role in befriending those at risk was acknowledged and was shared at a national level. We moved towards the strategy now in place that is based on a three-way partnership in the England and Wales Prison Service in particular, a partnership of care between prison staff, prisoners and Samaritans. This does not mean that other professional and voluntary organisations are not involved, they are, but it does recognise Samaritan volunteers' unique training and support structure, which enables them to ask about suicidal feelings and to encourage those at risk to really talk in confidence about their desperate dark feelings, in the knowledge that as volunteers they will be supported and cared for.

By the middle of 1993 we had reached a stage where all prison establishments, particularly in England and Wales, increasingly in Northern Ireland, Scotland and Eire were aiming to ensure that:

- All prisoners and staff have opportunities to contact The Samaritans.
- Prisoners experiencing severe emotional crisis can have emergency access to The Samaritans by phone or visit at any time of day or night.

An example of the partnership developing at a local level demonstrates how a positive partnership can develop. In 1989 the Putney Branch of the Samaritans joined Wandsworth Prison's then Suicide Prevention Committee and shortly afterwards helped to train all staff in basic suicide awareness and listening skills, alongside an officer from the Training Department in Wandsworth. Their involvement in these training sessions broke down some of the myths and misunderstandings shared by prison staff and Samaritan volunteers about each other and enabled the prison and the local branch director to look at how Samaritan befriending support could be offered to prisoners at risk. This began in the Health Care Centre where Samaritan volunteers visited on a regular basis seeing prisoners at both their request and on referral from Prison Health Care staff. Involvement in the prison's induction programme ensured that prisoners were aware that they could see a volunteer in total confidence and slowly the Samaritan support for those at risk increased.

Samaritan befriending is now available in all parts of the prison and staff are aware that they can make referrals when they are concerned, including phoning the local branch and asking for an emergency list. Confidential post boxes that can only be opened by the Samaritans are on every wing in the prison. Samaritan volunteers visit regularly and are seen on the wings befriending prisoners at risk and supporting staff in their care of prisoners they are concerned about.

The branch has also played a vital part in establishing their Prisoner Befriending Scheme, 'The Wandsworth Listeners' which has been in place for over 18 months now on three wings in the prison and it will shortly be helping to develop the service on other wings.

As part of the initial working party, the branch worked closely with prison staff and prisoners to develop 'The Listeners,' establishing the principles of the scheme, selecting the prisoners with prison staff and then training them as befrienders, using similar training packages to those used by Samaritan branches for their volunteers. Ongoing support is provided by the branch by telephone and at weekly support groups attended by all Listeners and two Samaritans. As the group of listeners has developed they themselves have become more involved in the selection and training of other prisoners working alongside the Samaritans.

The Samaritans' befriending involvement in the wings where listeners are available has decreased as prisoner befriending has increased. The Prisoner Befriending Scheme at HMP Wandsworth was the sixth scheme to be established and a fuller description of the Wandsworth Listeners from a prisoner's point of view follows on from this introduction.

Most of us who have worked in prison will be only too aware of the support prisoners offer each other. During the last three years their role has been formalised in an ever increasing number of establishments where befriending support is being offered by specially selected and trained prisoners to fellow prisoners at risk of suicide and self harm, as a supplement to the support offered by prison staff, Samaritans and other agencies. Based on the belief that Samaritan principles can be adapted to the prison setting, the first scheme was piloted and established in HM Prison Swansea during 1991.

In July 1991 Swansea Prison, in response to the devastating suicide of a 15 year old in 1990, were already well on the way to establishing a multi disciplinary approach to caring for the suicidal. Staff, prisoners and the local Samaritan branch were working closely together. Consequently they were asked by the Suicide Awareness Support Unit at Prison Service Headquarters and the Samaritans to consider piloting the scheme that could formalise prisoners' involvement similar to the one established by the Samaritans and Charles Street Jail in Boston, USA in 1979. HM Prison Swansea grasped the opportunity and established a working party to develop the scheme. Many obstacles had to be overcome, particularly that of confidentiality, but in September 1991 five prisoners had been carefully selected and the local Samaritan branch had trained them. The prisoners had decided to call themselves 'The Listeners'.

Early the following year developments at HMP Ranby created

the first 'Care Support Scheme' which again involved carefully selected and trained volunteers as Crisis Befrienders offering 24 hour support in a special care support suite, for fellow prisoners in an acute suicidal crisis.

These developments were shared at a series of seminars in early 1992, well attended by nearly 100 prisons in England and Wales. There was an enthusiastic response to the partnership and although quite understandably, there were anxieties about formalising the involvement of prisoners and Samaritans, many other establishments were quick to grasp the possibilities.

In April 1994 we now have 50 Prisoner Befriending Schemes in England and Wales and one in Scotland. Many combine the concept of a care or befriending room, most are called the 'Listeners', many of whom also offer the crisis support established by the care supporters. Care supporters are now very much involved in offering day-to-day befriending on wings and in units of the prison.

All these schemes are tailored to suit the needs of individual establishments but the main principles of the scheme are the same:

- Confidentiality of befriending.
- The Samaritans are involved in selecting and training the prisoners.
- Systems of referral, which ensure appropriate ongoing care and support to residential and Health Care staff, Samaritans and other agencies, and from prison staff to befrienders.
- The need for and feasibility of overnight support.
- Emergency and weekly support for prisoners befriending from the Samaritans.
- The need for a befriending room.
- Within the Samaritans branches a 'prison person' is appointed to liaise.
- Ground rules to deter and deal with abuse of the scheme.

Prisoner Befriending Schemes are proving valuable in numerous ways but above all they are ensuring that prisoners are confiding more readily with other prisoners, they are making good use of Samaritan resources, they are encouraging a sharing of information (without breaking confidentiality), they have improved prisoner staff relationships, they have increased the prisoners' self esteem and above all in some establishments they are now reducing the rate of self harm.

Further research has now been commissioned to evaluate the

work of Prisoner Befriending Schemes more formally.

Finally a quote, which for me, sums up the hard work of dedicated staff, prisoners and Samaritans with whom it has been a real privilege to work alongside. It is from a Governor responding several months after he had established a working relationship with his local Samaritan Branch and piloted a Prisoner Befriending Scheme:

> There can be very few better ways of illustrating our respect for human dignity than to provide opportunities for those in distress to have a empathetic ear and to give to those who provide the ear the credit and respect that they have merited.

# Eleven—Part 2

# The Wandsworth Listeners: Befriending in prison from a listener point of view

*Marc Carolissen*

As the author of these notes, the title suggests that I am an inmate, indeed, a serving one at HMP Wandsworth. My role as a Listener will become clearer as I progress but to portray an idea of what it feels like to enter prison as an inmate, I shall share with you the words of a fellow inmate, who upon reflection, remarked that on the very first day he entered a prison, an invisible notice 'flashed' before his eyes. It read, 'Hope ends here!' I feel it is safe to speculate that the psychological impact such an entrance into prison, and perhaps in custody elsewhere, too, has on anyone, who is confined to its walls for a short, medium or long term, can be damaging, leading to crisis.

When a crisis, such as the above, is on hand, we hope that the agents appointed to provide and care for prisoners will take immediate action to prevent any harm to the inmate concerned. Such prevention may take the form of psychological or medical help, but beyond the application of sciences to attend to a person's ills, lies a very common and sometimes neglected need of human kind. 'Man's real need, his most terrible need, is for someone to listen to him, not as a patient (or a prisoner) but as a human soul' (Lake 1986).

Literature elsewhere has already suggested that Prisoner Befriending Schemes under the descriptions of 'Listeners', 'Care Supporters', 'Stress Busters', 'Ears' are operational in some 50 prisons attending to that 'most terrible need' of every person in custody: to be listened to. In Wandsworth we are called 'The Listeners'.

Established in September 1992, the Wandsworth Listeners, under the aegis of The Samaritans, have provided a much needed service to inmates going through crisis and in imminent danger of harming themselves or taking their own lives. So who exactly are The Listeners and what is their function?

Set against a background when such schemes were unheard of listening is not a new phenomenon in prison. Inmates have always listened to each other's qualms, worries and fears. Invariably this has taken place when inmates shared a cell, walked together on the exercise yard, worked together in the workshops or where and whenever it was desired. When such concern is demonstrated one would expect confidentiality to be a vital ingredient in this process of care and support. A breach of confidence will lead to disastrous consequences but since inmates had little intention, if any, to share their problems with the very people who locked them up, the concern for another in confidence became very much an everyday aspect of life in prison. In fact, the bond of trust, confidentiality and concern amongst prisoners is a 'tradition' that is very much alive.

In recognising that prisoners have always cared for each other and are able to take on some of the responsibility for fellow inmates' welfare, Samaritans liaising with prison management pioneered the idea of what can be aptly described as 'prisoner-to-prisoner-care-schemes' based on the principles of The Samaritans.

In Wandsworth twenty four inmates volunteered to be trained as 'Listeners' after word was spread about such a scheme. Eventually twelve were selected by staff and Samaritans. The selection criteria were set by the Selectors (staff and Samaritans) but nowadays existing 'Listeners' are also referred to aid the selection of new volunteers. In volunteering to become a 'Listener' I had to question myself; just how much of an impact will it have on me to actually take on some of the responsibility of another person. Whilst I'm in prison, too? How will I deal with the delicate issue of suicide? Am I ready for all this? And it didn't stop there. During the training sessions - some twelve hours spread over six weeks - a number of issues were addressed, in particular, the fact that a person has a right to take his own life. As straightforward and liberal as it may sound it was initially difficult to comprehend that my role was not that of a suicide preventer but simply to 'be there' with the person who is feeling suicidal. Again I had to question myself about this. How do I help someone who wishes to take his own life? Is it not the ultimate act of humanity to be able to rescue a fellow human being? Surely we would all like to help someone in distress? True, but what we want and what those in crisis want is entirely different, bringing me back to the issue of right to life (or death). The ultimate act of humanity, then is not to impose my wants, hence my judgements, upon others, particularly those who are feeling suicidal. Just 'be there' for them.

It is important to stress that The Samaritans with their vast experience in the field of suicide, were a guiding force in my training as a 'Listener' and helping me in dealing with my uncertainties regarding suicide. However, not everyone is suicidally inclined and sometimes they require only a sympathetic ear. To this end The Samaritans initiated me in developing listening skills and by that I mean 'active listening': asking the 'right' questions, asking whether the person feels suicidal, dealing only with the person's feelings and 'mirroring' these feelings. Asking about suicidal tendencies, we believe, will not strike people who are not suicidal as a solution to their difficulties but will often enable those wanting to tell someone about their deepest of deepest feelings to do so. To put my role as a 'Listener' in perspective it means to 'Befriend' those in crisis, which in turn means listening and caring without being judgemental. My training was thus more than just an education in how to 'Befriend' but also a period of examining myself as to whether I feel comfortable with what I was being prepared for.

With an increased awareness I was eager to listen to inmates with problems. The range of difficulties that prisoners experience was brain-stormed and dealt with during training sessions. One problem that took me by surprise was the existence of barriers between inmates themselves as opposed to the well publicised barriers between inmates and staff. Listening and caring amongst inmates, which were once an everyday and unsung aspect of prison life, had all of a sudden been 'officialised'. All Listeners wear badges to be easily recognised and with it followed a plethora of derision and jibes to the tune of us being seen as 'undercover grasses' - that we are in cohoots with the staff. Sceptical inmates were not easily convinced but over time and with a lot of perseverance and sincere efforts we made our stance and continued to champion our cause. Surprisingly, a few of my very first contacts were those very sceptics!

With Wandsworth being a men's prison, the atmosphere is redolent with machismo. As someone once put it, 'Whenever I enter this place I can smell the testosterone!' And it is true to say that men do shy away from expressing their feelings. Like some of the sceptics many inmates preferred the macho-facade to save face in a world where only the toughest survive. It became apparent to me that, despite all the pretence, even the smallest of favours requested, e.g. helping with an application form, writing a letter or asking for a cigarette, could lead the inmate to actually wanting to talk about his difficulties. Occasionally I was approached to 'help' with this or that and in some circumstances it turned out that the inmate wanted someone to listen to him. The lesson here was to be a little more aware when inmates approached one, seeking assistance with the simplest of chores. However, let it be known that Listeners do not assist inmates with applications, letters, etc. as part of their training but are prepared to take these issues on and a step further if the inmate wishes to discuss any problems. We only listen and do not counsel.

The no-counselling policy was adopted by The Listeners because we are ordinary inmates with a lack of experience and training in that field and we do not have the necessary resources at hand to assist fully. That is left to the officers. Listeners can, in situations beyond their 'domain', gently lead the inmate to take up certain matters with their Personal Officer or other appropriate members of staff who will be better equipped to deal with it.

To date Listeners have maintained good relations with staff. Our scheme cannot operate without them for practical reasons, and in another sense Listeners have become a bridge between staff and inmates, particularly the ones in crises. But not all members of staff go along with the idea of Listeners. Wandsworth was once described by The Sobriquet 'Jurassic Park' - a reference no doubt to the fact that it is being dragged kicking and screaming into the twentieth century. A few dinosaurs still remain but we believe that their conversion is merely academic.

Apart from a lack of resources and having suffered the ill fate of ending up in prison, Listeners have their limitations in terms of 'befriending'. The single cell facility means that inmates spend at least twelve hours behind their doors, alone, and mainly at night. This is a dangerous period, especially for poor copers, who have time to entertain their depressed feelings and perhaps contemplate and even attempt suicide. Listeners, likewise, are locked up over this period and those in dire situations have no one to talk to. At the time of writing Wandsworth is considering an overnight 'Befriending Room' facility - the size of a double cell, completely fitted out with 'homely' amenities - so that 'Listeners' can continue befriending those in imminent danger around the clock.

It also goes without saying that as inmates 'Listeners' have their own problems, too. After all, it's people like us listening to people like us. We will be affected by the problems we listen to and from time to time we need to unload as well. So who listens to the 'Listeners'?

'Listeners' operate as a group and not as single entities. This allows individual 'Listeners' to 'befriend' each other. Alternatively, 'Listeners' can approach The Samaritans who uphold the same confidence as 'Listeners' do to their contacts. For this purpose we convene once a week to support each other, discuss and 'off load' the difficulties we encountered during sessions with our contacts. A 'Listener's' mental and emotional state needs to be balanced in the role of befriending and the sharing of experiences with contacts, during support meetings, is vital to maintain that equilibrium. Should a 'Listener' feel that he is incapable of performing his duties then he is at liberty to render himself 'temporarily inactive' until such time he feels it best to resume.

Although 'Listeners' take on some of the responsibilities of other inmates in crisis and the fact that those whom we 'befriend' live with us in such close proximity, means that we have to exercise some caution to prevent our contacts becoming dependent on us. A poor coper, for instance, can become easily dependent on a 'Listener' with whom he has shared his most intimate and private feelings, in confidence. The person is of course free to break contact at any time for we only stay with a person for as long as he wants us to be with him. But in the event of dependency a 'Listener' will kindly introduce the person to another 'Listener'. There is a set limit of times a 'Listener' can see a contact and if this limit is reached the contact will be referred to another Listener. This then allows a Listener to befriend many inmates in distress.

In one sense one can argue that prison deprives the inmate of his individuality and identity. Once inside, the system treats inmates en masse. No one is singled out for preferential treatment thus everyone passes under the same brush of the penal system. The loss of individuality and identity is closely linked to loss of expression of one's being and if 'Listeners' are trained to help those in crisis and perhaps those in search of individuality and identity to express themselves, albeit on an emotional level, then Listeners' Schemes operating at grassroots level, can be vital in breaking down barriers in prison that oppress and stifle human dignity.

Ultimately, the government is responsible for inmates' welfare, not Listeners (who are inmates themselves) since it was not elected to lock up people but has elected to do so. Listeners are then not the solution to incidences of self harm and suicide in prison but only a part of the solution. A notable researcher in prison suicides recently wrote that as someone, '... who has talked and listened through countless tears, some of them shed by officers and Governors but most of them by prisoners, over many years, who has seen the use of strip cells decline and attitudes towards self injury improve, who has witnessed the introduction of suicide awareness management teams in all establishments, and the provision of activity and support [by Listeners, Samaritans, etc] for those thought to be at risk, I cannot comprehend the purpose of this word `austere'. (Liebling, 1994).

# Twelve

# Women at risk

*Michael Jennings and Wendy Ratcliffe*

The purpose of this contribution is to ask two questions:

1. How different are women and men with regard to their 'pathways' to suicide?
2. How different do preventative measures employed in participants' workplaces need to be to cater for the needs of women and men?

Rates of suicide in the United Kingdom for men and women show a consistent pattern: more men than women take their own lives, by a ratio in excess of two to one. When parasuicide in the young (under twenty-fives) is looked at, the pattern is reversed: 80 per cent of young suicides are males, while 80-90 per cent of parasuicides are female. Thus, overall, women are more at risk of parasuicide/self-injury than males are, but are at less risk of completed suicide (Samaritans, 1993).

When trying to get comparable data for prisons, several difficulties present themselves. Women make up a small proportion of the prison population and, hence, a small proportion of completed suicides (Lloyd, 1990). Working out suicide rates for women to allow a comparison with males, of necessity, involves generalising from a very small number of cases. Some researchers claim that when consciously self inflicted deaths that did not receive a verdict of suicide are looked at, in addition to deaths recorded as suicide, the rate of suicide of women in prison is proportionally higher than that of men (Dooley, 1990a), which is the reverse of the situation in the community.

Some of the differences in suicide rates outside of prison are explained by the data on the variation in the methods men and women use to take their own lives. Men tend to use more lethal methods during suicide attempts, increasing the chance that an attempt will succeed (Samaritans 1993). In prisons hanging is by far the most common method for either sex; this is probably an effect of resources available in the immediate environment (Lloyd, 1990). The same writer commented that '... the alternatives to hanging, such as burning or wrist cutting are very unpleasant and therefore very difficult to carry through to completion'. Much of the gender difference in suicide methods, and presumably therefore rates, disappears.

Turning back to parasuicide and self-injury, when looked at in prison, there is a perception of this as a female problem. Lloyd 1990 concluded that, 'no studies have been carried out on exclusively male populations in the United Kingdom'. Both inside and outside of prison self-injury rates seem higher for women than men. Data from a closed male and a closed female prison, both in the North of England, revealed twice as much self-injury in the female prison, even though it had less than half as many inmates as the male establishment (Jennings, 1994). The data is often distorted by a few inmates being responsible for the majority of injuries.

So, the anomaly is that proportionately more women than men may well take their lives in prison. Whereas the opposite is true out of prison. Patterns of self-injury are similar, both in and out of prison.

The importance of the environment is clear; altering it is one of the methods used to try and prevent suicide and self-injury. Alterations can be made to the immediate physical environment: for example removing protuberances from cells (Kraus and Buglione, 1984) to remove some hanging points. Reports have recommended that inmate reception areas are made more welcoming (Home Office, 1988).

Other approaches have included staff training programmes to help staff identify those at risk, to assess the level of risk, and to monitor and seek help for them (Home Office, 1986). Contact between inmates and their families has also been encouraged (Geary 1980).

One relatively new way of addressing the problem in the United Kingdom is inmate listener schemes. The results of the evaluation of such a scheme at Styal Prison indicate that listener schemes can work in female establishments (McKeown and Jennings, 1993). Inmates were carefully selected and trained for this task. Monitoring and support indicated that they were heavily used. Surveys of staff, and individuals who had used the scheme, indicated a high degree of satisfaction; every inmate who had used the scheme felt that the experience had been beneficial. Listeners found the work demanding, but rewarding, and seemed to enjoy helping others. Procedures for listeners to refer 'clients' on to staff (with in all, except the most extreme cases, their consent) further integrates the scheme into an institution-wide approach to the protection of women at risk.

Groups of seminar participants at the conference discussed and gave some feedback on: vulnerability indicators and situational triggers, and stress induced by the immediate environment (the participants' workplace, if appropriate). They were asked to indicate those that applied especially or only to women.

With regard to vulnerability indicators, the only suggestions felt to fit the above criteria were concerns about children, Post Natal Depression, abuse as a child, and being 'menopausal'. The only situational trigger and stressor in the immediate environment that applied to women particularly, was lack of contact with the family. Of the extensive list of problems produced, very few of the problems of imprisonment applied to women especially. If these are accepted as forming an important part of a pathway to suicide, there is a clear similarity between those for men and those for women. This is a list of problems for women produced before the seminar:

- Care of children, fear of adoption (Mckeown 1994).
- There are only twelve prisons that take women, so they are further away from home, friends and resources (Grace 1990).
- Problems of accommodation; 12 per cent of inmates are of 'no fixed abode' and 27 per cent lose accommodation during their sentence (Posen 1988).
- High rates of anxiety and depression (Mckeown 1994).

Recent work by Mary Mckeown (1994) illustrates the first and last points well. She looked at a sample of 40 male and 40 women sentenced prisoners. Of the 26 male inmates with children, all of their children were in the care of their natural mother. In contrast, of the 28 women with children, just over 40% were with the children's natural father, a similar proportion were with grandparents and the remainder were with the Social Services. In the authors' experience, many inmates feel that once their children are involved with the social services, it is very difficult to regain custody of them. As a consequence, levels of anxiety regarding their children were higher amongst the women than the men. Use of the General Health Questionnaire (Goldberg and Williams 1988) showed that the women had a statistically significant higher amount of anxiety and depression than did the men. Thus, it might be that the problems leading to women being at risk are practical rather than psychological. Apparently, 'Whilst over 90 per cent of the suicides in the community are found to have a history of psychiatric illness in treatment, only a third of prison suicides are found to have such a history' (Dooley 1990, Backett 1987). Further evidence of the effect of custody is given by Liebling (1992): 'Amongst a comparison group of female young prisoners, thoughts of suicide, previous self injury and feelings of depression, were almost as common as amongst a group of suicide attempters'.

One way of addressing the problem of suicide and self injury, used extensively in the past, is the generation of prediction scales. Typical results of such attempts are that risk indicators for males are: being on remand; being early on in custody; a psychiatric illness; a charge of homicide; alcohol or drug misuse; previous self injury, and being on special location (Backett 1987, Dooley 1990a, Lloyd 1990, Liebling 1992 and Liebling and Krarup 1993; cited in Liebling 1994). In addition, a risk indicator for women is a history of arson or violence (Liebling 1992).

Although useful, there are two main problems with such scales: they give a largely static predictive score, and false positives makes cost-effective treatment of any at-risk population identified difficult (Pallis, Gibbons and Pierce 1984). Liebling 1992, and other researchers have identified more qualitative research as important, encouraging people to talk, and monitoring them for changes. This 'dynamic prevention' is epitomised by the EARS scheme. In addition the problems of prison *per se* for women need to be addressed, not just conditions within prions (Liebling 1992).

A list of protecting agents drawn from the literature in this field was presented: supportive supervision by staff; listening and befriending schemes; visits and frequent contact with home to allay fears; the making of future plans; constructive occupations; help with problems; good team-work and communications and, most importantly, people who listen.

# Thirteen

# The Howard League on Juveniles

*Sue Wade*

The Howard League has a long tradition of campaigning for prison reform and the abolition of capital punishment. It has also a parallel tradition of promoting reform in the treatment of juveniles, and through its international links, particularly at the United Nations, and an interest in reminding governments of the existence of conventions and international norms and standards. Three or four years ago, someone giving this seminar would have been entitled to be satisfied at progress in three of those four areas in the UK at least. Certainly not complacent, but satisfied that the imprisonment of juveniles had been reduced in most areas, that the remand in custody of children was beginning to be abolished by practice and would soon be removed from statute, and that in many respects the criminal justice processes for dealing with juveniles conformed to or exceeded international standards.

Who would have predicted that we are now facing the most repressive legislation aimed at juveniles that has been seen in this country since early this century. This statement is not an exaggeration, given the implications of children aged twelve locked up not just in so called 'Secure Training Centres' but in remand prisons and in 'overflow' sentenced prisons, and in police cells (as part of PACE changes). All this on top of a existing concern about the increased incidence of self harm and suicide among young people generally and particularly within prisons.

The basis of my seminar is a quote from Alison Liebling's 1991 paper:

> Young prisoner suicide is not an exclusively psychiatric problem; it is also a problem of coping. A lack of the necessary skills with which to endure a sentence of imprisonment may fall within the boundaries of 'normal mental health'.

My interpretation of her paper and subsequent writings is that the prevention of suicide is not the exclusive responsibility of medical services and indeed most prison department guidance for a number of years now has stressed the multi-disciplinary approach to prevention. A more robust interpretation could be that prisons are dangerous places and that you need pretty good coping skills to 'endure' or survive.

I think that we should add a very strong amendment to that approach; the problem of suicides in custody is not just a problem for the agencies working within the prison but the responsibility of all agencies and people that connect with the prison or with the criminal justice processes that can lead to prison. This approach does not discount the prison's highest duty to provide a safe regime for those whom the state imprisons, but does acknowledge the more complex relationships between various agencies and the provision (or not) of resources that affects who goes to prison in the first place, and who is remembered and who is forgotten when they are in prison. The Howard League's Inquiry into suicides at Feltham, led by Anthony Scrivener QC, spent some time looking at the outside world of the four young men who died in those seven months of 1991 and 1992, as well as examining the internal world of the prison. The recommendations of that report reflects this wider approach.

This conference has already heard in detail the various statistics that show an increase in the incidence of suicide since the mid 1980s particularly for young adult males, both in the general population and within prisons. Other studies have shown increasing social deprivation amongst the age and social group that is highly represented in court and prison workloads. Some have also shown the re-emergence of other health problems including diseases once thought eradicated from this country, and of course the continuance of drug, alcohol and other substance misuse. I will concentrate on giving you some details of the juvenile scene in England and Wales.

Table 1: Sentencing Practice England and Wales 1980 -1990:
Males (aged 14-16) sentenced to immediate custody, total and as
a percentage of all sentences. Indictable offences.

| Year | No. | % |
|------|------|------|
| 1980 | 7400 | 11.8 |
| 1982 | 7100 | 12.0 |
| 1984 | 6500 | 12.5 |
| 1986 | 4300 | 11.5 |
| 1988 | 3200 | 10.9 |
| 1990 | 1400 | 7.2 |

If we look at the use of imprisonment compared to both
sentences and formal cautions during the same period, the
reduction is even more marked. These figures also give some
indication of the juvenile crime trends over the same period
although followers of the Home Affairs Select Committee
hearings on juvenile offenders will know the problems faced by
conflicting evidence about crime statistics. We should also
acknowledge that generally, the 1980s were a period when the
numbers of the general population in this age range were
decreasing.

Table 2 Dispositional Practice England and Wales. 1980-1990
(Males aged 14-16)

| | Total known offenders | % Custody |
|------|------|------|
| 1980 | 94900 | 10.2 |
| 1982 | 94600 | 9.5 |
| 1984 | 94900 | 7.9 |
| 1986 | 81200 | 6.0 |
| 1988 | 72600 | 4.8 |
| 1990 | 63700 | 2.4 |

There was a significant decrease in the use of imprisonment
for juveniles particularly from the mid 1980s onwards, and the
reasons for this remarkable shift are attributed to several factors
including the influence of practitioners in all agencies.

The use of prisons for juveniles remanded in custody took
longer to change, partly due to lack of attention by practitioners,
until Nacro and the Association of Chief Officers of Probation
(ACOP) began surveys in the late 1980s and highlighted the
problems. The following figures are taken from ACOP/NACRO

1993 report 'Awaiting Trial'. By 1992, the average daily occupancy for prison remands had fallen to 56 from a total of 94 in 1989. Regrettably this improvement was not sustained during the 1993 moral panics of 'bail bandits' and 'persistent offenders', and the 1993 average daily figure has gone back to nearly 100, despite fourteen year olds having been removed from the remand procedure.

Table 3: Untried Juveniles Remanded in Custody

| Year | No. |
|------|-----|
| 1982 | 1544 |
| 1984 | 1436 |
| 1986 | 1568 |
| 1988 | 1493 |
| 1990 | 1159 |
| 1991 | 1080 |
| 1993 | 1200 (approx) |

We are expecting a similar pattern of increase in sentenced juveniles, despite the early promise of results from the implementation of the 1991 Criminal Justice Act. What appears to be happening is that some sentencers are anticipating legislation and reflecting a more punitive sentencing climate. However, the same characteristics of regional and race differences are also reflected in these increases, and it is likely that areas that traditionally have good links between agencies and a history of progressive practice will continue to use custody less, and those without that tradition will continue to send more children to prison. The remand survey highlighted 11 areas that were using a disproportionate amount of custodial remands. Some would also appear in a similar league table of custodial sentences. The result of these differences, other than the obvious injustice, is that juveniles are being imprisoned even further from home than is already required by the normal catchment areas of YOIs.

Suicide and self harm statistics are notoriously difficult to collect, and those involving juveniles particularly so considering the despair and trauma they represent. It is also of note that the other part of the state that locks up children, (the Department of Health through the Youth Treatment Agency) publishes less information than the prison service on this subject, and local authority secure unit figures are not all collated. Prison figures show that up to 5 per cent of prison suicides are juveniles and another 25 per cent are young adults (aged 17 to 20). The provisional 1994 figures already show 8 suicides in the first ten weeks, of whom 3 were under 21.

I hope to broaden the definition of who is responsible for the prevention of suicide in prisons, and will look at current problems from those two perspectives, the internal prison world and the outside context. The internal problems include regimes, bullying, groups and gangs, and isolation. The external ones include justice by geography and race, social services resources, education issues, and throughcare/aftercare arrangements.

Most juveniles are imprisoned in Young Offender Institutions (YOIs) or when remanded, in either remand units within YOIs or in local prisons. A great deal of writing has concentrated on regime issues and the separate but related problem of bullying. I am not going to replicate that discussion but connect it with Alison Liebling's comments about coping skills and with the findings of the Stewart survey 'Social Circumstances of Younger Offenders'. My concerns about some developments are that we may be concentrating too much on 'standard responses' to the problems. Time out of cells and special bully behavioural units sometimes seem like the only things that matter, when all our experience tells us that the children we are dealing with, all of whom are vulnerable in some way, need as many options as possible. We need to widen the choices available to solve the problems and possibly decide on different ones at different times. I hope that the sentence planning concept will help to introduce an individualised programme approach rather than institutional responses to institutional problems. Groups and gangs are part of the bullying scene, but a particularly difficult part as in some prisons at some times, race as well as region helps to form the allegiances. I have been to some YOIs where the existence of a larger group from Bristol, or south London, or Portsmouth, or wherever has caused real problems for others. The gang type behaviour is present on the streets and some children deal with it (those coping skills again) better than others, but there is a certain extra tyranny about being locked up with it. We may need to look to some of our detached youth work experience for better answers to this. And finally isolation, a factor in a number of the suicides we looked at in Feltham, and something Alison Liebling is best quoted on:

> Lack of contacts with outside, or lack of interest in the outside world are already well-established indicators of

risk. Lack of socialisation within the prison may be another (Liebling, 1991).

'So what do you do with yourself when you are banged up in your cell?' is a pretty good starting point for the most important relationship of all, the one between prisoner and prison officer.

On the outside, so much is changing in terms of policy and legislation that it is difficult to keep up. A new Circular Instruction a day was the going rate for a while. However some things seem never to change and those working in prisons may feel powerless to influence other agencies, particularly the resource decisions that are made that can help determine who gets to prison and who gets a reasonable service from the outside while they are in prison. Again, sentence planning and the new governor contracts may provide a route to make more consistent demands on the other agencies. I know of one probation area that is planning jointly with their social services colleagues, to set out a minimum throughcare programme that they will then negotiate with the relevant home area to ensure that the home agencies, the prison, and the prison probation area all meet their commitments. Eventually some funding arrangement that allows prison costs to be reflected in local authority budgets would also assist.

Future problems may dwarf our current concerns. We are likely to face an increase in the number of juveniles being sentenced to YOIs due to the change in sentencing climate and the change in statutory criteria. We will also face an increase in the length of sentence due to the doubling of the maximum YOI sentence to two years, and the extension of Section 53s to more offences and age groups, (including ten year olds). We also have the imminent prospect of a new sentence, for an age group many can't remember and most thought would never be in prisons again. The secure training order will be administered by private companies but with the ability to use any other establishment as an overflow on Secretary of State order. We are likely to see the use of remand centres for children as young as twelve, despite the announcement of an increase in secure places from 65 (already agreed in order to eliminate remands to prison custody) to 170. We are also likely to see an increase in the numbers being sentenced by courts as cautioning becomes less flexible and also less attractive to police officers. Most commentators predict an increase of custody as a result of increased business through the courts rather than any increase in seriousness of crime. And we are likely to see an increased rigidity in the enforcement of community sentences when the national standards review is completed.

So what impact will all that have, on prisons and juveniles in particular? Assume an increase in numbers, probably with the North and Wales, black people and travellers over-represented. Assume an increase in risk of and incidence of suicide and self harm as even more vulnerable children arrive and prisons have the same resources to deal with more people for longer periods, and assume some reduction in social services resources as ring fencing is removed from some core social services programmes and possibly as local government review changes start to impact.

Is there any good news? A recent Probation Inspectorate survey of partnership arrangements between social services and probation showed some examples of excellent practice, and those areas should be able to hold the line better than most. The opposition to Secure Training Centres or to the criteria for that sentence has produced some significant alliances, and the Howard League is still committed to campaigning against them rather than ameliorating their effects. The most important lesson of the 1980s was that practitioners did make a difference, and the Howard League among others, is spending a good deal of its time helping to support practitioners in all agencies to make a difference in these most difficult times.

# Part Three:

# Prevention

# Fourteen

# Custodial suicide: Overcoming obstacles to prevention

Three years ago I was honoured by the invitation to speak before the Institute for the Study and Treatment of Delinquency's first international conference on Deaths in Custody. It was then that I remarked that 'despite increased awareness of the problem, suicides continue to prevail within our jails while prevention efforts remain uneven. My experience in the field has bore frustration and impatience because I see the problem and its solution within arms' reach. When suicide prevention does occur within our jails, I find that its presence is piecemeal and often following the initiation of litigation'.

It is now 1994 and I was hoping to address this conference with both renewed hope and proof that we have begun to systematically reduce suicides in our jails. Unfortunately, I can not. What I can offer to you, however, are the reasons why we are perhaps not doing a better job in preventing jail suicides. The reasons might be numerous, but I believe they can be reduced to a simple phrase: *Obstacles to Prevention*.

## OBSTACLES TO PREVENTION

It has been this writer's experience that negative attitudes often impede meaningful suicide prevention efforts. Such attitudes form obstacles to prevention and they can be seen on both a local and universal basis. Simply stated, obstacles to prevention are empty excuses that jail suicides can not be prevented. For example, when a jail suicide is reported in the newspaper, it is often accompanied by a statement from the leading law enforcement official - normally the sheriff or police chief. Invariably, the response (or local obstacle) sounds something like this:

> We did everything we could to prevent this death, but he showed no signs of suicidal behaviour; *or*

> There's no way you can prevent suicides unless you have someone sitting watching the prisoner all the time, and no one can afford to be a baby sitter; *or*

> We didn't consider him suicidal, he was simply being manipulative and I guess it just went too far; *or*

> He didn't demonstrate any signs and symptoms of being suicidal; *or*

> We are not mind readers nor trained to be psychiatrists; *or*

> If someone really wants to kill themselves, there's generally nothing you can do about it.

Then there are universal obstacles to prevention: regressive attitudes that are far more dangerous because of their far-reaching ability to negatively influence correctional policy on a larger scale. We often find the roots of this attitude in the world of academia[1]:

> Statistically speaking, suicide in custody is a rare phenomenon, and rare phenomena are notoriously difficult to forecast due to their low base rate. We cannot predict suicide because social scientists are not fully aware of the causal variables involving suicide;

> Demographic profiles of custodial suicide victims are of little value for prediction because they often mirror the characteristics of typical jail inmates;

> Even those skilled mental health professionals, who have the time for extensive personal interaction with troubled individuals, either cannot forecast suicide or are unable to prevent patient suicide even if it had been somewhat anticipated; *and*

> Jail suicides are extremely difficult to predict due to their spontaneous nature.

There are various ways to defuse these local and universal obstacles. One could cite research which indicates that 'three factors (adequate staff, staff training and written rules and procedures) in combination would have a powerful effect on reducing problems of suicide[2]"; or another study which stresses that jail suicide profiles are not meant to be predictive but rather tools to sensitize jail personnel to those characteristics appearing most often in jail suicide victims[3]. And while it is questionable whether we are very good at precisely forecasting *if* or *when* someone will kill themselves, we maintain the ability to identify various predisposing factors in suicidal people. For example, at least two thirds of all victims communicate their intent sometime prior to death, and it has been consistently reported that any individual with a history of one or more suicide attempts is at much greater risk for suicide than those who have never made an attempt[4]. The key, of course, is *inquiry* and the above information is often readily accessible through the intake screening process. If obstacles to prevention discourage the inquiry, we  risk remaining ignorant to the potential risk for suicide.

One could also stress that while jail officials and their personnel are not (and should not be) held responsible for having credentials comparable to mental health professionals, nor judged as 'mind readers' or 'baby sitters', they should be required to take reasonable steps to identify suicidal inmates and prevent foreseeable deaths. Jails by their very nature are often conducive to suicidal behaviour, and jail officials (unlike mental health clinicians in the community) remain in a unique position to thwart suicides because of the 'captive' nature of the environment. A private therapist, for example, loses contact with his patient after each session; the jail official, on the other hand, maintains the ability to increase observation of (and remove dangerous items from) the potentially suicidal inmate, thereby reducing the likelihood of a successful suicide.

Finally, a straightforward way to defuse what I consider to be a premature response of 'we did everything we could to prevent this death' is to simply reply: *Show me your suicide prevention program!* Many can not.

OVERCOMING THE OBSTACLES

Perhaps the most powerful way to overcome obstacles to prevention is to cite examples of jurisdictions that have systematically reduced jail suicides. There are numerous illustrations of prevention occurring in small 'pockets' throughout the United States[5]. For example, a 130-bed county jail in suburban Illinois experienced three suicides during a 12-month period of 1980-1981, and yet 13 years and over 60,000 inmates later has not had another suicide. The principle reason is *attitude,* but not the regressive attitude of 'if someone really wants to kill themselves, there's generally nothing you can do about it'. Actually quite the opposite. As the sheriff told this writer: 'Inmates are human beings and we are taught an important lesson through those deaths. We simply will not tolerate it any more'. The sheriff contracted for mental health services, provided suicide prevention training to his staff, and implemented a suicide prevention program.

There are also larger examples. Three years ago I reported to you on the success of the jail suicide prevention efforts in the states of New York and Texas. Briefly, through the co-operative efforts of the New York State Office of Mental Health, Commission on Correction, Ulster County Community Mental Health Services and a statewise task force, the Local Forensic Crisis Service Model was developed and implemented across the state in over 300 county jail and police lockups between 1986 and 1988. The Crisis Service Model, designed to establish administrative and direct service linkages for suicide prevention efforts among county jails, police lock ups and local mental health programs, contained four major components: 1) jail policy and procedural guidelines; 2) suicide prevention intake screening guidelines; 3) an eight-hour training program; and 4) a mental health practitioner's manual.

During a six-year period of 1985-1990, the total number of jail suicides throughout the state of New York declined from 31 in 1985 to 17 in 1990. Most recently, the jail system experienced 11 suicides during 1992 and only *three* in 1993: a phenomenal achievement considering that total jail admissions for the state exceeded 310,000 per year. It would seem that the established success of New York's Crisis Service Model soundly overcomes the obstacles to prevention that suggest 'there's no way to prevent suicides unless you have someone sitting and watching the prisoner all the time' or 'we cannot predict suicide because social scientists are not fully aware of the causal variables involving suicide'.

In Texas, obstacles to prevention initially tried to defeat efforts by the state Commission on Jail Standards to implement stronger suicide prevention standards in county jails. Prior to final adoption of a requirement to implement an 8-step prevention program (developed by this writer) in over 255 county facilities, several sheriffs voiced their opposition to the

Commission:

> My overriding concern is just how far the state, and especially a police agency, should intrude into the lives of citizens. We are being placed in a position as police agencies of first determining that a person has suicidal tendencies, i.e. is mentally ill, and then spreading the word to his or her family and, through outside agencies, to the community at large. This, to me, is almost Orwellian and despite the good intentions behind it, borders on the police state;

> I find it hard to believe that the Commission, a county sheriff, or any of the medical persons that I have ever known would be blessed with the ability to detect a suicidal person when they see one; *and*

> I feel the requirement would serve no useful purpose. The only thing it might accomplish is to give lawyers a chance to hang us with our own paperwork.

The Commission, however, also heard from county sheriffs who genuinely embraced the new requirement, calling it 'an absolute necessity' and ' a valuable asset' as well as one confession that — 'We had to change a few procedures, and hardest of all, even *change a few attitudes we had about the subject*'. After much delay, the 8-step suicide prevention program (which included requirements for training, identification, communication, housing, supervision, intervention, reporting and follow-up/review) was finally adopted by the Texas Commission on Jail Standards in January 1992. To date, the Commission is beginning to see progress. In 1993, Texas experienced 19 county jail suicides, down from 26 such deaths in 1986—an admirable achievement considering that the average daily population in those facilities increased over 54 per cent during that time period.

While apparently successful, implementation of comprehensive jail suicide prevention services in New York and Texas provide differing examples of systemic change. In New York, change occurred through the collaborative efforts of the Commission on Correction and Office of Mental Health who, together with local mental health agencies, pooled their resources in an effort to provide comprehensive jail suicide prevention services throughout the state. In Texas, change occurred solely through the initiation of support and technical assistance of the

Commission on Jail Standards, which first promulgated the requirement and remained available to provide both technical support and training services to county jails in the development of their suicide prevention programs.

A key impetus for change, however, was the strong regulatory bodies that existed in both these states. Unfortunately, they are the exception rather than the rule throughout the United States. Although 37 states have jail standards, many are simply voluntary and do not include adequate suicide prevention procedures. In addition, several states have either eliminated or drastically reduced staffing of their jail inspection programs. Even in those programs that still exist, enforcement is either lax or non-existent. Finally, where state jail standards do exist, localities often lack the financial means to provide mandated services.

### PREVENTION THROUGH PERSUASION

The state of Mississippi offers a unique example of an unregulated system that has recently seen many of its county jails embark upon, perhaps reluctantly, the provision of suicide prevention programming. I refer to it as 'prevention through persuasion'. Mississippi does not have any state jail standards nor inspection programs, and offers little, if any, technical support to local jailers. Mental health providers are reluctant and often refuse to provide services to jail inmates. Not surprisingly, many of the 85 county jails in Mississippi are in deplorable condition, with underpaid and untrained staff, and few, if any, written policies and procedures. And, were it not for a recent investigative series by the state's largest newspaper (*'The Clarion-Ledger'*), the total number of jail suicides in Mississippi would still be unknown. The newspaper's investigation revealed that 41 county and city jail suicides occurred in Mississippi from 1987 through 1992 - almost 50 per cent of which involved black victims. Given the state's infamous civil rights history, the 'Clarion-Ledger' investigation rekindled suspicions that deaths of the black inmates - all by hanging - were lynchings disguised as suicides. In March 1993, civil rights leaders held two days of highly-publicized hearings in the state capitol of Jackson. Although no evidence was presented that the deaths were anything other than suicides, civil rights leaders persuaded the federal government to conduct a formal investigation.

In announcing that the U.S. Justice Department would

conduct a thorough inquiry of all the jail suicides, U.S. Attorney General Janet Reno effectively defused any potential obstacles to prevention in Mississippi when she declared on April 13, 1993 that 'those numbers of deaths are unacceptable' and that investigators will 'get to the bottom of' the question - 'How could that many people die?' The Special Litigation Section of the Department's Civil Rights Division was subsequently assigned to the Mississippi investigation, and was able to intervene under the legal aegis of the 'Civil Rights of Institutionalized Persons Act' (CRIPA). According to CRIPA:

> Whenever the Attorney General has reasonable cause to believe that any State or political subdivision of a State, official, employee, or agent thereof, or other person acting on behalf of a State or political subdivision of a State is subjecting persons residing in or confined to an institution ... to egregious or flagrant conditions which deprive such persons of any rights, privileges, or immunities secured or protected by the Constitution or laws of the United States causing such persons to suffer grievous harm, and that such deprivation is pursuant to a pattern or practice of resistance to the full enjoyment of such rights, privileges, or immunities, the Attorney General, for or in the name of the United States, may institute a civil action in any appropriate United States district court against such party for such equitable relief as may be appropriate to insure the minimum corrective measures... [6]

Launched in May 1993, the Justice Department's investigation would become unprecedented. Although the agency had previously investigated numerous alleged 'egregious conditions' at individual facilities throughout the country, it was rare to converge upon numerous jails within one state, as well as unusual to focus on suicide prevention procedures. And while the Justice Department's initial mission was to thoroughly investigate each of the Mississippi jail suicides that occurred during the past seven years, the inquiry was subsequently expanded to include general conditions of confinement (and suicide prevention procedures) at 18 local jurisdictions alleged to have the worst jail facilities. The investigative team comprised several Justice Department attorneys, as well as this writer and other national experts in the area of correctional management, medical care, and environmental safety.

The investigation, which included on-site inspections of each facility, thorough critique of jail procedures, review of suicide incident reports, and interviews with both staff and inmates, was conducted in May through July 1993. Pursuant to CRIPA, 'fact-finding' reports that detailed unconstitutional practices were subsequently forwarded to each of the 18 jails in late 1993. All of the 18 jails were cited for various grossly inadequate conditions ranging from maggot-infested cells to racially segregated drunk tanks and life-threatening fire hazards. Other deficiencies included insufficient staffing and poor training, infrequent inmate supervision, inadequate or non-existent medical and mental health services, and general lack of written policies and procedures. Many of the jails were also criticized for their 'pervasive filth, serious state of longstanding neglect, and significant deterioration.' In fact, the Justice Department called for the closing of four jails because they were found to be 'unfit for human habitation.'

In regard to suicide prevention, the findings in one jurisdiction was indicative of conditions in all 18 Mississippi jails:

> There is no suicide prevention program at the jail and mental health services are not available. As well, there is no detoxification program. There has been one suicide and three suicide attempts at the jail during the past two years. Inmates with mental disturbances or who are at risk to commit suicide are placed in one of three two-bed steel cages in isolation in an area called sick bay. The three 'sanity' cells each measure five feet by six feet with approximately half that space occupied by bunks, a toilet and a sink. Inmates and non-criminal mentally ill persons being held pursuant to Mississippi's commitment law, and awaiting admittance to a state psychiatric facility, can and have been incarcerated in 'sanity' cells for months. Our consultant found that such cage cells, with exposed, reachable overhead bars are 'absolutely suitable' for committing suicide.[7]

Although CRIPA provides clear authority for the Attorney General to initiate legal action in order to correct unconstitutional conditions, the Act also allows the Justice Department to avoid the need for litigation by encouraging 'the appropriate officials to correct the alleged conditions and pattern or practice of resistance through informal methods of conference, conciliation and *'persuasion'*. Therefore, in accordance with

CRIPA, each of the Justice Department's 'fact-finding' reports not only listed the egregious conditions, but also detailed the remedial measures necessary to voluntarily correct problems in the 18 jail facilities. For example, all of the jails were required to develop and implement a comprehensive suicide prevention program, and the following summarisation of an 8-step protocol was recommended by this writer to each of the facilities:

*Training*

The key to any prevention program is properly trained correctional staff, the backbone ingredient of any jail facility. Suicide prevention training, given to all staff who come into contact with inmates (i.e. correctional, medical, and mental health), should be approximately eight hours in length, and include instruction on why jail environments are conducive to suicidal behaviour, potential predisposing factors, high-risk suicide periods, warning signs and symptoms, as well as the components of the facility's prevention program.

*Screening*

Intake screening is also a crucial ingredient to any jail facility's suicide prevention efforts. It is imperative that every jail, regardless of size, screen each arrestee for potentially suicidal behaviour upon entry into the facility. Although an inmate can commit suicide at any time during incarceration, research shows that over 50 per cent of all suicides take place within the first 24 hours of incarceration, with almost one third occurring within the first three hours. Thus, suicide prevention efforts, particularly intake screening, rapidly lose their strength unless initiated during the early stages of incarceration.

Further, because many jail facilities do not have in-house mental health staff, intake screening becomes a vital prevention tool for correctional staff. The screening process also serves to regularly sensitise jail staff and increase general awareness to the potential of suicide within a facility, particularly in those jails lacking a mental health presence.

*Communication*

Suicide prevention begins at the point of arrest because the arrest scene is often the most volatile and emotional time for the arrestee - where potentially suicidal behaviour can be manifested, while previous behaviour confirmed by onlookers (i.e. family, friends, etc.). It becomes critical that any pertinent information regarding the arrestee's well-being is communicated by the arresting/ transporting officer to jail staff.

At a second level, effective management of suicidal inmates often comes down to how effective correctional officers are in transmitting relevant information amongst themselves and other professional staff. Because inmates can become suicidal at any point during their incarceration, correctional officers must maintain awareness, share information, and make appropriate referrals to mental health and medical staff. Finally, jail staff must utilize various communication skills with the suicidal inmate. These skills include: active listening; staying with the inmate if they are in immediate danger; maintaining contact (through verbalization, eye contact, and body language) and conversation; and trusting your own judgement (and avoid being misled by others into ignoring signs of suicidal behaviour).

## Housing

In determining the most appropriate location to house a suicidal inmate, there is the tendency of jail officials to both physically isolate and restrain the individual. These responses are often made for the convenience of staff, and to the detriment of the inmate. The use of isolation (which accounts for two thirds of all jail suicides) not only escalates the inmate's sense of alienation while feeding despair, but further removes the individual from proper staff supervision. To every extent possible, suicidal inmates should be housed within the general population of a facility and/or located in close proximity to jail staff. Removal of an inmate's clothing (excluding belts and shoelaces), as well as the use of physical restraints (e.g. handcuffs, straitjackets, etc.) should be avoided whenever possible, and only utilized as a last resort for periods in which the inmate is physically engaging in self-destructive behaviour. Housing assignments should be based, not on decisions that heighten depersonalising aspects of confinement, but on the ability to maximize staff interaction with inmates.

## Supervision

Two levels of supervision are generally recommended for suicidal inmates - close and constant. *Close supervision* is reserved for the inmate who is not actively suicidal, but expresses suicidal ideation and/or has a prior history of self-destructive behaviour. This inmate should be observed at staggered intervals not to exceed 15 minutes. *Constant supervision* is reserved for the inmate who is actively suicidal, either by threatening or engaging in the act of suicide. This inmate should be observed on a continuous, uninterrupted basis. Closed circuit television can be utilized as a supplement to, but never as a substitute for, these two levels of supervision.

*Intervention*

The policy regarding intervention should be three-fold; a) all staff who come into contact with inmates should be trained in standard first aid as well as cardiopulmonary resuscitation (CPR); b) any staff that discovers an inmate attempting suicide should immediately respond and initiate first aid while at the same time calling for back-up support and alerting other staff to immediately call for emergency services; and c) upon arriving at the scene of a suicide attempt, staff should never presume an inmate is dead, but rather initiate appropriate first aid and continue life-saving measures until relieved by arriving medical personnel.

*Reporting*

In the event of a suicide attempt or completed suicide, all appropriate jail officials should be notified through the normal chain of command. Following the incident, the victim's family should also be immediately notified. All staff who came into contact with the inmate prior to the suicide should be required to submit a statement as to their full knowledge of the inmate and incident.

*Follow-up / Review*

Following a jail suicide, misplaced guilt is often displayed by the officer who wonders - 'What if I had made my cell check earlier?' When crisis events occur and jail staff experience the effects of critical incident stress, a Critical Incident Stress Debriefing (CISD) may be appropriate. The trained CISD team, comprised of law enforcement officers, paramedics, fire fighters, clergy, and mental health professionals trained in crisis intervention and traumatic stress awareness, need to be called immediately. Because experience demonstrates that debriefings become less effective over time, CISD should occur within 24 to 72 hours of the incident.

Further, an administrative review and/or 'psychological autopsy' should also occur immediately following a jail suicide. The review should include a comprehensive examination of the incident, including: a) critical review of the circumstances surrounding the incident; b) critical review of jail procedures relevant to the incident; c) synopsis of all relevant training received by involved staff; d) pertinent medical services and mental health reports involving the victim; and e) recommendations, if any, for change in policy, training, physical plant, medical or mental health, and operational procedures.

To date, all of the 18 Mississippi jails have been persuaded to correct the unconstitutional conditions cited in the Justice Department's 'fact-finding' reports. In fact, several jurisdictions have already agreed to build new jails. The federal government, in turn, has agreed to provide training and other types of technical support to those jurisdictions requesting assistance in remedying the poor conditions. The Justice Department will also monitor compliance to the corrective action for an unspecified time period.

Although most jail officials in Mississippi welcomed (even invited) the Justice Department investigation, there were also those who criticized the federal intervention and resulting publicity. 'It's pretty apparent that Mississippi has been singled out,' said one sheriff. 'I can see the need for something to be done to solve the problems, but I really believe Mississippi caught a black eye on this that it didn't deserve.'

Notwithstanding the legitimate argument that Mississippi was 'singled out', and the fact that the state did not have the highest rate of jail suicides in the country (although it ranked approximately sixth); there was a general consensus that deplorable jail conditions and grossly inadequate suicide prevention procedures were pervasive and long-standing problems that had previously received little attention in Mississippi. As bluntly stated by one jail administrator whose facility was recommended for closure:

> We're not surprised. In fact we are relieved. No one really should have to be in our jail. We never have been able to get across just how serious a situation we have here. It took the Justice Department to come in and make it known to the world.

A key impetus for change was the strong regulatory bodies that existed in both these states. Unfortunately, they are the exception rather than the rule throughout the United States. Although 37 states have jail standards, many are simply voluntary and do not include adequate suicide prevention procedures. In addition, several states have either eliminated or drastically reduced staffing of their jail inspection programs. Even in those programs that still exist, enforcement is either lax or non-existent. Finally, where state jail standards do exist, localities often lack the financial means to provide mandated services.

CONCLUSION

The recent efforts in Mississippi, as well as the continuing efforts in New York and Texas, represent three diverse examples of jail suicide prevention through systemic change. And while not all jail suicides are preventable, these efforts prove that both local and universal obstacles to prevention can be effectively overcome through comprehensive programming. Unfortunately, however, suicide will continue to be the leading cause of death in our jails until such time as we decide to become more systemic in our prevention efforts.

Dr. Edwin Shneidman, an eminent psychologist and founder of the American Association of Suicidology once stated:

> Suicide, I have learned, is not a bizarre and incomprehensible act of self-destruction. Rather, suicidal people use a particular logic, a style of thinking that brings them to the conclusion that death is the only solution to their problems. This style can be readily seen, and there are steps we can take to stop suicide, if we know where to look.[8]

In applying this observation to the area of jail suicide prevention, we are left with two simple choices: either continue to look for excuses regarding what we can not do, or work toward implementing suicide prevention programs that better enable us to 'know where to look'. And while much needs to be done to reduce jail suicides throughout our country, the path will be clearer if we remove the obstacles to prevention.

**Notes**
1. For an academic account of jail suicide that typifies various universal obstacles to prevention, see Kennedy, Daniel B., 'Rethinking the Problem of Custodial Suicide,' *American Jails*, January/February 1994, pp. 41-45.
2. Kimme Planning and Architecture, *The Nature of New Small Jails: Report and Analysis,* Washington, D.C.: National Institute of Corrections, U.S. Justice Department, October 1985, p. 59.
3. Lindsay M. Hayes, 'National Study of Jail Suicides: Seven Years

Later,' *Psychiatric Quarterly*, Volume 60, Number 1, Spring 1989, pp. 11-13.

4. David C. Clark and Sara L. Horton-Deutsch, 'Assessment in Absentia: The Value of the Psychological Autopsy Method for Studying Antecedents of Suicide and Predicting Future Suicides,' in Maris, et. al. (Eds.), *Assessment and Prediction of Suicide*, New York: The Guiford Press, 1992, pp. 144-182.

5. For an in-depth discussion of five model jail suicide prevention programs, see *Jail Suicide Update*, Volume 3, Numbers 1 through 4, 1990-1991. In addition and as previously noted, many comprehensive jail suicide prevention programs are the result of litigation. For a recent example, see *Jail Suicide Update*, Volume 4, Number 1, Spring 1992, pp. 1-8.

6. Civil Rights of Institutionalized Persons Act,' Title 42 U.S.C. Section 1997, 'Public Law 96-247, 96th Congress May 23, 1980, 94 Stat. 349-354.

7. *Jail Suicide Update*, Volume 5, Number 4, Spring 1994, p. 2.

8. See Edwin Shneidman, 'At the Point of No Return,' *Psychology Today*, March 1987, pp. 55-58.

# Fifteen

# Prevention of deaths in custody: A worldwide problem

*Joseph R Rowan*

Detention and correctional facilities throughout the world are facing serious problems regarding deaths in custody. Such deaths may be caused by suicide, AIDS, drug-resistant strains of tuberculosis and Hepatitis B. In talking about deaths in custody, we must differentiate between *detention* or pre-trial facilities and those for sentenced inmates confined in *correctional* facilities. Further, differentiation is needed in a country like the United States where our more than 3,000 county jails house *both* pre-trial detainees and sentenced misdemeanants.

I talk about differentiation because *causes* and *rates* of death *differ* by category of institution. For example, AIDS is rapidly becoming the Number One cause of deaths in US prisons or correctional institutions for felons or serious offenders. Suicide is the second highest cause of prison deaths, but has been *decreasing* over the past three years. In 1992 AIDS deaths were almost *six* times greater than suicides in prisons.

Until 1992, *suicide* had always been the Number One cause of death in USA jails or remand centres. During that year, reports from 164 facilities housing over 200 prisoners each (mean = 1,386) indicated that deaths from AIDS surpassed those by suicide. Since 88 percent of jail suicides in the USA in 1986 occurred in urban and suburban facilities, future deaths by AIDS can be expected to continue to rise and outnumber suicides in jails.

183

My presentation on deaths in custody will pertain to suicide, its identification and prevention.

Based on systems which have already had *significant decreases* in the rate of deaths, we see great hope for the decrease of suicides in US facilities. This includes some facilities which once had *extremely high* suicide rates.

### Chicago Police Department

The CPD has reduced completed suicides by *75* per cent during the past 10 years. In 1982 *training* in suicide prevention was conducted for 650 lockup officers, and *health screening* was initiated for all arrestees. I was one of the trainers - my first experience in training police.

### Cook County Jail (Chicago)

CCJ has reduced completed suicides by 80 per cent since 1980, at a time when its average daily population rose from 3,700 to *9,600* inmates.

### Philadelphia Police Department

Since 1989, when I trained 450 lockup keepers in suicide prevention, and *health screening* was initiated on all arrestees, the PPD has had a *90* percent *reduction* in completed suicides. It took a $1,104,000 jury verdict *against* the City (concerning one of its 20 suicides in six years) to get its attention. The case went through the US Court of Appeals all the way to the US Supreme Court which upheld the verdict of the US Court of Appeals. Cost of training was only $4,000. Had the City spent that money on training *before* the suicide, it would probably have been spared the $1,104,000 verdict.

### State of New York

The 57-county/regional jails and over 300 police lockups servicing over 900 police departments and 62 county sheriff's departments within the State of New York have reduced completed suicides from 26 in 1984 to *three* in 1993 - an *88 percent* reduction. New York State regulations require not only *eight hours* of suicide prevention training for all direct service workers, but also health screening upon admission and *constant* or close monitoring of those prisoners who are either considered at high risk for suicide or intoxicated.

During those 10 years that New York State jails were experiencing an 88 per cent reduction in suicides, their average daily population increased 80 per cent. Based on statistics from approximately 200 urban and suburban jails nationally, there has been a 12.6 per cent decrease in the suicide rate over the past three years - a very hopeful sign.

Based on the national survey which Lindsay Hayes and I co-directed in 1987, there are 870 per cent more suicides in *US jails* than in the community. During the past three years the rate of suicides in *prisons* has risen just slightly more (about 28 per cent) than the rate in the general community. This is dramatically less than jail suicides. The Native American Indian suicide rate is five times greater in jails than in the community.

### CANADA

The Canadian federal prison system has responsibility for inmates with sentences of over two years. In 1991 the suicide rate in Canadian federal correctional institutions was *94* per 100,000 - about *four* times that found in the general Canadian population. This was a *six* times greater rate than found in US prisons during the same year.

### AUSTRALIA

Statistics on custodial deaths in Australia show that 44 per cent pertain to *suicide*. Although only 17 per cent of the offender population were remandees during 1990-91, they constituted 31 per cent of the prison deaths. Again, persons awaiting disposition are at greater risk than sentenced inmates.

The *rate* of prison deaths *stabilized* during 1990-91, compared to the previous 10 years. The suicide rate in prisons during 1990-91 was 109 per 100,000 inmates. Two-thirds of the deaths of Aboriginal people occurred in police custody during 1980-89, but during 1990-91 that percentage *decreased* to 25 per cent. This is a significant reduction, reflecting a firm commitment by the police to change their practices. I witnessed this during and after training police from Australia's six states and two territories and after representing the New South Wales Police Department as an expert witness in its two successful suicide lawsuits.

Although Aboriginal people make up less than one per cent of the Australian general population of 17 years and older, they make up *14 per cent* of the prison population and 20 per cent of prison *deaths*. Hence, they are more than 14 times over-represented in the offender *population* and 40 per cent more among prison *deaths*. Aboriginal people make up almost 29 per cent of police custody cases, an over-representation by more than *26* times that of non-Aboriginals. In my training sessions last year police told me that there were now greater efforts at releasing Aboriginal arrestees to responsible adults or on their own recognizance, or not charging them in the first place. Such practices are in line with recommendations by the Royal Commission Into Aboriginal Deaths in Custody and are key reasons for the significant reduction of those deaths as outlined earlier.

NEW ZEALAND

New Zealand's National Police operates 110 watchhouses located throughout its three islands. The average number of suicides annually over the past 13 years has been four. National Police Headquarters, concerned with a higher than average suicide rate during recent years, asked that its top personnel and trainers be trained. Following the training, which I provided, there were some important developments. A working committee of the top six division heads was immediately appointed by Commissioner MacDonald, and the committee developed plans for a 'major overhaul of policies, training manuals, general instructions, operating guidelines and physical holding facilities.'

'Suicide-proofing' the cells and equipping them with needed sanitation facilities, where absent, were included in the planning. Implementation of the proposed plans has been significantly effected.

What factors changed New Zealand watchhouse operations so much faster than would be accomplished in the US and perhaps other countries? Capable, committed *administration* was one. Another was the *extremely high level of entrance training* required of new officers (higher than any I have seen anywhere in the world): *32 weeks* of *classroom* training, six weeks of on-the-job training, and a *two-year* probationary period. Not one police or corrections department in the USA requires this, nor do many other countries.

About 80 per cent of the 86,000 arrestees annually are out on bail within one to four hours - a very high percentage compared to other countries. Arresting constables have broad powers of releasing on bail without sureties - a key element in suicide prevention.

The rate of suicide in the general population of New Zealand is 16.5 per 100,000 residents. Based on their two largest prisons which I surveyed earlier this year, the suicide rate in prison is approximately 100 per 100,000. During fiscal year 1992-93 there were four *remand* suicides and no correctional suicides in all of New Zealand's detention/correctional institutions. With an average daily population of 4,500 inmates, the prison suicide rate would be 89 per 100,000, or over *five* times greater than in the community. It must be remembered that, like Australia, New Zealand confines both remandees and sentenced inmates in the same system and institutions.

### RUSSIA

In surveying several custodial, police and mental health facilities in 1992, we learned that suicides in the community throughout Russia are approximately 60 per 100,000, or five times that found in the USA. Young soldiers were reported to have the highest suicide rate. Statistics were unavailable for custodial suicides, although corrections, police and mental health officials reported that they were very high and of serious concern. There were no training materials for custodial suicide prevention, and our training manual was eagerly accepted for translation and the training of trainers.

### CHINA

Last year I was one of the fortunate few of a small, international group comprising the first criminal justice officials invited to survey several of China's detention and correctional institutions as well as a metropolitan police operation.

Statistics on suicide deaths in custody were not available, but officials conceded there was a serious suicide problem. We provided one suicide training manual, which was welcomed for translation by the Chinese Ministry of Justice.

Our entire delegation was surprised to learn that each inmate is tested for dietary/chemical deficiencies and given a computerized diet printout for implementation. The future may tell whether this unique practice will have an impact on physical and mental well being, which could impact suicide.

The maximum recidivism rate in Chinese correctional

institutions is 10 per cent, with a three-year follow-up.

Strong *family unity* characterized by a reported divorce rate of only five per cent (compared to 55 per cent in the USA) and a 94 per cent agrarian/agricultural economy appear to be influential factors.

DENMARK

The suicide rate in Danish custodial facilities from 1977-86 was an amazingly low *19* per 100,000 prisoners. This is particularly noteworthy since the Department of Prisons and Probation operate both the prisons for sentenced inmates and the local prisons (jails); these are under the supervision of the chief of police, where *pre-trial* prisoners are confined.

ENGLAND

During 1988-89 and 90, suicide deaths in English correctional facilities rose each year until 1991 when there was a significant *reduction*. Reductions were noted among *young offenders* and inmates in local prisons and remand centres, *contrary* to the experience in all other countries with which I am familiar.

The greatest rise was among lifers, who had a *fourfold increase*. The number in training prisons remained *constant* over the four years, while dispersal prisons had a noticeable *increase* in 1991. In 1993 the prison service in England and Wales had 47 suicides, giving a rate of 104 per 100,000 inmates.

THE POSITIVES OF SUICIDE PREVENTION SEEN IN VARIOUS COUNTRIES

*Top administration*

Suicide prevention and reduction are only as good as *top administrators understand and firmly support* what many of us know reduce suicides in custody.

*Institutional climate / environment*

The total institutional climate and environment influence suicide, either positively or negatively, and the top administrator who does not even trust his/her own staff enough to involve them meaningfully in policy, program, procedure and facility changes, cannot expect to have a TEAM operation. An absolute must is *participatory management,* but, at least in the US, about half of the administrators don't practice participatory management. There are some good points about the para-military style of management, but it needs to be significantly modified.

Inmates/prisoners are generally treated by officers and other direct service workers the same as their supervisors treat them. An unhappy staff person, who does not feel that s/he is a true team member, does not make a good suicide prevention worker.

A new, highly capable top administrator at Cook County Jail in Chicago was responsible for starting the jail on its uphill course from being possibly the worst urban jail in America - one with a shocking suicide record - to one of the best today.

## Training of all direct service staff

Good staff training starts with the top *administrator* who then inculcates supervisors under him with his *m*otivation, *a*ttitude and *p*hilosophy. This MAP training is then passed on to direct service staff through day-to-day supervision. Most job learning in detention and corrections does not come from a classroom. Rather, it comes from the *immediate supervisor,* going back all the way to the governor, superintendent, warden or director.

HM Prison Service is to be commended for putting in so much time, effort and expense in training its top institutional managers and supervisors in suicide prevention in 1991. The New Zealand National Police force followed the same approach by bringing top managers from throughout the country into its academy for suicide prevention training. All too often in the US administrators and top supervisors do not participate in the training, even though we strongly encourage them to be involved. When line officers see only peers at training sessions they ask where their supervisors are. Effective suicide prevention is unlikely in those facilities.

New York State's mandate of *eight hours* of suicide prevention classroom training should be the goal and practice of all systems. Recognized, progressive systems provide refresher training at least every *two years*. Some do a few hours of re-training *each year*.

## Suicide screening at intake / booking

Most police, jail/remand centre and prison facilities which *do* screening do *total* health screening, of which suicide identification is one part. In about 85 per cent of US jails, screening is done by trained correctional/jail officers. Both the American Medical and Psychiatric Associations clearly declare that officers can be trained to identify health problems. Experienced intake/admissions staff believe that 75-90 per cent of potential suicides can be identified by *trained* personnel who do health screening at admission.

There appears to be agreement among the different countries that suicide victim *profiles* should never be given *priority* in identifying a potentially suicidal prisoner. Instead the person's comments and actions at arrest, transportation to the facility, at intake and while in confinement are the most important. Some time-proven signs/symptoms which clearly demand consideration are: sudden mood and behaviour changes, current and past mental illness, past suicidal gestures/ideations, feelings of helplessness/hopelessness, extreme anxiety, unusual agitation and being under the influence of alcohol and/or drugs.

*Suicide prevention by teamwork*

Among the various countries, most agree that effective suicide prevention can only be effected through *team* work. This may involve:

- Unit Management process;
- Suicide Prevention Management Groups;
- Case Management concept;
- Classification as part of the team;
- The living unit or housing officer - the backbone of suicide prevention - with medical and mental health services as backup;
- Peer inmate support such as the Listener/Befrienders Scheme used in England/Wales and similar methods used elsewhere ('buddy watch' in the US);
- Peer staff support teams such as the staff care team concept in England/Wales, unfortunately missing in the US;
- Involving outside suicide crisis line support agency such as the Samaritans, who are used heavily throughout the custodial institutions in England and Wales.

*Suicide assessment - miscalculations by professionals*

A common problem I find in the different countries where I have trained is when correctional or living unit officers disagree with the medical or mental health assessment of 'not suicidal'. I have become acquainted with a number of such cases in the States while serving as an expert witness. Tragically, deaths occurred when officers followed *policy* and mental health recommendations with which they disagreed. Trained officers who live with the prisoner sometimes have a better assessment of suicide potential.

The New York State Office of Mental Health, joining with the New York Commission of Correction, has taken the lead in supporting correctional officers as follows:

If you believe a detainee is suicidal, YOU SHOULD trust your own judgment. If you believe someone is in danger of suicide, act on your beliefs. Don't let others mislead you into ignoring suicidal signals.

This courageous and credible policy position of top mental health personnel in New York State has been one of four reasons for the dramatic suicide reduction in that state. The agency which I direct has taken on the job of getting this policy adopted nation-wide. A national seminar involving approximately 100 key mental health and medical personnel resulted in their full support for the policy change. The *American Jails* journal prominently featured our research on this subject, and it is available from our agency at no cost.

*Obsessions with security can hinder more effective suicide prevention*

In various countries the para-military mindset and reliance on untested myths about what constitutes good security in a prison or remand centre, works against normalizing custodial environments. I am convinced that this impacts on suicide prevention. The US, as well as other countries, still have a number of prison and jail systems in which there are few, if any female officers working in male, maximum security institutions. A mailed survey of all 50 US state prison systems compared male and female officers who directly supervise maximum security *male* inmates. Returns from 36 of the prison systems showed the following:

Assaults on female officers occur only 29 per cent as often as against male officers. An interesting second aspect of the survey showed that 7.1 per cent of the female officers used disciplinary segregation as dispositions, compared to 5.2 of male officers. Conclusion: *Female officers enforce prison rules more strictly than do their male counterparts, but they must do it in a more positive manner than do the men, because of the low number of assaults made on them.*

I am also convinced that future research will show that institutions where female officers make up at least 40-50 per cent of total staff will be providing the type of climate and environment which will result in fewer suicides.

The same principle applies to female nurses in male institutions. Only 15 years ago Texas male prisons had *no* female nurses. Now, they make up approximately *90 per cent* of nursing staff; furthermore, they do not get victimized like some of the wardens/governors predicted when we surveyed those institutions before one female nurse set foot into a facility.

*One man or woman with courage can constitute a majority and help to effect better suicide prevention*

A. When a new administrator took over at Cook County Jail in Chicago, he was told that his budget, which would include monies for increasing new officer training from 400 to 800 hours, would *not* be approved. Only when he publicly threatened a lawsuit against his own County Board of Commissioners did he get the budget he requested. The high calibre of training for all officers at that facility, plus an additional 120 hours of mental health training for officers working in the mental health units is a big reason for the 80 per cent suicide reduction and accreditation by two national agencies since 1980.

B. A female deputy sheriff in Mississippi 'blew the whistle' on reported abuses in the jail, and got fired. Eventually she and other ex-officers testified before the Mississippi Commission on Human Rights Abuses, which led to the US Civil Rights Commission asking the US Justice Department to investigate conditions in Mississippi jails. The US Justice Department entered the scene and so did Lindsay Hayes, as he described earlier. That was followed by the Mississippi Department of Corrections' request for me to conduct two days of suicide prevention training for state and northern Mississippi county and city officers last summer. Participants at those training sessions, with little or no prior training, were very positive and eager to learn. I expect their practices to change and suicides to decrease.

A senior jail officer in the southern part of the state drove 200 miles to attend the northern training, liked it and returned to southern Mississippi to convince his sheriff to arrange training for jail staff from the southern counties. I trained them last fall. Recently, at a national meeting, the Director of Corrections in Mississippi said there had been a noticeable decrease in suicide attempts since the training.

Research by our agency showed that, while Mississippi did have a serious problem with suicides, due in great part to what

Lindsay Hayes and I have already described, five other states in the same region had an even *higher* rate of suicides. This matter was formally presented to the US Justice Department, and last week I was notified in writing that the Department will expand its investigative activities into other states as needed. The whole process of change in Mississippi and neighbouring states was brought about when the firm convictions of one young woman with courage demonstrated that one person can constitute a 'majority.'

C. An urban jail which never trained its staff in suicide prevention, did no screening, had 15 suicides in five years and reportedly the same number in approximately the same number of years prior thereto. The psychiatrist there said nothing until subpoenaed to testify in a lawsuit involving 'his jail,' where he finally laid bare the facts about faults in the system. The result of the lawsuit changed the system significantly; there are now few suicides, and the psychiatrist was NOT fired! Based on my earlier comments about the various jails which have achieved at least a 75 per cent reduction in completed suicides, 10-12 of those 15 suicides could have been *prevented* if the psychiatrist had had the courage to use his professional position to speak up years before.

D. In my travels around the world I find that there are some lives being lost because we professional people don't stand up to be counted. Part of the problem is that we don't make the effort to find out if suicide prevention may be working better elsewhere. In saving lives we need to reach out more. I am indebted to some of you here for new approaches that I am selling in the US.

I commend all who have been responsible for organizing and developing this Second International Conference on Deaths in Custody. I look forward to the Third one.

# Postscript

# After dinner speech by Terry Waite

*Delivered extempore*

INTRODUCTION BY ANDREW COYLE

*Vaclav Havel, the former President of Czechoslovakia, spent several years in prison and from there he wrote frequently to his wife, Olga. In one of the letters he managed to get past the very strict censor he wrote:*

> *I never feel sorry for myself, as one might expect, but only for the other prisoners and altogether, for the fact that prisons must exist and that they are as they are, and that mankind has not so far invented a better way of coming to terms with certain things (Havel 1990, p.270).*

*It seems to me that at a conference like this we can discuss the pains of imprisonment and the effect which it has on those who are imprisoned, but none of us can really know what it is like to be in prison. Terry Waite has unfortunate and unrivalled knowledge and we are indeed highly honoured that he has agreed to come here this evening to speak to us.*

## TERRY WAITE

Andrew, ladies and gentlemen, thank you very much indeed for your welcome. It is a great privilege for me to be here with you this evening. During the course of the meal I was asked how long I would be speaking and I said 'Well, about 15 minutes', and then

I was asked if I would take any questions, and I said, 'To me that would be the most valuable part of the evening', so if anyone would like to ask me questions when I have concluded what I have to say, I would be more than happy to answer them. If you have no questions then I am sure the bar is open!

People have said to me, 'After spending four years in strict solitary confinement, aren't you nervous about coming out again and meeting people and speaking on public occasions?'. I confess to a certain nervousness from time to time, although I try and suppress it because I remember that too much nervousness can get people into serious trouble. For example, Moses was feeling rather low on one occasion, and God recognised that Moses was feeling low and he called him into his presence. He said 'Moses, I gather you are not too happy at the moment'. Moses said 'No'. God said, 'Well in that case', he said, 'I will give you any land you want. Name it, Moses, and it is yours'. Moses came increasingly nervous at this remarkable offer. He began to stutter. He said, 'Oh well, CCCCC' and then God anticipated what he was going to say, and he said 'Canaan, Moses? Well, if that is what you want, it is not much to write home about, you can have it'. Moses went away and he got Canaan, went back to his wife. His wife said 'How did you get on?'. 'Eh', he said, 'I was so nervous I got Canaan. What I was really trying to say, was California'. That is a joke I think that will be appreciated by our American friends.

The years of captivity are I suppose what you will be interested in hearing about. And so therefore, this evening what I will try and do, is three things. First of all give a little background to the hostage saga. Secondly, speak about the years of captivity itself, and thirdly talk about release. To do that properly would take a long time and therefore I am going to abbreviate certain things and if there are any things that you wish me to elaborate on please ask me a question afterwards.

The reason the Church ever became involved in hostages was simply because we received at Lambeth Palace when I was on the staff of the Archbishop of Canterbury, responsible for his international responsibilities, we received there requests from relatives of people who had gone missing in different parts of the world. And the reason they turned to the Church was because this was a last resort. They had tried to have communication with a variety of agencies or groups, and in particular with the government of the day, through the foreign office, and the response they had received was to their mind, not particularly satisfactory. They turned to the Church for help. In the first instance, of course, our first involvement was in Iran during the days of the Iranian revolution. When in fact members of the Anglian Church in Iran disappeared, the leaders of the church disappeared, and their relatives in this country and in other parts of the world turned to us for help. Here was an occasion where we had really a very legitimate argument for trying to do something. Because the Archbishop of Canterbury as primus inter pares, (first amongst equals) of the Anglican communion, had a general overall moral and spiritual responsibility for the Anglian church in that country. There are many things I could say about that experience but simply to say for the purposes of this evening I went out there and was able to through a long series of discussions and negotiations to bring home hostages.

That gave a certain profile to myself and to Lambeth Palace. When another group of hostages were taken this time in Libya, again relatives turned to us because they felt that nothing was happening. Our initial response always was wait a while, try and see what could happen through official government channels. Eventually when nothing appeared to be happening, again I went out to Libya, had conversations with Colonel Gadaffi and his colleagues and again was instrumental in bringing home British hostages.

Two hostage encounters and two seeming successes, again increased the profile. So it wasn't surprising that when the whole Beirut saga blew up, again relatives of those who had been taken hostage turned to Lambeth Palace, and in particular the relatives and colleagues of the Rev. Benjamin Weir who was a Presbyterian minister working in Beirut who had disappeared. And when his colleagues and relatives came to Lambeth, my first reaction was to say no to their requests. I felt that two hostage events in which I had been involved immediately previous to the request coming from Beirut were quite enough and the third one with our slender resources and the demands that were being made on our time was far too much to take on board. Our advice to those who came to see us was to hold off and try and see what could be done through other channels. Nothing seemed to happen. More hostages were taken, more requests were made and again we said no. And it was the third visit by the group from the United States who came to appeal on behalf of Ben Weir that led our saying well at least we will try and see what can be done.

Now, one doesn't say yes to a request like that lightly, because I knew very clearly that once you say yes we will try and do something, and once you begin to raise the hopes of desperate relatives, then you do not let go the matter easily, you have to stick with it. It seemed to me to be totally irresponsible and it still seems to me irresponsible to raise hopes and then to say, 'Well I am sorry, it is getting too difficult and I have to let it go now'. I remember a colleague at Lambeth saying to me 'Be careful before you take on this problem, it is likely to run on for six or seven years'. His prophecy proved to be exactly right.

When having agreed to take on the problem, one had to make another very difficult decision. Whether to, in fact, go public and bear the heavy cost and burden of going public on a mission such as that or whether to try and find a way of entering the situation quietly and privately. Now if you can cast your mind back to the mid-80s when American hostages, French hostages, German hostages, British hostages were taken in Beirut, you may remember that the picture was extremely complicated. No-one knew at all with any clarity who was taking hostages. And no-one knew at all with any clarity what demands were being made. There was general feeling that this was a politically inspired activity with one or two exceptions, one or two one might say 'criminal gangs' who got into the act purely to extract money from relatives or from others. But no-one knew with any degree or certainty at all who was holding hostages and why. And we took a conscious decision to go public not, I hasten to say, not so that we could be seen to be clever, ecclesiastical politicians strutting confidently across the world's stage, but to try and make it clear to whoever was holding hostages that there was an independent third part willing to talk and willing to try and find the way through the problem, whatever that problem was.

That strategy was a dangerous one to take. I knew very well from previous dealings with the media, that if you go public you have to go along with the consequences of that. You can't suddenly turn it on at your own convenience and then turn it off. You have to run with it whichever way it goes. But it had a result. It in fact led to a letter being received at Lambeth Palace signed by four American hostages, Terry Anderson, Tom Sutherland, David Jacobson and Martin Jenco. The way in which communications came initially from the kidnappers was as follows: they would get a message written on a piece of paper, they would wrap it round a brick or stone, they would then drive at great speed past the AP - Associated Press - Headquarters in Beirut and throw the stone through the doorway around which the message was wrapped. A.P. would then collect it, read it, pass it on to us at Lambeth, that is how we got the message. The message in fact signed by these four hostages was clearly written by their kidnappers and it came as a result of the publicity we took initially. It invited the Archbishop of Canterbury to actually intervene and to make his good offices available to try and find a solution to the problem. It was as good, in fact, as getting a visa. Acting on that I went out to Beirut. There have been many stories about these journeys and there has been film on T.V. screens which could be misleading. I am seen, for example, sitting in a Landrover surrounded by armed guards as though that was the way I went to be kidnapped. What happened was this. Exactly this.

The kidnappers sent another message via that route and they said, bring with you a short wave radio and we will communicate with you on that. And Associated Press brought me a short wave radio. I went out and established myself in Terry Anderson's flat, rigged up the radio, tuned into the frequency that they gave me and waited. Nothing happened. And the phone rang, one evening, and a man came on the phone and he said 'Meet me', and he named a certain petrol station; Well of course, anyone can ring up and here lies, of course, one of the problems that faces anyone who has to do negotiating in this way. How do you make your tests? There are so many people in that field who are out for a variety of motives, the number of people who come to you wanting this, that and the other, wanting money, making spurious claims, a legion. I put a question to this particular man on the phone and said, 'Will you bring me the name or give me the name of the girlfriend of a personal friend of Terry Anderson's?' It was a nickname, and it was a name that only Terry Anderson himself would know. And if I got the correct name back over the phone at least I would know that the person who was speaking to me had some contact in one way or another directly with Anderson, the former A.P. journalist who was a hostage. Half an hour later the phone rang, the correct name was given and I decided on the basis of that rather thin strand, to go and meet this particular man. The story about armed guards is - that one goes with armed guards to the end of the street, and then says good-bye to then go the last of the journey alone. This time it wasn't a petrol station but it was a doctor's surgery in which we met. And the doctor greeted me and told me that I had to be blindfolded, for the discussions. The discussions made it clear that I was in touch with the right people. I first of all asked them to take me to see the hostages and they refused. I gave them a polaroid camera and they said before we have any discussion bring me back this evening pictures of the hostages with whom you have contact.

They agreed to that and within an hour they'd returned and there were pictures of Anderson, Jacobson, the four Americans, each holding a copy of the Wall Street Journal which I had signed and given to the kidnappers. And there was positive proof that I at last was in touch with the right people.

Then we began to try and find out what the demands were. And the demands were, as you might expect, partly political, partly as a result of having blood relatives who were imprisoned in Kuwait, held on a variety of terrorist charges. The claims of these men in Beirut were that these men were being held in appalling conditions, they wanted better conditions, they wanted these men released, eventually, they wanted them to have communications with their families which they claimed they were not having. I said that I would be perfectly prepared to try and visit the men, to ease the situation, to take messages from their families and see eventually what could be done about their release. Because of course, as you will appreciate, in a situation like this, an extraordinary, delicate, difficult, volatile negotiating situation one has to try and ease the situation, try and calm it, try and play for a little time, try and see that the feelings that are so high and so potentially dangerous can be calmed. And they accepted this offer. And I went away to try and work on the problem.

The details of what happened in those intervening months are in fact recorded in the book, that's not a plug to buy the book, I am simply saying that time is going by and I can't give you all the details, suffice to say that one got nowhere and I could not understand why I was not getting the political support that I felt I ought to have got both from my own government in this country and from the United States. And then of course the bombshell broke. What became known as the Iran Contra affair. I was in Wiesbaden, someone came in to see me and said 'You heard about Olly North and his visits to Iran?' And of course it broke to me for the first time then as it broke to the world, that there was another agenda altogether. A broad political agenda about which one knew nothing.

Putting these pieces together now over the years, what happened is clear, or reasonably clear to me. Two agendas: one, the Lebanese agenda concerned with their blood relatives in Kuwait, and two, the broad political agenda of Iran fighting the Iran/Iraq war and seeking to benefit from the hostage crisis by gaining weapons and muscling in on that crisis also. And of course Iran was in cahoots with Beirut in trying to spread the

Islamic revolution and gain political influence in that part of the Middle East.

It faced me with probably the most difficult decision I have ever had to make in my life. Do I at this stage pull out or do I return, try and pick up the pieces? And there have been many commentators who have made all sorts of comments on reasons for returning. I think I am the only person who can really know my motives for that. And they were as follows. And I knew very well that at that point these men, these hostages were utterly demoralised by seeming political collapse. Secondly, it seemed to me entirely wrong that when there had been a collapse like that, the church of all groups, and I as a representative as I was in those days, should pull away, say 'I am sorry, it has got too difficult'. And thirdly, there was the question admittedly, of personal integrity. My integrity, and the integrity of the Church had seemingly been compromised. And it was a case of either walking away and hoping for a better day or going back and try and pick up the pieces. And I decided to return.

When I got back, I made the rounds of Beirut, visited all the principal leaders in the city, trying to get some sense, some feel of what was happening in this dissolving crazy situation. The kidnappers got in touch with me by phone again, and invited me to go and see them. And I went, again alone, and a man whom I recognised as my principal contact said to me as follows: He said, 'Last time you were here, you asked to see the hostages', I said 'Yes'. He said 'We didn't allow it then' (that was the time they gave me the photographs). He said, 'This time you can see them, because with Anderson and Sutherland, they 're ill and we think one even may die. As a member of the church you can come and see'. And I said what I am sure anyone in this room would say: I said 'But you will keep me', and he said 'No'. I said 'Give me your word on your faith you won't'. He gave me his hand and I looked at my watch, it was about 11.30 at night, and I said, 'I can't come now, give me time to think'. 'Alright', he said.

And I went away, took advice, the advice was the advice that again I knew, and it was this: if someone gives you a word in that way it ought to be kept. True, it ought be kept, would it be kept? There was a high high doubt in my mind that it wouldn't be kept I have to admit. And yet at the same time, there was something driving me within that said this, and this is probably the element of personal pride, or whatever you might call it entered into it: If you walk away and the man is telling the truth, and someone does die, what does that say about your faith? It is one thing to stand around and pronounce truths but the day comes when you will be asked to step down from that and actually put into practice what in fact you have been proclaiming, namely that the real matters of this world are fought in the moral and spiritual realm. On the other hand, you might say, a perfect trap had been set. Whatever, I went back. There have been stories of course, pictures of the last journey in that Land Rover, that certainly wasn't the last journey. I went out of the hotel, into a car with my bodyguards, to the end of the street, said goodbye to the bodyguards, deliberately, went the last two hundred yards, went into the doctor's surgery, the doctor excused himself because he said he had an engagement at the hospital, the kidnapper came up into the flat, he asked me if I was armed, I said no, he gave me a body search, quickly, we went down together into the car; I expected to be away five or six days, I expected to be moved from place to place for obvious security reasons: I knew that I would be subject to the most rigourous search, there were stories, and had been stories about locator devices: Anyone who writes such a story has no idea what it means to meet with kidnappers; every tooth examined, to see if anything is concealed beneath the filling, every scar of the body probed to see if anything has been implanted in the body, a complete change of clothing, constant movement from house to house, and then after six days, being told that I would now be taken to see the hostages, still having a very grave doubt in my mind, being driven across Beirut in the back of a van, and then finding myself in a garage blindfolded, I could see beneath the blindfold a trapdoor that I was told to jump down and pushed across the room. The door closed behind me and I was in a cell that was completely tiled. And I knew that that was it. That the promises that had been given were empty. I cursed myself for my stupidity and then I said, 'Well, stand by three things: no regrets, because you need not regret doing what you honestly believed to be right, in hindsight, you could have made different decisions, alright, but no regrets, don't allow regrets to gnaw at you. Secondly, no self pity because self pity will kill, and thirdly, no over sentimentality'. In other words, thinking back across life and saying, if only one had been a better husband, a better father, spent more time with the children, over sentimental...you cannot allow it, do not allow it. And somehow these three resolutions which perhaps in a different context look a bit pious, and a bit pompous, actually at that moment meant an enormous amount and somehow I was able to stand by them. With increasing fear, because I knew that certainly I was in for possibly a rough interrogation. One knows that cells of that kind are tiled because they are easier to clean up after torture. One knows that. And one had the eerie experience of knowing that there were prisoners in this underground block, goodness knows who they were, I tried to communicate with them and got no response whatsoever from them, from tapping on the cell wall. To this day, I don't know who my fellows in this underground prison were. Most bizarre place. Yet afterwards, or before I had heard of these underground prisons, but afterwards I learned that Beirut was riddled with them. Especially built places under apartment blocks right across the city, and in some cases it was rumoured that people had been kept there for years. Certainly my fellow European hostages, Terry Anderson who will be here in London next week, John McCarthy, Tom Sutherland, Martin Jenco, they were all kept in such places. Incidentally, prior to my captivity, it was no coincidence that the first two hostages to be released before I was captured were both clergymen: Jenco and Ben Weir. The kidnappers told us they were releasing these men as a sign to the Church to keep up our activities. It was no surprise to me that when the interrogations did come, when one was woken in the middle of the night, when one was beaten on the soles of the feet, when one was chained for twenty four hours a day by the hands and feet and constantly blindfolded and left lying in a corner. In one instance for as long as nine months in those conditions without any book, any paper, any conversation except with an interrogator, it was no surprise that the whole interrogation centred around the activities of Colonel North. I at the time had difficulty understanding what was going on. Years later, perhaps I begin to piece together a story. Whether one would ever know the whole truth I know not. At the moment its my belief that the Beirut kidnappers who had their agenda in Kuwait found it something of a surprise themselves when the Iran-Contra affair broke. And they wondered themselves what was going on in the broader political arena. And in some areas it was known that I had had contact with North, in the way I had contact with so many people who had been involved in this business. They took me to see what I knew. The final, although I didn't know it at the time, part of the interrogation involved a mock execution, when I was told I had five hours to live. At that point I was so exhausted that when the interrogator went out of the room, I simply laid down, I was in chains of course, blindfolded, closed my eyes and slept. Five hours later they returned and said 'Anything more to say' I said 'No'. They said

'Well, do you want anything to drink?' and being British I asked for a cup of tea, which I got. I said 'I would like to write a letter'. I said I would like to write several letters, to my wife, my family, my friends. They said you can write one letter. And I wrote it and I addressed it to the Archbishop first, then to my family and friends. I addressed it to the Archbishop first, because I thought it might stand a chance of getting out if it was addressed to him. Then they said 'Stand'. My hands had been released from the chains, my feet were still chained. I stood, I faced the wall, I felt a pistol against my head. I said a prayer and then the pistol was dropped, they said, 'Another time'. That was it. No more interrogation after that point. There was nothing at all useful that I could say about the political events which interested them. And then one experienced after one year of this type of interrogation three more years of complete solitary. Occasionally books. And the way, I suppose, one survived during those years was first of all, a fundamental conviction that I would, a determination that I would not be beaten. There was no way that I was going to be beaten in a battle that I had willingly taken on on behalf of the cause I believed in. And secondly, I suppose, a fundamental simple religious conviction that they had the power to break my body, they had the power even to bend my mind, but my soul was not theirs to possess. That somehow somewhere I could retain that sense of inner self-worth, inner self-being, integrity, I find this difficult to put into words, it wasn't theirs to take hold of. And even if I lost my sanity, my soul still wasn't theirs to possess. Because it belonged to God. I can't claim at all great religious feeling, great religious comfort even, just a steady determination to hold on. There were times when I said to myself physical death would be preferable to this living death. And yet, and I suppose this is to do with my own personality and character, I never felt tempted to commit suicide. Some hostages did, whether it was a serious attempt or whether it was an attempt to draw attention and get some easing of their conditions, I don't know. Some simply banged their heads against the wall, one managed to get hold of a plastic bag and tried to suffocate himself. Some died as a result of simply giving up, their spirit gave out, and some died as a result simply that their bodies became totally exhausted and they died of disease, something which nearly overtook myself, when I was in a room where there was a generator outside the door and fumes came under the door which destroyed the lining in the lung and gave me a chronic bronchial infection which meant that I very nearly died.

The years of solitary though were kept going by the fact that I was able to develop a lively inner imagination. And being able to draw on a lifetime spent on reading. And here I can understand some of the things that Alison has been researching and writing about in such an intelligent way, whereby those who have been brought up in a culture that simply they depended upon the visual image, the T.V. screen or film or what have you, and have never had for one reason or another the opportunity or ability or encouragement to develop the mind in the way where by you can store up in your mind that which you have read. Those who have been impoverished in that way have in such extreme circumstances and in a situation of deprivation, relatively little to draw on. I am so fortunate to have spent a lifetime reading, not only to draw on those experiences but can actually begin to write in my head this book which has been afflicted on you now during those years. And some people have said in reviewing it, but why didn't you mention X, Y and Z and political ends. Simply fact, it is the book that was written in my head in captivity, with events not mentioned there because I didn't know them. I wrote as I went along, recalling the past, bringing the past into the present, and beginning to recognise that in some strange and curious way time in those circumstances of great solitary, great isolation takes on a new meaning. And you find in some way that the past, present and future are lived out in the moment, and one has to learn to live for the moment.

The experience which I haven't written about in detail in this book of moving to be with others after spending years in solitary was difficult. And I intend to write about it more completely at some point. The reason that I haven't written about it in this book is because when I moved to be with others the inner writing process stopped in a way and took on a new form and the book that I was writing in my head stopped virtually at the point where I was moved to be with others. I had had to survive by becoming in a way rather self-centred, but I don't mean selfish, I mean centred on self and centred on survival. They who had lived together as a group had found patterns and ways of relating to each other and unconsciously had adopted these patterns over the years, seven years some of them had been together, and one had to find then how to match the experience of being solitary coming back into the group and finding a new relationship. And that is a whole subject in itself and a subject of a whole other book which I shall write in the future.

Coming out, I shall be brief now because I have gone on far too long, coming out of the experience, yes one has been made vulnerable, even more vulnerable, not a bad thing in itself; yes, it's sometimes difficult to trust in the way that one would like to trust, probably one could then realise as a result of this experience just how treacherous human beings can be and are, and therefore there is the tendency also as a result of that type of insight and also as a result of living in the way one had to live over those years a tendency to want to retreat, to want to go back, to want to go back into isolation, back into solitary, back into those years when you are not bombarded with the demands of inter-personal relationships. I mean, for example, when I came home and went to Lynham, I couldn't immediately sit down with my family to a meal. It took me two weeks before I could sit down with just my own immediate family and share a meal with them. Not because I didn't want to but because the simple emotional demands were actually overwhelming. And how grateful we all were, not just myself, but all our family were, that we were able to have such thoughtful and helpful counselling and advice when we came out, not the counselling of telling you what to do, but of course the counselling advice so clearly demonstrated in the work of the Samaritans by having helpful, willing and sympathetic listening.

I believe more firmly than ever that suffering which is part of the human condition which effects us all to a greater or lesser degree, need not destroy. It will always be painful, every human being will face it in one way or another, but it can be made creative. Something creative can come from it and will do so providing that it is approached and understood in an appropriate way. And thirdly and finally, I think my experience has given me a little more positive direction as to the orientation of life for myself, and as I say it I talk without any way being pious. And it can be summed up very simply, because in expressing what I now express I am sure that I express what each and every person in this room in their own way is attempting to achieve in their professional lives. To enable the weak to be strong, to enable the strong to be just and above all, the enable the just to be compassionate. Thank you very much.

Andrew Coyle:
*Terry, thank you very much for allowing us to share in such a personal way your intimate experiences. There is really very little to be said after that. We are very privileged. The attention you were given and the response at the end underlines how much we appreciate what you have given to us. I think if I may suggest that*

*in view of the fact that Terry has spoken to us for so long and in such an impressive way that it would be unfair to impose on him with further questions. With your agreement I think we will conclude the official part of the evening and thank Terry again very much for everything he said.*

# References

Aboriginal Deaths in Custody: Overview of the Response by Governments to the Royal Commission, AGPS, Canberra (1992).

Allardice, G. Goldberg, D. J. Raab, G. M. and Gore, S. M. (1994) HIV testing in Scotland: who, where, when, why and with what result? *Lancet* (in preparation).

Amnesty International (1989) *When the State Kills... The Death Penalty v. Human Rights*, London: Amnesty International.

Amnesty International (1992), *South Africa: State of Fear*, London: Amnesty International, International Secretariat.

Amnesty International (1993) *Report 1993*, London: Amnesty International.

Amnesty International (1993), *Australia: a Criminal Justice System Weighted Against Aboriginal People*, Australian Section, Sydney.

Amnesty International (1993a) *Proposal for an Inquiry into Deaths and Ill-treatment of Prisoners in St. Catherine's District Prison*, London: Amnesty International, International Secretariat.

Amnesty International (1994) *"Disappearances" and Political Killings: Human Rights Crisis of the 1990s - A Manual for Action*, Amsterdam: Amnesty International.

Australian Bureau of Statistics, 1993, *Causes of Death, Australia 1992*, Cat. No. 3303.0, ABS, Canberra.

Backett, S. (1987) Suicides in Scottish Prisons, *British Journal of Psychiatry* 151:218-221.

Backett, S. (1988) Suicides and Stress in Prison, in Backett, S; McNeil, J; and Yellowlees, A. (Eds.) *Imprisonment Today*, London: MacMillan.

Bagshaw, M. (1988) Suicide Prevention Training: Lessons from the Corrections Service of Canada *Prison Service Journal* 70 5-6.

Barraclough, B. M., Birch, J., Nelson, B. and Sainsbury, P. (1974) A Hundred Cases of Suicide: Clinical Aspects, *British Journal of Psychiatry* 125: 355-373.

Barraclough, B. M. and Hughes, J. (1986) *Suicide: Clinical and Epidemiological Studies*, Croom Helm: London.

Basedow, M. (1990) *A Review of Suicide Prevention Procedures used by New South Wales Police Department* NSW Police Research Department, Sydney.

Benn, M. and Worpole, K. (1986) *Death in the City*, Canary Press.

Biles, D. (1991) Deaths in Custody in Britain and Australia *Howard Journal* 30 (2):110-120.

Biles, D. and MacDonald, D. (1992) *Deaths in Custody in Australia 1980-1989: The Research Papers of the Criminology Unit of the Royal Commission into Aboriginal Deaths in Custody*, Australian Institute of Criminology: Canberra.

Bird, A. G., Gore, S. M., Jolliffe, D. W. and Burns, S. M. (1992) Anonymous HIV surveillance in Saughton Prison, Edinburgh in *AIDS* 6:725 - 733.

Bird, A. G., Gore, S. M., Jolliffe, D. W. and Burns, S. M. (1993) Second anonymous HIV surveillance in Saughton Prison, Edinburgh: prisoners give a lead to other heterosexuals on being HIV tested in *AIDS* 7:1277 - 1279.

Bird, A. G., Gore S. M., Burns S. M. and Duggie J. G. (1993) Study of infection with HIV and related risk factors in young offenders' institution in *BMJ:* 228 - 213.

Burtch, B. E. and Ericson, R. V. (1979) *The Silent System: An Inquiry into Prisoners who Suicide and Annotated Bibliography*, Centre of Criminology: University of Toronto.

Bornasco, W., Kerkhof, A.J.F.M., v d Linden, B. (1988) *Suicidal gedrag van gedetineerden in Nederland. Tijdschrift voor Criminologie*, pp 61-75.

*Commissioner of Police of the Metropolis Reports 1983 - 92* Metropolitan Police.

Christie, B. (1993) HIV outbreak investigated in Scottish jail, *BMJ*: 307:151.

Bowker, L. H. (1980) *Prison Victimization*, New York: Eklsevier.

Broadhurst, R. G. and Maller, R. A. (1990) 'The recidivism of prisoners released for the first time: reconsidering the effectiveness question' *Australian and New Zealand Journal of Criminology*, 88-103.

Brown, D. (1989) *Detention at the Police Station under the Police and Criminal Evidence Act 1984*, London: HMSO.

Coggan G. and Walker, M. (1982) *Frightened for My Life: An Account of Deaths in British Prisons*, London: Fontana

Colvin, M. (1982) 'The 1980 New Mexico Prison Riot', *Social Problems*, 29, 449-63.

Council of Europe (1991) *lst General Report on the CPT's Activities Covering the Period November 1989 to December 1990*, Strasbourg: Council of Europe.

Council of Europe (1991a) *Report to the United Kingdom Government on the Visit to the United Kingdom from 29. 7.90 to 10. 8.90*, Strasbourg: Council of Europe.

Council of Europe (1992) *Public Statement on Turkey: Adopted on 15.12.92*, Strasbourg: Council of Europe.

Council of Europe (1993) *Rapport au Government de la Republic Franscais relatif a la visite effectuee par le CPT en France de 27.10 au 8.11.1991*, Strasbourg: Council of Europe.

Cowlishaw, G. (1991) 'Inquiring into Aboriginal Deaths in Custody: The Limits of a Royal Commission', *Journal for Social Justice Studies*, vol. 4: 101-115.

Cox, J. F; McCarty, D.W; Landsberg, G. and Pavarata, M.P. (1987) *The Mental Health Resource Handbook for Human Service Personnel Serving the Local Correctional Population*, Office of Mental Health in New York State.

Christie B. (1994) Report recommends drug agency for Scotlnd *BMJ* 308:1318 - 1319

Danto, B. L. (1973) *Jail House Blues: Studies of Suicides Behaviour in Jail and Prisons* Epic Publications: Michigan

Dell, S., Grounds, A., James, K. and Robertson, G. (1991) *Mentally Disordered Remand Prisoners, Report to the Home Office*, Cambridge: University of Cambridge.

Department of Health *Guidance for Staff on Relations with the Public and the Media.*

Dexter, P. (1993) *Suicide Attempts at Highpoint Prison* unpublished M.Sc. Thesis submitted to Birkbeck College.

Dooley, E. (1990a) Prison Suicide in England and Wales 1972-1987, *British Journal of Psychiatry*, 156: 40-45.

Dooley, E. (1990b) Non-natural Deaths in Prison, *British Journal of Criminlogy*, 30(2): 229-34.

Edwards, C. and Read, P. (eds.) (1989) *The Lost Children*, Doubleday: Sydney.

Eldrid, J. (1988) *Caring for the Suicidal*, Constable: London.

Evans, M. and Morgan, R. (1992) 'The European Convention for the Prevention of Torture: Operational Practice' *The International Comparative Law Quarterly*, 41, 590-614.

Foucault, M. (1967) *Madness and Civilization: A History of Insanity in the Age of Reason*, Pantheon, Tavistock.

Foucault, M. (1977) *Discipline and Punish: The Birth of the Prison*, Allen Lane.

*Freedom of Speech in the N.H.S.* M.S.F., Park House, 64-66, Wandsworth Common North Side, London SW18 2SH

Gaba M. (1993) Glasgow inquires into drug fatalities *BMJ* 307:822

Geary, R. (1980) "Deaths in Prison", *NCCL Briefing Paper*, October, London: National Council for Civil Liberties.

Gilligan, C. (1982) *In a Different Voice: Psychological Theory and*

*Women's Development*, Harvard University Press: Massachusetts.

Global Programme on AIDS (1993) Who guidelines on HIV Infection and AIDS in prisons World Health Organization: Geneva, March.

Goffman, E. (1961) *Asylums: Essays on the Social Situation of Mental Patients and Other Inmates* Anchor Books Doubleday, New York.

Goldberg, D. and Williams, P. (1988) "A Users Guide to the General Health Questionnaire", Windsor: NFER-Nelson.

Goldstone Commission (1994) *Interim Report on the Incidence of Political Violence and Elements within the South African Police and the Kwazulu Police*, Commission for the Investigation of Political Violence: Johannesburg, SA.

Gore, S. M., Jolliffe, D. W., Bird, A. G. (1992) Prisoners' uptake of confidential, named HIV testing, *Lancet* 339:1491 - 1492.

Gore, S. M., Basson J. Bird, A. G. and Goldberg D. J. (1993) Uptake of confidential, Named HIV testing in Scottish prisons, *Lancet* 340:907 - 908.

Gore, S. M. and Bird, A. G. (1993) No Escape: HIV transmission in jail. Prions need protocols for HIV outbreaks *BMJ* 307:147 - 148.

Gore, S. M. and Bird, A. G. (1993) Transmission of HIV in prison *BMJ* 307:681

Grace, S. (1990) "The Needs of Women Prisoners", Home Office Research and Planning Unit No. 29.

Graham, D. (1989) *Dying Inside*, London: Allen and Unwin.

Green, C; Kendall, K; Andre, G; Looman, T. and Poliv, N. (1993) A Study of 133 Suicides among Canadian Federal Prisoners *Medicine Science and the Law* (2) 121-127.

Gunn, J. Maden, A. and Swinton, M. (1991) *Mentally Disordered Prisoners*, London: Institute of Psychiatry.

Haney, J. (1990) *Report on Self-Injurious Behaviour in the Kingston Prison for Women*. Unpublished Report to the Correctional Service of Canada: Ontario.

Hankoff, L. D. (1980) *Prisoners Suicide*, International Journal of Offender Therapy and Comparative Criminology 24(2): 162-166.

Hatty, S. E. and Walker, J. R. (1986) *A National Study of Deaths in Australian Prisons*, Australian Centre of Criminology: Canberra.

Hawton, K., Osborn, M., O'Grady, N. and Cole, D. (1982) Classification of Adolescents who take Overdoses, British

Journal of Psychiatry, 140:124-131.

Hawton, K. and Goldacre, M. (1982) Hospital admissions for adverse effects of medicinial agents (mainly self-poisoning) among adolescents in the Oxford region, British Jounral of Psychiatry 141:166-70.

Hayes, L. (1993) Suicidal or Manipulative? Does it Really Matter? in *Crisis* Vol 14 No. 4 pp 154-156.

Hayes, L. (1994) Developing a Written Program for Jail Suicide Prevention, in *Corrections Today* Vol 56 No. 2 pp 184-187.

Hayes, L. (1994) Jail Suicide Prevention in the USA; Yesterday, Today and Tomorrow, in Liebling, A. and Ward, T. (eds.) *Deaths in Custody: an International Conference* Whiting and Birch: London.

Hayes, L. (1994) Juvenile Suicide in Confinement: An Overview and Summary of One System's Approach in *Juvenile and Family Court* Journal Vol 45 No. 2.

Hayes, L. (1994) Jail Suicide Prevention in the U.S.A: Today and Tomorrow, in Liebling, A. and Ward, T. (eds.) *Death in Custody: An International Conference*, Whiting and Birch: London.

HMCIP (1990, 1992, 1993) see Home Office

Home Office (1986) *"Report of the Working Group on Suicide Prevention"*. London: HMSO.

Home Office (1988) "H.M. Remand Centre Risley. Report by H.M. Chief Inspector of Prisons. London: HMSO. In Lloyd 1990.

Home Office (1990a) Report by Her Majesty's Chief Inspector of Prisons *YOI Feltham*, London: Home Office.

Home Office (1990b) *Report on a Review by Her Majesty's Chief Inspector of Prisons for England and Wales of Suicide and Self-Harm in Prison Service Establishments in England and Wales.* HMSO: London.

Home Office (1992a) Report by Her Majesty's Chief Inspector of Prisons *HM Prison Acklington*, London: Home Office.

Home Office (1993a) Report by Her Majesty's Chief Inspector of Prisons *The Disturbance at HM Wymott on 6. 9.93*, Cm 2371, London: HMSO.

Home Office (1993b) *Report of Committee of Inquiry into Complaints about Ashworth Hospital: Vol 1 and 2* HMSO: London.

Hood, R. (1989) *The Death Penalty: A World-wide Perspective,* Oxford: Clarendon Press.

House of Commons Scottish Affairs Committee (1994) Report - Drug abuse in Scotland, HMSO: Edinburgh and London.

Hopes, B. and Shaull, R. (1986) Jail Suicide Prevention: Effective Programmes Can Save Lives, *Corrections Today* 48(8): 64-70.

House of Commons Home Affairs Committee (1980) *Deaths in Police Custody* HMSO.

Howard League (1993) *Suicides at Feltham*, London: Howard League.

*Jaarverslagen Commissie van Toezicht voor de Amsterdamse Politiecellen 1989-1993* Amsterdam.

Jack, R. (1992) *Women and Attempted Suicide*, Lawrence Erlbaum Associates: Hove.

Jennings, M. (1994) Unpublished Research.

Johnston, E. (1991) *Royal Commission into Aboriginal Deaths in Custody: Report of the Inquiry into the Death of John Peter Pat*, AGPS, Canberra.

Kemp, C. and Morgan, R. (1990) *Lay Visitors to Police Stations: Report to the Home Office*, Bristol: Bristol Centre for Criminal Justice.

King, R. D. and Morgan, R. (1980) *The Future of the Prison System*, Farnborough: Gower.

King, R. D. and McDermott, C. (forthcoming) *The State of Our Prisons*, Oxford: OUP

*Knight* v *Home Office* (1990) 3 All ER 237

Kraus, R. A. and Buglione, N. J. (1984) "Suicide in Massachusetts Lock-ups 1973-84. Report of the Special Commission to Investigate Suicide in Municipal Detention Centers. In Lloyd (1990).

Laing, R. D. (1960) *The Divided Self*, Tavistock.

Laing, R. D. (1967) *The Politics of Experience and the Bird of Paradise*, Penguin.

Langlay, G. E. and Bayatti, N. N. (1984) Suicide in Exe Vale Hospital, 1972-1981, *British Journal of Psychiatry*, 145;463-467.

Lawyers' Committee for Human Rights (1992) *Critique: Review of the U.S. Department of State's Country Reports on Human Rights Practices 1991*, New York: Lawyers' Committee for Human Rights.

Lennane, K. J. (1993) Whistleblowing - a Health Issue in *BMJ* Vol 307 pp 667-670.

Liebling, A. (1991) Suicide in Young Prisoners: A Summary presented to the Home Office, published in a revised form in Liebling, 1992, Suicide in Young Prisoners: A Summary, in *Death Studies*.

Liebling, A. (1992) *Suicides in Prison*, London: Routledge.

Liebling, A. and Krarup, H. E. (1993) *Suicide Attempts in Male Prisons* Home Office: London.

Liebling, A. (1994) Suicides Amongst Women Prisoners *Howard Journal* 33 (1):1-9.

Liebling, A. and Ward, T. (1994a) *Deaths in Custody: International Perspectives* Whiting and Birch: London.

Liebling, A. and Ward, T. (1994b) A History of Prison Suicide, in Hiostry of Prison Medicine, Wellcome Trust: London, forthcoming.

Livingstone, S. and Owen, T. (1993) *Prison Law: Text and Materials,* Oxford: OUP

Lloyd, C. (1990) *Suicide in Prison: A Literature Review* Home Office Research Study 115 HORPU: London.

Massachusetts Special Commission (1984) *Suicide in Massachusetts Lock-ups 1973-1984.* Unpublished Final Report Submitted to the General Court: Massachusetts.

McConville, M., Sanders, A. and LENG. R. (1991) *The Case for the Prosecution*, London: Routledge.

McDonald, D. and Howlett, C. (1993) *Australian Deaths in Custody 1991*, Deaths in Custody Australia, No. 4, Australian Institute of Criminology, Canberra.

McDonald, D; Walker, J. and Howlett, C. (1994) 'Trends in Aboriginal and Torres Strait Island Deaths in Custody and Incarceration: Annual Report 1992-93', in *Implementation of Commonwealth Government Responses to the Recommendations of the Royal Commission into Aboriginal Deaths in Custody) First Annual Report 1992-93*, Royal Commission Government Monitoring Unit, Aboriginal and Torres Strait Islander Commission, Canberra: vol. 1:1-41.

McDonald, D. and Whimp, K. in press 'Australia's Royal Commission into Aboriginal Deaths in Custody: Law and Justice Issues', in K. Hazlehurst (ed.) *Indigenous People and the Application of the Criminal Law.*

McKeown, M. (1994) "A Study of the differences in the effects of incarceration on the psychological well being of females as opposed to males". Paper presented at the Prison Service Conference for Women, 1994.

McKeown, M. and Jennings, M. (1993) "An Evaluative Study of the EARS scheme at HM Prison/YOI Styal", Paper presented at the Prison Service Psychology Conference, 1993.

Morgan, R. (1993) Prisons Accountability Revisited in *Public Law* pp 314-332.

Morgan, R. (1994) Imprisonment, in Maguire, M. Morgan, R. and Reiner R. (eds.) *The Oxford Handbook of Criminology*, OUP: Oxford.

Morgan, R. and Evans, M. (1994) Inspecting Prisons: the View from Strasbourg *British Journal of Criminology* and in King, R. and Maguire, M. (eds.) *Prisons in Context*, OUP: Oxford.

NACRO (1994, forthcoming)*Developing Community Prisons: Report of a Working Party*, London: NACRO.

Noone, A., Gore, S. M. and Curran, L. (1994) Pilot survey of HIV and Hepatitis B infections in men received into three London prisons. Communicable disease Report (submitted).

Northern Ireland Prison Service (1990) *Inmate Suicide: An Awareness and Prevention Manual*, NIO: Belfast.

Office of Corrections Resource Centre (1988) *Suicide and Other Deaths in Prisons including Victorian Results from the National Deaths in Corrections Study* Research Unit, Office of Corrections: Canada.

O'Mahony, P. (1990) *A Review of the Problem of Prison Suicide* in Liebling, A. and Ward, T. (1994).

Orwell, G. (1949) *1984* Penguin.

Pallis, D. J., Gibbons, J. S. and Pierce, D. W. (1984) "Estimating Suicide Risk among Attempted Suicides II. Efficiency of Predictive Scales after the Attempt. *British Journal of Psychiatry*, 144, 139-148.

*Palmer* v. *Home Office*, The Guardian, 31. 3.88

Paxman, M. (1993) 'Aborigines and the Criminal Justice System: Women and Children First!', *Alternative Law Journal*, vol. 18, no. 4 (August): 153-7.

Posen, I. (1988) "The Female Prison Population" in Morris, A. and Wilkinson, C. (eds.) "Women in the Penal System", Cambridge: Cropwood Conference Series, No. 19.

Potier, M. A. (1993) Giving Evidence: Women's Lives in Ashworth Maximum Security Psychiatric Hospital in *Feminism and Psychology* Vol.3 (3) pp 335-347.

Power, K. G. and Spencer, A. P. (1987) Parasuicidal Behaviour of Detained Scottish Young Offenders, *International Journal of Offender Therapy and Comparative Criminology*, 33 (3): 227-235.

Prasser, S. (1992) 'Public Inquiries: Their Use and Abuse', *Current Affairs Bulletin*, vol. 68, no. 9 (February): 4-12.

*Pratt and Morgan* v *Attorney General of Jamaica and the Supt. of Prisons, Saint Catherine's Jamaica*, Judgement of the Lords of the Judicial Committee of the Privy Council, 2.11.93.

Prison Service (1992a) *Report of the Work of the Prison Service April 1990-March 1991* HMSO: London.

Prison Service (1992b) *The Way Forward: Caring for Prisoners at*

*Risk of Suicide and Self-Injury*, An Information Paper, Home Office.

Prison Service (1993) Caring for Prisoners at Risk of Suicide: An Information Pack DIA1: London.

Ramsey, R. F., Tanney, B. L., Searle, C. A. (1987) Suicide Prevention in High-Risk Prison Populations *Canadian Journal of Criminology* 29 (3): 295-307.

Raab, G. M., Burns, S. M., Scott, G., Cudmore, S., Ross, A., Gore, S. M., O'Brien, F. and Shaw T. (1994) HIV prevalence and risk factors in univiersity students *AIDS* (submitted).

Richardson, G. (1985) 'The Case for Prisoners' Rights' in Maguire M., Vagg . and Morgan R. (eds.) *Accountability and Prisons: Opening Up a Closed World*, London: Tavistock.

Richardson, G. (1993) *Law, Custody and Process: Prisoners and Patients,* London: Hodder and Stoughton.

Royal Commission into Aboriginal Deaths in Custody (1991a) *National Report*, 5. vols, Canberra: Australian Govt. Publishing Service.

Rowan, J. (1994) The Prevention of Suicide in Custody, in Liebling, A. and Ward, T. (1994) (eds.) *Deaths in Custody: An International Conference*, Whiting and Birch: London.

Royal Commission into Aboriginal Deaths in Custody, *National Report, 5 Volumes* (1991a) Commissioner Elliott Johnston, Australian Publishing Service: Canberra.

Royal Commission into Aboriginal Deaths in Custody (1991b) *Report of the Inquiry into the Death of John Peter Pat*, Canberra: Australian Govt. Publishing Service.

Samaritans (1993) Unpublished Document.

Sanders, A. (1994) 'From Suspect to Trial' in Maguire, M., Morgan R. and Reiner. R. (eds.) *The Oxford Handbook of Criminology*, Oxford: OUP.

Scarry, E. (1985) *The Body in Pain: the making and unmaking of the world*, New York: Oxford University Press.

Scottish Home and Health Department (1985) *Report of the Review of Suicide Precautions at H.M. Detention Centre and Young Offenders Institution Glenochil* HMSO: Edinburgh.

Scottish Prison Service (1988) *Custody and Care: Policy and Plans for the Scottish Prison Service* HMSO: Edinburgh.

Scottish Prison Service (1989) *Scottish Prison Service Business Plan 1989-1992* SPS: Edinburgh.

Scottish Prison Service (1990) *Opportunity and Responsibility: developing new approaches to the Management of the Long-Term Prison System in Scotland* SPS: Edinburgh.

Scottish Prison Service (1992a) *Suicide Prevention Strategy*.
Scottish Prison Service (1992b) *Suicide Prevention Strategy Training Pack*.
Scraton, P. and Chadwick, K. (1987) *In the Arms of the Law* Pluto Press.
Shengold, L. (1989) *South Murder* Yale University Press.
Shneidmen, E. (1987) At the Point of No Return, *Psychology Today*, March 1987 pp 55-58.
Sim, J. (1990) *Medical Power in Prisons: The Prison Medical Service in England 1774 - 1989*, Open University: Milton Keynes.
Skegg, K. and Cox, B. (1993) Suicide in Custody: Occurrence in Maori and non-Maori New Zealanders *The New Zealand Medical Journal* 106 (948) 1-3.
Sparks, R. (1994) Can Prisons be Legitimate? Penal Politics, Privatization and the Timeliness of an Old Idea, in *British Journal of Criminology*, 34:14-28.
Sperbeck, D. J. and Parlour, R. R. (1986) Screening and Managing Suicidal Prisoners *Corrective and Social Psychiatry* 32 (3): 95-98.
Sykes, G. (1958) *The Society of Captives*, Princetown: Princetown University Press.
Szasz, T. S. (1983) *Law, Liberty and Psychiatry: An Inquiry into the Social Uses of Mental Health Practice*, Macmillan, New York.
Szasz, T. S. (1970) *Ideology and Insanity: essays on the Psychiatric Dehumanization of Man* Anchor Books Doubleday, New York.
*The Whistle* Freedom to Care, PO Box 125, West Molesey, Surrey KT8 1YE
Thomson, N. 1991, 'A Review of Aboriginal Health Status', in Reid, R. and Trompf, P. (eds.) *The Health of Aboriginal Australia*, Harcourt Brace Jovanovich, Sydney.
Thomson, N. and McDonald, D. (1993) 'Australian Deaths in Custody 1980-1989: 1. Relative Risks of Aborigines and Non-Aborigines', *Med J Aust*, vol. 159: 577-581.
Thornton, D. (1990) *Depression, Self-Injury and Attempted Suicide Amongst the YOI Population*, in Fludger, N. I. and Simmons, I. P. (eds.) Proceedings of the Prison Psychologists' Conference DPS Report Series 1 34:47-55.
Toch, H; Adams, K. and Grant, D. (1989) *Coping: Maladaptation in Prisons* Transaction: New Brunswick.
Toch, H. (1992) *Mosaic of Despair: Human Breakdowns in Prisons* (Revised Edition) Easton Publishing Services: Easton.
Topp, D. O. (1979) *Suicide in Prison*, British Journal of Psychiatry, 134: 24-27.

Turnbull, P. and Stimson, G. V. (1994) Drug use in prison *BMJ* 308:1716

Walmsley, R., Howard, L. and White, S. (1992) *The National Prison Survey: Main Findings*, Home Office Research Study No. 128, London: Home Office

West, D. (1965) *Murder Followed by Suicide* Heineman: London

*White Paper on Open Government*: CM2290 of 15. 7.93

Winfree, L. T. (1985) American Jail Death Rates: A Comparison of the 1978 and 1983 Jail Census Date, paper presented at the Annual Meeting of the American Society of Criminology, San Diego, California.

Woolf Report (1991) *Prison Disturbances April 1990: Report of an Inquiry by the Rt. Hon. Lord Justice Woolf (Parts I and II) and His Hon. Judge Stephen Tumim (Part II)*, Cm 1456, London: HMSO.

Wootten, H. (1991) '99 Reasons... The Royal Commission into Black Deaths in Custody', *Polemic*, vol. 2, no. 3: 124-8.

# Index

# Participants

**Abbott WJ** Prison Governor Pentonville Prison

**Aggelopoulou Katerina** Post graduate Fellow in Criminology University of Athens

**Anderson Dr James** Senior Registrar in Forensic Psychiatry Broadmoor Hospital

**Astill MB** Head of Vulnerable Prisoners Unit HMP Dartmoor

**Atkins DW** Head of Custody and Regime HMP Featherstone

**Barnard Grenvil** Prison Governor Thorp Arch

**Bates Andrew** Senior Psychologist HMP Grendon

**Batten Nikki** Prison Researcher

**Beeston Tim** Governor 4, Health Care Manager HMP Holloway

**Bentley RJ** Probation Officer HMYOI Swinfen Hall

**Bhatt Dr R** Senior Medical Officer HMP Cardiff

**Biggar Kathy** Senior Probation Officer, HMP Wandsworth Samaritans

**Biggs Marilyn** Prison Officer HMP Cookham Wood

**Bignell RJG** Health Care Principal Officer HMYOI Aylesbury

**Bingley William** Chief Executive MHAC

**Bird Dr Graham** Consultant Immunologist

**Bishop Dave** Senior Officer HMYOI Portland

**Black Dorothy** Mental Health Act Commissioner MHAC

**Blackburn Stuart** Deputy Principal Orchard Lodge

**Blom-Cooper Sir Louis** Chair, Mental health Act Commission

**Booth Andrew** Probation Officer HMP Kirkham

**Bosworth Mary** Postgraduate Student Cambridge Institute of Criminology

**Bradley Gail** ISTD

**Braggins Julia** Director ISTD

**Bray Margaret** Samaritan HMP Wandsworth

**Brookman Simon** Sergeant Metropolitan Police

**Bullens Pauline** Hospital Officer HMP Hindley

**Burnett Dr. Frances** Senior Registrar in Psychiatry Douglas Inch Clinic, Glasgow

**Burrows Mike** Health Care Officer HMP Ashwell

**Carney Fred** Director of Training National Schizophrenia Fellowship

**Carolissen Marc** Prison Inmate HMP Wandsworth

**Carr Gordon** Senior Probation Officer HMYOI Thorn Cross

**Castle Diana** Regional Co-Ordinator, Prisons Samaritans
**Chiemeka Uju** Postgraduate Student Cambridge Institute of Criminology
**Childs Geoff** Prison Officer HMP Wandsworth
**Coles Deb** Inquest
**Connell Patricia** Postgraduate Student Cambridge Institute of Criminology
**Cope Dr Rosemary** Consultant Forensic Psychiatrist Raeside Clinic
**Cromie R** Prison Governor HMYOI Hydebank Wood
**Crookston Y** Scottish Prison Service Scottish Prison Service
**Da Costa Anne** Senior Probation Officer Devon Probation Service
**Dendy MR** Health Care Officer HMP Down View
**Dixon Dr Terry** Senior Medical Officer NI Prison Service
**Dunbar Ian** Director Inmate Administration HM Prison Service
**Dunn Bob** Post Graduate Research Student Edgehill University
**Dunne Patrick** Governor, Arbour Hill Prison Department of Justice, Republic of Ireland
**Eaton Alice** Hospital Officer HMP Exeter
**Etheridge Paul** Police Sergeant Metropolitan Police
**Eustace Len** Prison Inmate HMP Wandsworth
**Fico Dr Robert** Law Institute, Ministry of Justice, Slovakia
**Fitton Terence** Board of Visitors HMP Belmarsh
**Fraser Dr Kim** Forensic Psychiatrist Newcastle mental Health NHS
**French David** National Committee Police Federation
**Frost Irene** Administrator ISTD
**Gajdus Dr Danuta** Assistant Professor of Criminology Warsaw University
**Gallagher T** Senior Health Care Officer HMP Norwich
**Gee Kenneth** Judge Serious Offenders Review Council, Australia
**Geller Jozsef** Assistant Professor Law Budapest University
**Ginn Bill** Prison Governor HMYOI Deerbolt
**Gobeil Remi** Deputy Commissioner Correctional Services of Canada
**Godschalk JG** Area Manager Ministry of Justice, Netherlands
**Goodison Clem** Prison Governor HMP Everthorpe
**Goodwin W** Suicide Awareness Trainer HMP Stafford
**Gore J** Director Social Developments Ltd
**Gore Dr Sheila** Medical Research Council
**Griffiths Richard** Senior Probation Officer, HMP HIndley Probation Service
**Groombridge Nic** ISTD
**Gunchenko Alexander** Deputy Chief, International Department Interior Ministry of the Ukraine
**Haley Roger** Governor HMP Wandsworth

**Hall Guy** Visiting Fellow Edith Cowan University, Australia
**Hannant Jan** Senior Social Worker Rampton Hospital
**Harding Richard Professor**, Director of Crime Research Centre University of Western Australia
**Harrison RP** Principal Health Care Officer HMP Brixton
**Hartley David** Senior Social Worker Rampton Hospital
**Hayes Lindsay** Assistant Director NCIA, Mass. USA
**Haynes Ruth JP** Parole Board Member Parole Board
**Heng Jian Pang** Interpreter Foreign Affairs, Hebei Province, China
**Heyes J** Prison Governor HMP Swansea
**Hickman John** Treasurer ISTD
**Hosking Penny** Associate Tutor Bethlem and Maudsley Hospitals
**Jackson Keith** Clinical Manager Premier Prison Services
**Jacques Roderick** No 1 Governor HMP Liverpool
**Jennings MW** Higher Psychologist HMPYOI Styal
**Johns Tom** Chaplain Prison Service College
**Jones Alan** Grade VIII Officer HMP Erlestoke House
**Jones Alun** Senior Officer HMP Bedford
**Karabee Dr Zdenek** Director General Czech Prison Service
**Kolodyazhnly Mikhailo** Interpreter Internat Department of Interior Ministry of Ukraine
**Koulouris Nikos** Post-Graduate Fellow in Criminology University of Athens
**Lawrence B** Designer, Directorate of Works Prison Service
**Lee Michael** Manager Butler Clinic, Regional Secure Unit
**Leslie FA** Nursing Advisor Scottish Prison Service
**Lewington Dr Frances** Medical Training Organiser Metropolitan Police
**Liebling Dr Alison** Senior Research Associate Cambridge Institute of Criminology
**Liu Shenzun** Chief, No. 1 Labour Relations Team Foreign Affairs, Hebei Province, Lockett RW Head of Nursing Services Prison Service
**MacFarquhar Rod** Governor 5 HMP Hedon Road, Hull
**Maden Tony** Institute of Psychiatry
**Maguire P** Prison Governor HMP Belfast
**Martin G** Principal Officer HMP Belfast
**Martin Carol** Conference Co-Ordinator ISTD
**Mateer Pauline** Board of Visitors HMP Belfast
**McCann A** Board of Visitors HMP Cookham Wood
**McDonald David** Senior Criminologist Australian Institute of Criminology
**McGregor Dr J** Medical Officer Scottish Prison Service
**McGuigan Dr Kevin** Head of Healthcare Isle of Wight Prisons Group

**McHugh Martin** Suicide Awareness Support Unit HM Prison Service
**McKinstry Thomas** Health Care Officer HMP Durham
**McLean Dr Gillian** Senior Psychiatric Registrar NHS
**McNally Paul** Governor V HMP Magilligan, NI
**McNamara WP** Hospital senior Officer HMP Kirkham
**Memery Paul** Assistant Principal Officer Department of Justice, Republic of Ireland
**Mihalik Professor J** Dean, School of Law University of Bophuthatswana
**Miller Christina** Staff Nurse The State Hospital, Carstairs
**Mjeda Silvana** Prison Inspector Albanian Prison Administration
**Moore Mike** Probation Officer West Sussex Probation Service
**Morgan Rod** Professor, Criminal Justice University of Bristol
**Morgan Gethin** Professor, Mental Health University of Bristol
**Motah Hemduth** Vice-Chair National Association of Black Law Students
**Moyle Paul** Research Fellow Crime Research Centre, University of Western Australia
**Neal David** Suicide Awareness Support Unit HM Prison service
**Neal Malcolm** Hospital Senior Officer HMP Long Lartin
**Newell J** Prisoner Governor HMP Magilligan
**Newell Tim** Prison Governor HMP Grendon
**Novikov Evgeny** Chair Belarus League for Human Rights
**O'Dea V** Prison Governor HMP Featherstone
**O'Gorman Dr P** Board of Visitors HMP Belmarsh
**Ord Derek** Prison Inmate HMP Grendon
**Payn-James Dr Jason** Editor Journal of Clinical Forensic Medicine
**Pearce J** Area Director Scottish Prison Service
**Piggott Clive** Head of Custody HMP Norwich
**Pope Steve** Assistant Director Regimes NI Prison Service
**Potier Moira** Consultant Clinical Psychologist St Chad's Clinic
**Potts Harry** Health Care Manager HMP Everthorpe
**Power Dr K** Clinical Psychologist Scottish Prison Service
**Ratcliffe Wendy** Suicide Awareness Trainer HMPYOI Styal
**Representative** SHSA Rampton Hospital
**Robinson Lynda** HMYOI Deerbolt
**Rodgers Brian** Area Manager NI Probation Board
**Rowan Joe** Executive Director Juvenile And Criminal Justice International, Minn, USA
**Rowe T** Health Care Senior Officer HMYOI and Remand Centre, Brinsford
**Rubenstein Paul** Co-Ordinator, Prison Support Team The Samaritans

**Russell Peter** Senior Probation Officer West Midlands Probation Service

**Sagal-Grande Dr Irene** Criminologist Rijks University, Netherlands

**Seed David** Principal Training Officer HMP Preston

**Shapira Naomi** Ministry of Police Israel Police

**Sharpe Bobie** Federation of Prisoners' Families Support Groups

**Shaw Dr Stephen** Director Prison Reform Trust
China

**Sheppard David** Custody Inspector Avon and Somerset Police

**Sherratt Samantha** Projects Officer Howard League

**Siddons Peter** Assistant Director, HMP Blakenhurst UK Detentions Ltd

**Slater EJ** Head of Inmate Activities HMP Moreland

**Snijder S** Investigator Bureau of National Ombudsman, Netherlands

**Stevenson V** Senior Medical Officer, Prison Department HMP Brixton

**Stevenaon Neil** Suicide Awareness Instructor HMYOI Glen Parva

**Stewart Derek** Health Care Principal Officer HMP Swaleside

**Tate Alex** Probation Officer Southwark Crown Court

**Taylor C** Suicide Awareness Instructor HMP Featherstone

**Thomas Peter** Officer/Instructor HMP Blundeston

**Thompson A** Senior Nurse Officer Scottish Prison Service

**Thorpe Sandra** Law Student University of Central England

**Todhunter Michael** Board of Visitors HMP High Down

**Tweedie June** Inquest

**van der Meer F** Deputy Governor, House of Detention Ministry of Justice, Netherlands

**Vardy Derek** Principal Officer, Health Care HMP Grendon

**Wade Brian** Chief Inspector Metropolitan Police

**Wade Sue** Assistant Chief Probation Officer Hampshire Probation Service

**Walker D** Care Support Trainer HMP Ranby

**Wallace DWF** Senior Probation Officer HMP Littlehey

**Ward Tony** Lecturer in Law de Montfort University/Inquest

**Wells David** Principal Health Care Officer HMP Channing Wood

**Welsh John** Governor 5 (Nursing) Scottish Prison Service

**West Tessa** Inmate Services Manager Group 4

**Whitty Joseph** Governor HMYOI Feltham

**Woods James** Governor Department of Justice, Republic of Ireland

**Wortley Dr Richard** Lecturer Griffith University, Australia

**Wright Mandy** Principal Psychologist Northern Ireland Prison Service

**Yisa MA** Senior Medical Officer HMP Pentonville